TWO RIVERS

TWO RIVERS

Travels in West Africa on the Trail of Mungo Park

PETER HUDSON

CHAPMANS

Chapmans Publishers Ltd
141–143 Drury Lane
London WC2B 5TB

0071258979

BRITISH LIBRARY CATALOGUING IN PUBLICATION DATA

Hudson, Peter
Two Rivers: travels in West Africa on the
trail of Mungo Park.
I. Title
916.604328

ISBN 1-85592-528-1

First published by Chapmans 1991

Photoset in Linotron Garamond by
Rowland Phototypesetting Ltd
Bury St Edmunds, Suffolk

Printed and bound in Great Britain by
Butler and Tanner Ltd, Frome and London

For the Africans

Acknowledgements

To the people of small towns and villages in places such as the Gambia and Mali hospitality is a way of life, and profuse offerings of thanks are not only regarded as unnecessary but also somewhat unseemly: it is ungracious to presume that the hospitality one receives is a special favour and not the natural way of things. As it was, however, the people I met throughout my journey gave me not only the warmest of hospitality but also their friendship and goodwill, and so I shall indulge myself and let my gratitude to them be known, for friendship and goodwill are the bread and butter of the traveller's diet; without them he soon withers.

I should also like to thank the Society of Authors for a grant that helped towards my travel expenses, Vikki Tate for her patience in typing up my work, Veronica Hudson for her drawings, Marie Rudas for daily listening to my literary frustrations, my parents for their support, Serafina Clarke for being such a resourceful agent, and Mark Crean, my editor, for untangling my manuscript so adroitly.

The day that I finished writing my book the corrupt regime that had endured for so long in Mali was overthrown in a military coup. Although for the time being this will have little effect on the ordinary people of Mali, one can only hope that the new regime implements a mode of government that is not only honest but also fitting to the African way of life, and so in the long run may benefit those people who are far from the centres of power. For reasons of security it is still best for many of the people I write about to be anonymous, and so I have changed their names.

Contents

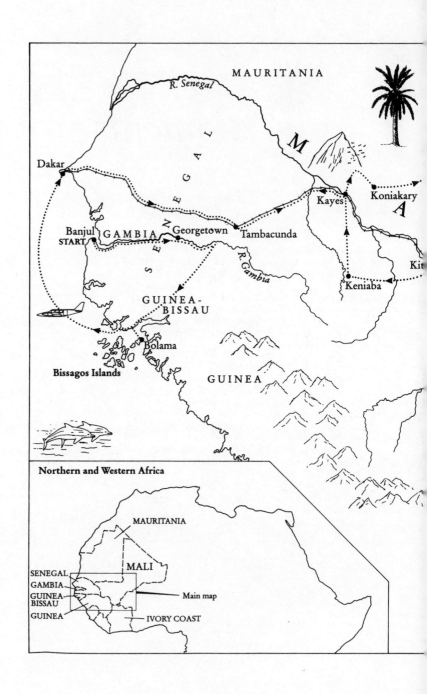

MAURITANIA

R. Senegal

Dakar

S E N E G A L

Banjul
START

GAMBIA

Georgetown

Tambacunda

Kayes

Koniakary

M

A

Keniaba

Kit

R. Gambia

GUINEA-
BISSAU

Bolama

Bissagos Islands

GUINEA

Northern and Western Africa

MAURITANIA

MALI

SENEGAL
GAMBIA
GUINEA-
BISSAU

GUINEA

Main map

IVORY COAST

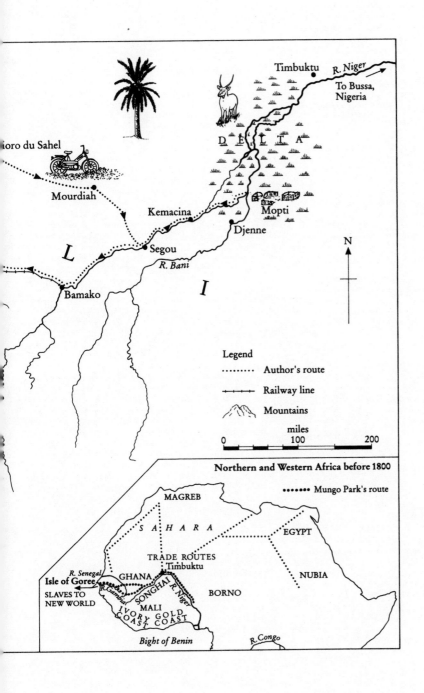

Timbuktu

R. Niger

To Bussa,
Nigeria

ioro du Sahel

Mourdiah

D E L T A

Kemacina

Mopti

Djenne

Segou

R. Bani

L

I

N

Bamako

Legend

.... Author's route

+—+—+ Railway line

⛰ Mountains

miles
0   100   200

Northern and Western Africa before 1800

•••••• Mungo Park's route

MAGREB

S A H A R A

EGYPT

TRADE ROUTES
Timbuktu

NUBIA

R. Senegal
Isle of Goree

GHANA

SONGHAI

R. Niger

BORNO

SLAVES TO
NEW WORLD

R. Gambia

MALI

IVORY GOLD
COAST COAST

Bight of Benin

R. Congo

Preface

THERE ARE FEW things more relaxing and therapeutic than a sea voyage: watching the swell and dip of an ocean day after day; the clean cut of the bow as it divides the waves and curls them down the side of the boat; the turbulent wake as it drifts off behind in the direction of your home that you know each second becomes more distant, and so your destination closer. A sea voyage hardens you up, acclimatizes you and prepares you for the place you are going to: the wind and salt, and the sun that browns your skin. You do not arrive all pasty-faced and awkward. And it is exciting. Each day brings new sights: migratory birds coming from, or going to, the same exotic lands you are perhaps headed for; strange and rare seabirds that dive into the water from great heights; some dolphins, maybe even a whale; and, best of all, those glimpses of distant land, sometimes almost indistinguishable from the horizon, but at others quite clear, with the dark swellings of mountain. All these things, along with the change of climate and the smell of the wind, remind you that you are off somewhere new and maybe exciting, and begin to turn that savoury knot of anticipation and nerves in your stomach.

And then the day of your arrival comes. You draw closer to the land: it takes on shape and texture, a long strip of the colours of the country which, like a barrier, prevents you from seeing what is hidden behind it. At least this is how the far western coast of Africa looks and how it must have looked to the Scottish explorer, Mungo Park, when he sailed along it in the June of 1795, seeing first the mountains of Mogadore in southern Morocco, then the heavy vegetation that hugs the coast near the estuary of the Gambia river. Perhaps with a strong eye-glass he might have been able to pick out a village or two, but other than that the coast told nothing of what it hid behind it, for in those days there were no cities to break its silence.

That Scottish explorer, Mungo Park, was the first known European to travel deep into the heart of West Africa and return with news of what he had found, and I was going on a voyage to follow the first of the two journeys he made there. This was a journey that had taken Mungo Park into a land, in his day, of myth and legend, a land in which the people and beasts were rumoured to be little more than barbarians and hobgoblins. In reality, though, it was a land that had been the arena of successive empires and kingdoms whose sophistication and wealth would surprise most people even today. What Mungo Park found there is as interesting to read about today as it must have been in 1799 when *Travels into the Interior of Africa*, the book of his first journey, was published.

This journey would take me first to the small West African country of the Gambia, and then from there, passing briefly through Senegal and Guinea-Bissau, into Mali. It is in the area of what is today the modern nation of Mali that the majority of Mungo Park's travels had been conducted, for the principal object of his journey had been to explore the course of the Niger, West Africa's largest and most majestic river that passes through the heart of Mali. This was a country which, through previous visits there, I had acquired a great liking for. Here, for me, could be found all that is so hypnotic about Africa. Here was that special blend of poverty and grace, and that almost mystical proximity with nature which is the essence of much of Africa. I hoped this journey would give me the opportunity to immerse myself in Africa more than I had ever done before. I would abandon myself to it, let it take me in its grasp, run me through its course of events and deposit me on the morrow as it saw fit.

Mungo Park had travelled with a similar attitude and it was this that had attracted me to him. He, it seemed from a reading of his book, did not travel to Africa on this journey to prove anything to himself or others, nor to conquer or convert, nor to confirm the popular belief in the barbarity of the place. He was independent of the current beliefs and fashions of his day and sets a good example in comparison to the style in which later explorers and travellers were often to approach their subjects. Park's personal reason for going to Africa was merely, he says, 'a passionate desire to examine into the productions of a country so little known and to become experimentally acquainted with the modes of life and characters of the natives'.

Mungo Park travelled by ship from England to the estuary of the Gambia river and this I should also like to have done. Sadly, it was not possible. So, instead of enjoying the gentle transformation of a sea voyage, I committed myself to the abrupt and sudden arrival of an aeroplane trip. This is something that is, to me, little different from walking through a door. There is no connection drawn between the place you have left and the one you are going to: no continuity between the two different realities. What your aeroplane ticket guarantees just suddenly pops up before your eyes.

Peter Hudson,
London,
June 1991

I
The Coast

W HEN I STEPPED out into the night, what struck me most was the smell, the smell of Africa: a combination of dust and vegetation and dirt. It is a smell that to someone who knows Africa well conjures up a hundred other smells that in their turn swamp you with memories as a single chord of music can sometimes take you back to a place and time where the smells and feelings are as real as if they were happening all over again. As I walked down the aeroplane steps and across the tarmac towards the terminal building, into an almost tangible wall of humidity, I was assailed by feelings of nostalgia. I was nervous and excited, and happy to be back in Africa.

The airport terminal building was small and badly lit. Although it was the early hours of the morning, the air was hot enough to make everybody sweat: within minutes clothes were damp and hands clammy and dirty. The customs and immigration men looked tired and dishevelled, as though they had just woken from sleeping in their clothes. But they were polite and as the passengers filed through their posts they wished many of them a happy stay in the Gambia.

Outside the front of the terminal building there was a tall wire-mesh fence. Behind the fence, and in fact pressed right up against it, was a crowd of people with lanterns, taxis and carts, and small portable stalls. There was no transformation between the air-conditioned sterility of the aeroplane and this Africa. There was just the terminal building, then a small clear space, then this fence holding back the horde. There was a soldier at the gate in the fence and then many people were shouting at me and hands were tugging at my clothes. I followed, or rather was pulled along by, a man shouting, 'Taxi, taxi'. When we arrived at his car my bag disappeared from my hand, a door, bent and battered, was forced open, and I found myself in the front seat. Then followed the slow, agonized turning of the engine until it

3

fired, and we were off, careering away from the light and turmoil of the airport into darkness.

The drive was long because the road, although tarmacked, was badly broken up. There were no houses, no lights, just the outlines of the dark bush on either side. About half-way there we had a puncture. For ten minutes whilst the wheel was being changed I stood in the silence and immensity of the African night. There were crickets in the bush and the sky overhead was bright with stars.

I had been recommended a hotel in Banjul, capital of the Gambia, and we were suddenly there, the humming darkness still surrounding us, the town seemingly non-existent, just the hotel and a few dim lights further off, down the road. I hammered on the hotel door until I woke up the nightwatchman who gave me a room in which to sleep.

★

The Gambia is a small, tropical country consisting of only a thin ribbon of land at no point more than 50 kilometres wide. It hugs the banks of its namesake river following it from its estuary on the Atlantic Ocean to nearly 500 kilometres inland. It has often been described as a thorn in the side of Africa because, geographically, this is how it looks. But to be more precise one should say that it is a thorn in the side of Senegal because it is this large West African country that is nearly cut in two by the Gambia penetrating deep into the heart of it.

In this case, however, the comparison is not only visual, because Senegal feels the pain of having the Gambia dug into its side as if it were indeed a thorn. In order to travel from the north to the south of the country one has either to take a long detour to the east of it and so slip around the end of the Gambia, or take the trans-Gambian highway. But taking this highway means having to go through the Gambian border formalities twice and having to depend upon the efficiency of the Gambian ferry service as there is no bridge on which to cross the river. Senegal is a fast-moving, competitive and well-developed country whereas the Gambia is a slow-moving, underdeveloped country. As a result the Senegalese often opt for the long detour rather

4

than having to cope with the Gambian border formalities and the ferry service to make a trip that, without the presence of the Gambia, would be so quick and simple.

There have been many attempts made to give life to a concept of a unified Senegambia, as the region between the Senegal and Gambia rivers is known. For a long time the Gambia flirted with the idea, even to the extent of allowing Senegal to post some of its army within their frontier. But it has always come unstuck, essentially because the Gambia has its own separate cultural identity and does not want to lose this by being merged with a much larger and more forceful one. The result is that the Gambia, although very poor, is one of the more charming West African countries where, despite the fact that you are never more than 25 kilometres from Senegal, you feel as though you were on a small, tropical island. More than once I have heard one of the many tourists who visit the country asking in which part of Africa Senegal is to be found.

★

The hotel in which I spent my first four days in Banjul, the capital, had not been recommended well. It was dim, dank, seedy, and too expensive. I seemed to be the only person staying there and passed my evenings sitting in the common room drinking beers and eating greasy chicken and chips in the company of the hotel staff. The staff were friendly but the monotony of their jobs, hanging around the empty hotel day and night, had reduced them to a state of such torpidity it was difficult to raise any reaction from them. Each evening, it being the rainy season, there was a thunderstorm and the television set which the staff spent a lot of their time watching would not work. Sometimes these storms were accompanied by power cuts and then we would all sit in an abject silence in the light of oil lamps until someone dropped in to socialize. Then there would be a bit of laughter. In fact, at these times a great effort was made to joke and laugh.

Not that Banjul was a dull place, by day at least. There is a long main road that, by way of a bridge, links the city to the mainland. It runs right to the centre of town, and down this road, each day, come all the thousands of people who do not live in Banjul but who work there or need to go there because this is where the port and the Albert market are, and where anything official is to be found. The road is in the most appalling state of repair and, when it rains, is little better than a quagmire lined with one pothole after another, each one quite big enough, one would think, to stock fish. The fleet of minibuses and cars which bring all these people to town is obliged to use this one route and so the road quickly becomes jammed up as vehicles try to avoid the worst of the potholes by driving down the wrong side of the street and mounting the pavements. Each vehicle is filled to capacity with Gambians dressed in the colourful materials of West Africa and any dry patch of the street is also filled to capacity with street sellers and squads of bureaucrats and workers trying to negotiate a dry route to the centre of town. What with the noise of car horns and shouting, the scene makes quite an impression as you step out of your hotel door on your first morning in Africa.

At first, I found it delightful. I picked and weaved my way along the road to the centre of town, enjoying all the sights, sounds and smells around me. But this did not last long. In Africa it is easy to become badly self-conscious. You can get the impression that everybody is staring at you because you are white and they are all black. This feeling can build up until you become para-noiac and walk around with your eyes fixed firmly on the ground. Then, when someone says something to you, you jump like a startled toad and give them a suspicious, even aggressive, look. Of course it is true: everybody is looking at you; but, hopefully, you discover later on that this is generally just curiosity on their part and if they encounter an open and more friendly visage on the stranger, he immediately, whether he wishes it or not, slips into the role of being just another ordinary human being. When you discover this, it is like waking on a fresh and clear morning after a night of bad dreams – on my first morning it was not long before my jaunty step became a little duller and I found myself hurrying around the town trying to be as inconspicuous as poss-ible until I eventually bolted back to my hotel room, closed the door and lay down to try to compose myself.

The beach at Banjul ran all the way down one side of the

town, and each evening became a gymnasium for many running, hopping and bending athletic young men. But like the streets, the beach had its drawbacks. There was a large tourist hotel on it and each day the tourists would lie out on the sand in front looking, in all essence, like a colony of large, pink seals. Because of the presence of these tourists, everybody on the beach, with the exception of the self-absorbed athletes, was what I came to know as the 'wanting boys': 'You want Gambian friend? You want woman? You want best Colombian grass?' they would greet you the moment you set foot on the beach, and persist until you left; one time even, 'You want my friend, here?' one small boy said to me, indicating another small boy, 'the white ones sex him, you know, like Boy George.'

I even made a friend of one of these people. He was a young man who had grown his hair into dreadlocks like a Rastafarian. He was very obliging and kind and his favourite expression was 'No problem'. He picked me up at my hotel and trailed me around town for a couple of days to see things he thought I might like to see, such as the fishermen and dope smokers on the beach. He took me to his home and introduced me to his family and I sat with his friends listening to reggae music and getting stoned, and we pretended that we were great friends. Then he asked me for some money for a dental operation for his sister and I gave him some and never saw him again.

'But this is just the beginning,' I kept saying to myself. And, anyway, not all was bad in those first few days. There were evenings on the beach watching the sunset and the seagulls squabbling, and the high-flying swallows, and the fisherwomen shrouded in smoke from the fires on which they smoked their fish. And there were all the many small experiences and sights that pass unnoticed but cheer one all the same: the smile and laugh of a market woman; a small boy coming up and shaking one's hand; a man from whom you have asked directions taking ten minutes to lead you all the way to your destination.

I remember one old man dressed up like a Rastafarian, standing in the middle of the street shouting, 'Babylon will curse you, you blood-sucking vermin,' and none of the passers-by ignoring him but throwing jokes at him and laughing in a kindly way, as though he might have been their senile grandfather.

7

There was the Director of Tourism who gave me a lift in his Mercedes but then discovered that he was nearly out of petrol, obliging us to go around all the petrol stations trying to find one in which he had not run out of credit: the pump attendants were not very helpful because they were tired of men in Mercedes who never had any money to pay their bills. He was a round, jolly man and was apologetic to the attendants and explained to me the complexities of his domestic arrangements with two wives and too many children who ate up all his money.

Such was the run and mill of the place, a small and not-very-hard jungle where a new stand was being built by the Chinese in the central MacCarthy Square from which the President could give speeches, even though the terrible road that ran past it had not even had a pothole filled in and was gradually destroying the fleet of minibuses that used it; everybody accepted this as a not unreasonable state of affairs. There were good times in those first days but I was pleased when I found out that Banjul was not a place in which people stayed through choice, and left it.

★

In Mungo Park's day Banjul, or Bathurst, as it was known before the Gambia gained independence from its British colonizers, did not exist because Park came to Africa over eighty years before Europeans were to begin to call parts of Africa their own and build their towns on them. But even in his day the process that was to lead to this was already in motion. In fact it had been in motion for a long time and it came in the shape of trade.

For many centuries, long before the first Europeans were to sail down the west coast of Africa, there had been a lucrative and flourishing trade between the lands of black Africa, south of the Sahara Desert, and the lands to the north of it. This trade had been carried out by camel across the desert and was conducted with the peoples of the interior countries rather than those who lived on the coast. When Europeans began to notice that North African merchants grew rich from this trade, and when they began to hear rumours of supposedly fabulously rich cities such as Timbuktu, and of the great quantity of gold to be found in those interior countries, they started to explore down the coast of West Africa for the purpose of trading with the coastal peoples, hoping, through them, to be able to tap some of this wealth for themselves.

Two of the most useful things needed when trading by ship with an unknown and possibly hostile country are rivers and islands. Both of them can give shelter to ships from the open sea. An island is an easily defendable place and by means of a river one can conduct trade with peoples who live far inland. It was therefore the islands and rivers that are found on the coast of West Africa that were to give Europe its first foothold and a means by which to trade with and eventually penetrate the interior. The Senegal river, just south of the Sahara, the island of Goree, opposite what is today the capital of Senegal, Dakar, and the Gambia river with an island 30 kilometres up its estuary were among some of the first places to have contact with Europe. The Portuguese landed on the island in the Gambia river estuary in 1456. They traded in such things as salt, iron pots and firearms for ivory, ebony, beeswax, gold and slaves. Later the Germans, Dutch, British and French all arrived on the coast and squabbled over the prize islands and rivers. But gradually the trade began to centre on one item only, and that was slaves.

The principle of slavery, of one man owning another, had always existed in Africa, and slaves had always been traded, not only between the people of black Africa, but also north across the Sahara to serve the wealthy nobility of the Mediterranean states and the Middle East. This trade, though, took on a whole new scale when the Europeans began to import slaves to work the mines and plantations of their new colonies in the Americas. Vast numbers of slaves – it has been estimated that from the sixteenth to the nineteenth century fifteen to twenty million slaves were carried away from West Africa – were brought down from the interior of West Africa by African middlemen who sold them to the Europeans to be shipped across the Atlantic. The Europeans continually squabbled amongst each other to monopolize this trade but by the end of the eighteenth century, when Mungo Park arrived on the scene, the situation had settled. By then the slave trade had dwindled as a result of new sources of slaves having been found in other parts of Africa, the French were established with their spheres of influence based upon the

Senegal river and the Isle of Goree, and the British controlled the Gambia river and the island 30 kilometres up its estuary which was now called James Island – spheres of influence that remain strong up to today.

★

When I left the hotel I had been recommended in Banjul I moved to a small town called Bakau a few miles up the coast. Here I found lodgings with a man called Ali Bah who had a large compound with many rooms to rent. The one I rented was a tiny square box with a foam mattress on the floor. There were no windows and the walls were of unpainted, flaky cement.

At first I could not stand all the insects that shared my room, and sometimes my bed, especially the ones that looked like black cockroaches with wings and made a loud screeching noise all night long, but I soon got used to them and no longer noticed the noise of the 'screechers'. The ants fascinated me. They had little, busy motorways up and down the walls and across the floor. Whenever they met each other on the motorways, they would bump heads as if they were greeting each other. And if I dropped a crumb of food on the ground, only seemingly a miraculously short time later I would see it moving across the floor and, on closer inspection, discover a team of ants underneath it.

There were a lot of the smaller forms of life in Ali Bah's compound. Along with the ants and spiders and mosquitoes and the many other types of insects that appeared in my room from time to time, there were a few frogs that lived in the yard outside my door. The yard was small and square with a shady kola nut tree in the middle of it, and the ground was sandy. The frogs were much the same colour as the sand and so sometimes I would accidentally tread on one of them. They were amazingly rubbery, however, and seemed to be able to flatten out with no visible harm, and then slowly puff up again. Between the rains the frogs would become dry and sad-looking; but when the rains came, thundering on the corrugated iron roofs of the compound and flooding the yard, they would join together in a cacophony of croaking, as if filled with elation at once again being wet and slimy.

Gerhart, a German medical student who rented the room next to mine, had geckos on his wall. These are a type of lizard with large round eyes. They are shy and have, one feels, good characters. They eat mosquitoes and are believed by some people to bring good luck, although Seydou, a young Gambian who lived in another of the rooms in Ali Bah's compound, hated them and said that they were evil. But then for Seydou almost anything you cared to mention had some sort of spirit, good or bad, lurking in it.

The most delightful animal life in Ali Bah's compound, though, were the birds that nested in the kola nut tree and the tall palm tree that hung over from the compound next door. Often Seydou, Gerhart and I would hear their dawn chorus before we went to bed; the nights were too hot and our rooms too airless for sleep, especially as Ali Bah insisted that we lock ourselves in because there were supposed to be many thieves in Bakau.

'Africa is a dangerous place, you believe me,' he'd often tell me. 'And Bakau. The thieves here are especially daring. They will even come into your room when you are asleep and steal the very sheet from on top of you.'

'Pah, Ali Bah,' Seydou retorted on one of these occasions. 'You like to scare your foreign visitors too much. You know that Bakau is filled with honest people like yourself. It's only down by the big hotels on the beach that thieves can be found.'

'Say what you like, Seydou,' Ali Bah replied. 'But I advise your friends to *shut* and *lock* their doors at night. It would grieve me too much if they had any of their expensive things stolen.'

'Ali Bah, you make me laugh,' Seydou answered. 'You like to think all men are bad and that Africa is the most dangerous place on earth. But this is not the truth.' Still, Seydou would make a point of seeing that Gerhart and I locked our doors when we went to bed at night. 'Just to be on the safe side,' he'd say.

I was always amazed at how, when the big wind swept in just before each rain, the birds in the palm tree managed to survive. They were small, yellow weaver-birds and their nests were round balls of woven grasses that hung by threads of grass from the palm fronds. They looked so fragile, and when the wind howled and ripped through the palm fronds, bending the tree, I was always sure that they must all be blown away. Of course occasion-

11

ally the odd one was, and sometimes even one of the coconuts would be blown down. Seydou, who lived in the room nearest the palm tree, wore charms against the possibility of one of the coconuts falling on his head. This seemed to me the extremity of caution but most people in the Gambia wear charms against many kinds of evil, such as knife wounds and snake bites, and when you consider how big a coconut is and how high it grows, if you lived beneath a palm tree it would make sense as a direct hit would surely be fatal.

I passed three weeks in Bakau before I headed inland on the trail of Mungo Park. I became involved with the place, as had Gerhart, and he had already been there for three months. But it was also very hot. Sometimes the afternoons would be so hot all one could do was lie down and sweat and I knew it would be even hotter inland. The thought of the rain and mud and mosquitoes, and the clammy heat of upriver, deterred me. The Europeans on the coast referred to upriver as 'upcountry', and to many of them it was far away, wild and to be avoided, especially at this time of year. The coast was like an island with Europe closer to it than inland Africa. An aeroplane could take you there faster than a bus could take you to the other end of the country, and with considerably less fuss. And as for such places as Mali, they were in a different universe, and the thought of the burning savannahs there made me quail. I knew that sort of heat, the sort of heat that makes crossing the road a major task, let alone traipsing off into the bush on the heels of an explorer. And so I delayed leaving, waiting either to get more acclimatized or for the rainy season to end and so the temperature to fall.

★

Ali Bah was a waiter in one of the many large tourist hotels which were on the beaches near to Bakau. His job there was only seasonal as during the long quiet season from April to October when there were few, if any, tourists, many of the hotels closed down and laid off the staff without pay. This season was referred to as 'the hungry season', though in truth the term was more to do with agriculture than the tourist industry. This was the time of year when the staple crops of the Gambia, groundnuts and millet, were planted and grew to maturity, and by the end of it the stocks of last year's harvest were running low or were even finished.

To combat this, Ali Bah had built his compound and rented out the rooms. There were eight of them and Ali Bah, his wife and young son lived in the biggest one. Ali Bah was, himself, a cheerful man who went to the nearby mosque regularly and at this time of year passed his days sitting with friends on a wooden bench beside the doorway to his compound. Whenever you came or went through the doorway he would have polite things to say to you.

'Ah, Mr Peter,' he might say, 'how was your night? I see you're going.' Or if you were coming it would perhaps be, 'So hot today, so, so hot. Yes, I see you're coming.'

His wife seemed to pass much of her day carrying water from the standpipe down the road, and his young son made himself at home in the lodgers' rooms fiddling with their possessions and chatting away to them even if, as was the case with myself whose room seemed to be of particular interest to him, they did not understand a word of the language he spoke.

In the same area as the tourist hotels which were near to Bakau, there were also a great many Western embassies, aid organizations, projects and businesses. This area was known as 'tubab land', *tubab* being the local word for 'white man', as indeed in many respects it was very like a piece of Europe transported to the coast of Africa. The buildings there were modern and often beautiful, many of them surrounded by luxurious vegetation on the cliff tops looking out over the sea. There were supermarkets, smart restaurants and bars and the roads were well paved.

Many of the people of Bakau found employment in 'tubab land' in the same way that Ali Bah did, and the rest of the rooms in Ali Bah's compound were occupied by people who had connections with it in some way or another. There were two hotel cooks and an assistant to a European dentist. There were myself and Gerhart, both of us travellers. There was Seydou who acted as a part-time guide-cum-helper-cum-friend to travellers and tourists, and there was Seydou's friend Mamadou. Mamadou was an artist who worked for a Government rural development

13

programme, drawing the picture-stories that taught illiterate peasants such things as new methods by which to grow crops. But he also made extra money designing T-shirts for tourists and selling pieces of art to them.

Although Seydou and Mamadou were close friends, they could not have been more different from each other. Where something like corruption in the Government would make Seydou angry, Mamadou would comment on it in a way that would make us all laugh. Mamadou liked the absurdity of things. When one day we heard on the radio that 'a board of managers is to create an association in alliance with members of the Government to meet each week in a newly constructed conference hall for dialogue over the situation of the retailing of foodstuffs', he laughed and said, 'Discussions. Discussions. They discuss all the time, but never do they actually *do* anything.' And when another time he came back from a conference of professors that he had been involved in because of his job, he remarked that many of the professors had got their doctorates in universities that nobody had heard of and were barely literate.

'You should have been there today,' he said to me. 'There was a lady who wore spectacles on the end of her nose and a black professor's gown draped over her shoulders as though she was the very mother of learning. She had a large black briefcase and when she opened it I saw the only things inside were a large gold pen and a hairdryer. "Madam," I said to her, "I see you have a large gold pen, but I bet you cannot even sign your name." And how furious she was,' he laughed, 'but I was not fooled by her.'

When Seydou heard Mamadou tell this story he became quite indignant. 'Those sort of people are a damn shame,' he said. 'They ought to be exposed and punished for their deceit. But they will get their due. We all have to face God in the end.'

Where Mamadou was easy-going, Seydou was very proud. He was proud of the way he had been brought up and proud of his religion, Islam. 'Each year,' he once said to me, 'in the month of Ramadan, I fast. I take no food or drink between sunrise and sunset. Towards the end of the month I am just skin and bones and can only lie on my bed and think of death. When I was only ten years old,' he continued, 'my father made me work in the docks at Banjul. He could not afford to support me and all my brothers and sisters. I had to spend the nights sleeping on the quays because my village was too far to go back to. Sometimes it was very cold. And then at the end of each month I had to give all my money to my father. In this way, I learnt to always put others before myself and to help others whenever possible. This I have not forgotten.'

Gerhart liked doing tricks. He was very good at them and could do things like put a coin into his mouth and then make it reappear behind someone's ear; or tear a banknote into many pieces and then make it whole again. He had quick, agile hands and when he did a trick he would give his audience a mischievous look and then when it was done burst into laughter. He was a natural and soon gained a reputation and people were often asking him to do one of his tricks. The Gambians were especially fascinated by his tricks because many of them believed in magic and thought that he was a magician. He did nothing to disillusion them of this but he did not cultivate it and only did his tricks occasionally, and then to people he knew well. It was only once that I saw him do a trick to two complete strangers. They were two youths who had come up to us to hustle for some money. Gerhart, to their astonishment, tore up a note, then remade it and offered it to them. They were so impressed that they did not take the money but instead passed the rest of the evening sitting by his side proclaiming him to be a very special, even holy, person.

Magic was a difficult subject between Europeans and Gambians. When somebody you know well and with whom you think you have an understanding tells you suddenly, out of the blue, that a few weeks ago he saw two boys walking along the road and one of them suddenly turned into a goat, it leaves you speechless. And when he continues by saying that a passer-by then said that the goat was his and he wanted to take it away and eat it, and the boy clung to it crying that it was his brother, until a crowd gathered and a kindly, passing holy man turned the goat back into the brother, you do not know how to react.

'But did you see this with your own eyes?' you ask, trying not to sound sceptical because your friend is telling you the story as

15

if he were describing the meal he ate yesterday. And when he replies that he did see it with his very own eyes you might wonder why this friend who you thought you knew so well was lying to you, because you do not believe in magic, or at least not in magic which is quite so obvious.

Seydou was a person like this. He used to tell us stories of magic, and he was a very good storyteller. He would create an atmosphere around his story by the way in which he told it. As he progressed, he would become more and more involved. He would be poised on the edge of his chair, his hands stretched out in front of him designing the significance of what he was saying, copying the movements of his story. His voice would become hushed at important bits, as if in respect, and then shout out the action sequences as if they were actually happening. His eyes would become fixed, as if looking at some distant place, and when he had finished he would sit back with an expression, not of satisfaction, but of awe. There were stories of people who could fly and stories of people who could turn themselves into hippopotamuses. There was a hippo hunter who could go underwater for three months at a time, and a hippo who was an evil spirit who turned himself into two beautiful women who seduced the hippo hunter and so destroyed his magic. But Seydou also liked to tell stories that were puzzles to be worked out. One of them went like this:

'Once upon a time,' he began, 'there were two men who were in love with the same beautiful young girl. The father of the girl invited the two young men to come and eat a meal with him in order to decide which of them should marry his daughter. When they had finished their meal the father said, "Whoever can pick the fruit of that tree before I finish saying this," and he indicated a tree nearby, "can marry my daughter." And immediately,' cried Seydou, flinging his arms out either side of him, 'before he had finished saying it, one of the men had already climbed the tree and picked the fruit. But the other,' and here Seydou lowered his voice dramatically, 'had plucked the whole tree out of the ground.

'Who,' he asked me as he peered intently into my eyes, 'should marry the girl?'

16

'The first man of course,' I answered. 'It was he who picked the fruit.'

But Seydou only laughed at my answer and said, 'Ah well, that could be.'

Gerhart and I used to talk about the magic that was so prevalent in Africa. Because he did tricks himself, he had a theory that magic, like tricks, was just a kind of hypnosis. You create an atmosphere that partially hypnotizes your audience in the way that the smallest things from a calm, deep voice to a back massage can put one into a minor trance, and then you make people believe they are seeing something that has not actually happened, it just seems as if it has. That is the art of doing tricks, or magic if you like. Gerhart and I would analyse and rationalize many things like this, in the way that we found being in Africa made us: there was so much here that was new and, at first, inexplicable. Nothing escaped our sceptical hammer, from the existence of God, to magic, to the ways and beliefs of people. Seydou would often be with us on these occasions but generally he would not join in as we hacked our way into the mysteries of life. He would, other than tell us his stories that gave us all the more material, sit silently, often looking a little unhappy at our talk.

Then one day Seydou suddenly stood up and shouted, 'Look, I can fly.' And blew out the candle on the table in front of us. 'Look,' he said, with defiance in his voice, 'can't you see me go out of the door with the smoke, or are you blind, blind like a man lost on a dark night?' And, with that, he marched out of the door and for the next day was in a strange, aggressive mood.

★

The strange atmosphere in Bakau of Europe and Africa trying to come to terms with each other had me in its clasp and I put off my departure day after day. I was acclimatizing, getting my feet. Mungo Park had done something similar when he first arrived in Africa. He spent five months at an English trading factory 330 kilometres up the Gambia river, waiting for the end of the rainy season, after which it was much cooler and so the best time of year in which to travel. The factory was called Pisania. Today it has disappeared but there is a monument on the site upon which it once stood in remembrance of Mungo Park, for it was from this spot that he set off on his two voyages to the Niger. There is another monument in remembrance to Mungo Park in Nigeria, near the man-made lake that now covers the rapids of Bussa, for it is at Bussa that Mungo Park met his sad and unhappy death. But Bussa is a place to which I never went. That was the end of Park's second disastrous voyage and I was following his first successful one.

Park was said to be bookish and introverted as a boy, a dreamer perhaps. His father was a tenant farmer in the borderlands of Scotland near the town of Selkirk. It was in the family home of Foulshields that he was born on 10 September 1771. Opposite Foulshields, on the far bank of the small Yarrow river that ran in the valley below the house, were the ruins of Newark Castle, a reminder of the days of Scottish and English conflict, fierce days that have shaped to some extent the hardy and proud characters of the borderlands.

This was a romantic land filled with the ballads and poems that Park so liked. Sir Walter Scott, the famous poet and novelist, was a Selkirk man and a friend of Park's. The country is a gently rolling lowland of pretty valleys and solitary moors. It was and still is sheep-farming land, and it was sheep that the Park family farmed. Their house was small, a stone cottage of three rooms, some lofts and one fireplace. There were eight children who had survived from the thirteen born to Park's mother and the whole family lived in this one small house. Not that the Parks were poor. Mungo Park's father, an upright, Calvinist Protestant, could afford to employ an instructor to live with the family and give lessons to his sons, all of whom were educated well. But it must have been a tough upbringing and one can see the young and serious-minded Mungo escaping from the cramped conditions of his home to wander on the moors, dreaming perhaps of adventure: Britain was at this time entering the Industrial Revolution and there was more affluence in the country than there had been for a long time; it was the beginning of Britain's imperialist era and a young man from the borderlands who was getting a good education must have had a desire to be a part of it.

Mungo Park's early choice of career was medicine and it was

whilst he was apprenticed to a surgeon in Selkirk that he met and went on a tour of Scotland with his brother-in-law, James Dickson, who was a botanist and wanted to collect plants. Dickson had the friendship and patronage in London, where he worked, of the by then important and influential Sir Joseph Banks. Sir Joseph was also, amongst other things, a botanist and it was in this capacity that he had travelled on Captain Cook's first voyage to Australia, an experience that not only cemented his reputation as an explorer and a scientific observer, but that also inspired him to devote much of his life to the patronage of exploration and science. He had noticed and befriended Dickson when Dickson was working as a gardener at a large nursery in London. And Dickson, having befriended Park, introduced him to Sir Joseph Banks, the man who was to give Park all that his ambitions could desire. Banks must have quickly been impressed by Mungo Park because it was not long after Park had finished studying medicine at Edinburgh University that he found him a place as assistant surgeon on an East Indiaman bound for Sumatra.

Sir Joseph Banks was the Treasurer and one of the most prominent members of the African Association, a newly founded body whose objective was to promote the discovery of the interior of Africa; its membership consisted of intellectual and influential gentlemen who had a common interest in science and exploration, inspired by Britain and Europe's new industrial wealth. The oceans of the world had by now mostly been charted and there were few lands about which there was not a good deal of knowledge. Africa was the vast and obvious exception. Just recently, parts of Ethiopia had been explored and the source of the Blue Nile had been discovered, and there was much movement into southern Africa from Cape Town by the hardy, farming Boers. With this encouragement the African Association turned its eye towards the area south of the Sahara Desert in West Africa. There was already a small and tantalizing amount of knowledge about the lands to be found here, but it was mostly rumour and hearsay: patchy and unreliable stories gleaned from people who had talked to Arab traders and travellers and to captives of many descriptions, and from the explorers and traders who had been sailing down the coast of West Africa for a long time, penetrating small distances up the rivers.

The best information to be had about these lands was that written by two of the greatest and earliest of travellers, the Arab, Al-Idris, and the Moorish Christian convert, Leo Africanus, who had visited sub-Saharan West Africa in the early twelfth and sixteenth centuries respectively. Even in their accounts, though, there was much that was confused and contradictory. There were names like Houssa, Kawkaw and Songhay, supposed to be great kingdoms or cities. There were rumours of imperial civilization, steady trade and vast quantities of gold, conflicting with those of cannibalism and sacrificial murder. And there was most importantly a great river, the Niger, but there was as much confusion about where it came from, and where it went to – some thought it joined up with the Nile, some with the Congo, some that it dried up in the desert – and, because it made a huge loop, about its course, as there was about the many peoples who lived on its banks. It was time to put all this to rights, and the African Association was looking for men to travel to the interior of West Africa to discover the truth with their own eyes.

There came a series of attempts to fulfil this ambition, mostly by men who approached West Africa from across the Sahara. All ended in near or total failure until a Major Houghton was sent to approach the area by means of the Gambia river, as Park was to do. But although Houghton managed to travel further inland than any known European before him, his notes and discoveries were lost in the silence that closed over him and his fate. And so the African Association was on the lookout for a new man at about the time Mungo Park arrived back from the trip Sir Joseph Banks had arranged for him to Sumatra, eighteen months after his departure.

Sir Joseph must have been impressed at how Park conducted himself on that voyage to choose him as the next of the African Association's employees. He had shown that he could observe and convey the results of his observations by the botanical work he did on the voyage. He was, to add to this, a seasoned traveller, unattached and of a sober and resolute character. He was twenty-four years old and, having been instructed by the African Association to explore the course and, if possible, the rise and termination of the Niger, and to use his 'utmost exertions to visit the principal towns or cities in its neighbourhood', he set sail from Portsmouth on the 22 of May 1795 and six weeks later found himself beginning his five months' wait for the end of the rainy season at Pisania, 330 kilometres up the Gambia river.

The first place Mungo Park set foot in Africa, before he sailed up the Gambia river to Pisania, was a small town called Jillifree which was 30 kilometres up the Gambia estuary on the north bank, near to the old European trading settlement of Albreda and opposite to James Island: two places that have a long history of French and British rivalry and through which many thousands of slaves passed on their way to the Americas. Although Jillifree no longer exists today, near to its old site on the banks of the Gambia river is a village called Jufureh which has become famous because it is the very village to which Alex Haley, the author of the book *Roots*, traced his ancestry. In the final episode of the film which was made of *Roots*, it is to this village that Alex Haley takes a boat from Banjul to embrace the descendant of the brother of his ancestor, Kunta Kinte, who was taken as a slave from Jufureh. The book and the film have brought Jufureh fame, and many tourists visit it. I also decided to visit it and so in the company of Seydou one day took the ferry from Banjul, across the Gambia estuary, to the town of Barra on the north bank, from where we could get a bus to the village.

★

By day the estuary of the Gambia river, seen from the beaches of Banjul, is a swathe of bright raw blue, and the far shore is often lost in the mist of fine sea spray. The sun beats down upon it and in the layer of condensed heat that wavers on its surface the cargo ships lying off Banjul's port seem to buckle.

The Gambia river, after running smoothly and quietly for nearly 1,000 kilometres from its source in the Fouta Djallon mountains of Guinea, matches its power here in the estuary against the tides of the Atlantic. For a long time, though, it will have felt the presence of the sea, for even at Georgetown, nearly 300 kilometres upstream, there is a small tide and not long after

21

this the river tastes the first of the sea salt. But in the estuary the sea prevails. The large Atlantic rollers easily breach the banks of sediment deposited at the estuary mouth. They break over them in a line of continuous surf, washing into the estuary and joining their swell with the turmoil of conflicting currents and ebbing and waning tides.

The morning that Seydou and I took the ferry across the estuary the boat was filled to, or probably well past, capacity. The passengers, as is always the case in West Africa, had a great quantity of baggage with them. They were mostly the people of the villages in the thin strip of country that runs down the far side of the river. With them they had the goods and supplies brought from Banjul to take back to their families or to sell in their local markets. There were people leading goats and pushing bicycles, and people with suitcases and calabashes. There were baskets of tomatoes and yams, and baskets of rice, millet and groundnuts. It was as if a whole market had suddenly got up and run off. Cans of Coke and oranges and small hot potatoes were for sale; money-changers hustled their trade right up to the gangplank. Some children were dressed in rags and bare feet and some dressed smartly and neatly. Every woman of the right age had a baby at the breast or swaddled to her back with a piece of material that matched the material of her dress, so the baby's little body was lost in its mother's moving form, only its head sticking out and lolling from side to side.

The ferry pulled out slowly from the port, past the tugs and barges moored at the quays which were so rusty and abandoned-looking one was surprised to see crews asleep on their decks. Banjul grew small and became lost in the curves of the coast and I stood at the prow in the sun and salty wind watching the far shore that did not seem to grow. The passengers settled down like a pie, children squabbling and playing around their mothers. I noticed some Europeans amongst the throng of people. They wore shorts and floppy hats and had small nets and binoculars in their hands. They were busy peering at patches of the sea which they pointed out to each other. They were smiling and filled with exhilaration and, I discovered later on, were the British Dragonfly Association off for a hunt in the bush on the far shore. That shore suddenly became large. The ferry overshot the quay in order to be washed down upon it by the tide. The gangplank was lowered and the passengers swept over it in a wave and dispersed to their separate destinations.

Barra, the town that Seydou and I now found ourselves in, was named after the old kingdom of Barra. Mungo Park remarks that its king was more formidable to Europeans than any other chieftain on the river. He did good trade with the peoples who lived on the higher reaches, exchanging salt panned from lagoons with them for rice. Because of the large numbers of canoes the king owned, he could extract duties of £20 on any vessel, big or small, of any nation that wished to enter his territory.

On disembarking from the bus Seydou and I took from Barra, we went first to visit the old town of Albreda. Today it was just a village, the only relics of its past being a stone warehouse and a large, iron cannon. In the middle of the village there was a tall baobab tree. Baobab trees are one of the most common trees to be found in the savannahs of West Africa and are called by some 'the upside-down tree', because they look like a tree that has been pulled up and put upside down with its roots sticking in the air. Their trunks are immensely thick, quite out of proportion to their spindly and contorted branches, and have a silvery, almost spongy bark. The one in Albreda had hundreds of weaver-bird nests hanging from its branches and was alive with their bright, yellow inmates. I saw a flock of these birds flying far out over the river whilst I was in Albreda. They flew close together in a single, tight, dark ball. The ball changed shape as it moved, thinning out at one end, bulging in the middle, transforming itself as though it was a single entity.

The people of Albreda were not very friendly. Too many tourists visited their village and those tourists made the villagers feel like artifacts in a museum as they wandered about photographing anything that took their fancy. They treated the village like a public space and so there was none of the traditional hospitality meted out to strangers here. The villagers resented the tourists, not only because of the way they behaved, but also because they were hardly profiting from them. They remained poor while the money of these, to them, immensely rich people went to Western tourist agencies and the Gambian Tourist Office. They were not,

I discovered, even allowed to rent their boats out to take people to nearby James Island. Only one man had permission to do this and he had to charge a set and expensive fee, 80 per cent of which went to the Tourist Office.

I saw a tour arrive whilst I was in the village and it was a pitiful sight. The villagers swarmed around the camera-clad tourists trying to sell wooden sculptures or simply begging for money. But the tourists already had too many wooden sculptures and by now had ceased to give money away to beggars so ignored them or brushed them aside, like flies.

The same sort of fawning abjection took place in Jufureh. Here the villagers also held a grievance against Alex Haley who was the reason the tourists came to their village. He, they claimed, had not done enough to help the village: he should have done much to improve the conditions there. Tourism had ruined these two villages. The people were aggressive and discontented, the order and harmony of their lives broken down by too blunt a contact with Westerners.

There was one old woman in Jufureh, though, who was happy about the tourists. She was the descendant of the brother of Alex Haley's ancestor, Kunta Kinte. In the yard outside her house she had a large shaded area where there were many benches and it was to here that the tourist pilgrimage led. The old woman had a photograph of herself with Alex Haley and another that she told the tourists was of Kunta Kinte, although in fact it was only of the man who acted Kunta Kinte in the film of *Roots*. She related with great pride the story of how Kunta Kinte and her ancestor, his brother, were collecting firewood near the village one night when some slavers abducted him. She then held out her hand for tips. 'Give her nothing,' was Seydou's advice when my turn came to give something. 'These people are bad people and deserve nothing.'

★

The days passed remarkably quickly in Bakau and so the rainy season began to draw to an end. There would be longer periods between the downpours and sometimes, for whole days, lightning could be seen flickering on the horizon, moving from one part of it to another, circling around, but never coming closer. Sometimes it was sheet-lightning flashing across the bottom of the clouds, but at others great cracks stabbed the earth like jagged pieces of glass. Between the downpours the temperature would rise steadily until everybody was sitting on the edge of their seats and then, for a short time, when the rain came with a sudden, deafening *swoosh*, it would become even more humid as the water turned to vapour on the baked earth. The thunder would roll around the town and out over the sea like somebody rolling an empty drum down a cobbled alleyway and soon the storm drains down the sides of the streets would flow in torrents and pour out into open spaces to form temporary ponds. When it rained the electricity would be cut off as transformer boxes fused and smouldered, and at night-time the transformer centre in Bakau would look like a fireworks display with trails of sparks leaping high into the air. Then people would gather around candles in their homes and at the bars as water leaked through their roofs.

I had been making enquiries about the possibility of going upriver by boat as Mungo Park had done, but it was a bad time of year for this. There was no commercial traffic on the river at the moment with which I could perhaps hitch a lift because the crops of millet and groundnuts that the barges transported had not yet been harvested. The one ferry boat that had used to run between the town of Basse Santa Su, far at the other end of the country, and Banjul had sunk a few years previously, and the tourist cruises had not yet started business. This left me with the option of renting a fishing boat, but after many and protracted enquiries I discovered that no fisherman was prepared to take me any distance upriver for a price I could contemplate. I would have, instead, to take a bus.

The evening before I was to leave the coast Seydou took me to see a spectacle that Mungo Park had also witnessed, shortly after he had set off inland from Pisania. It was a kind of traditional wrestling that had been and still was popular amongst the Wolof and Mandingo tribes of Senegal and the Gambia, and it took place in Serecunda in an arena inside of which were three rows of benches encircling a large patch of sand.

An integral part of the wrestling was drumming, performed

here by three groups of Wolof drummers. They started playing a long time before the wrestlers arrived. They held their wooden drums between their legs and waddled around the circle of benches literally drumming money out of the audience by stopping in front of people and raising their tempo to such a high crescendo that the spectators were embarrassed into giving them something.

A few beggars had got past the ticket man and also went around the audience asking for money. One of them had no arms so bobbed his head back and forth to indicate the people from whom he was begging. His face was a toothless grin and he fixed you with his glinting eyes without saying a word until you gave him something. Then he bent his torso forwards as though he was bowing so you could tuck your offering into his shirt pocket. Another man was deformed in such a way that he could only walk sideways; he shuffled around the audience like a cardboard cut-out.

The wrestlers appeared slowly. They were well-built young men, naked except for a coarse pair of pants with colourful ropes and tassels tied about the waist. Their skins were oiled to a high and glossy shine, and they strutted about the fighting area flexing their muscles and puffing out their chests. Each one of them was a champion, each one unbeatable. They held themselves exaggeratedly erect and their chins they pointed high.

In the end there were about twenty wrestlers and now and again two of them would choose each other for a fight. They would circle around, staring intently into each other's eyes, but then break off and stride away with an air of disdain as if saying, 'He's not good enough for me.' Gradually, however, small skirmishes began to break out. The object was to throw one's opponent to the ground on his back. The best way to do this was to lift him up high and then dash him to the earth, but in order to do this one had to get a good hold. Much of the fight was therefore devoted to a grappling of the hands in order to find this hold or to ward off the other's advances. They would, after a short time, lock together, their heads pressing against each other like rutting rams. They would get themselves into tight knots, their arms and legs entwined, each one straining in the strategy of movements that if successful could break the other's hold. They could be locked together in these stalemates for long periods, their bodies streaming with sweat and their feet grinding up a cloud of dust as they twirled slowly round and round like dancers at a ball; then, if the stalemate went on too long, they would break off again.

Soon the couplings became more frequent until there were three or four going at one time. Some fights were fast and spectacular but many were of the slower, more strategic kind. The first man to be thrown was small and lightweight. His challenger quickly found his holds and then lifted him up high above his head like a modern-day Samson and dashed him to the ground. Then the audience leapt to their feet shouting and whistling, wild with excitement, and the victor made a round of the arena with a group of drummers. He danced and pounded his feet and flexed his muscles to their rhythms and spectators threw him money.

The fights went on for an hour. Occasionally there were disputes about who the winner of a bout was. Then the referee would come over and decide, but often the defeated person would not agree and do a victory round all the same.

There was another spectacle that Mungo Park witnessed that I also saw in my time in Bakau. This was a ritual the name of which, because of Park's description of it in his book, has become a phrase in the English language. It is 'Mumbo Jumbo' and it was a ritual that Mungo Park describes as being 'an indecent and unmanly revel'. The Kafirs – an Arabic word meaning unbeliever and referring to those who have not taken the religion of Islam – of the villages, Park writes, on account of being able to have as many wives as they wished, often had matrimonial problems and Mumbo Jumbo was invented to deal with these problems. The husband would dress himself in a masquerade habit made of tree bark and arm himself sternly with a rod. He would announce his coming to the assembled villagers by loud and dismal screaming in the woods nearby and when it was dark appear before them. Up until midnight everybody would sing and dance, all the women, Park points out, nervous because it was never known whose husband it was behind the mask of Mumbo Jumbo. At midnight the woman who had been causing matrimonial problems was seized, stripped naked, tied to a post and severely beaten with Mumbo Jumbo's rod. It was the women in the audience, Park again points out, who shouted their derision the loudest at the unfortunate victim.

Although this practice may well still go on in some of the more remote and traditional villages, in Bakau where I just caught a glimpse of it when returning home one evening, Mumbo Jumbo was a dance for entertainment only. Many men had dressed themselves in the tree bark and mask of Mumbo Jumbo and the dancing and singing went on far beyond midnight with no woman being so 'inhumanely scourged'.

★

There is a good tarmacked road beside the river from the coast of the Gambia to the town of Basse Santa Su at the other end of the country. On leaving the coast my intention was to go to Georgetown, 300 kilometres upcountry on an island in the middle of the river called MacCarthy Island. By boat it would have taken me two or three days to reach Georgetown. By road it would take me five or six hours. This was a depressingly short time.

On the day of my departure Seydou and I found a taxi in the nearby town of Serecunda that was going to Soma from where I could get a bus to Georgetown. It was a Peugeot with three rows of seats for nine passengers. As it was not ready to depart immediately, Seydou and I went off to get something to eat. When we came back, as was Seydou's habit, he insisted on carrying my bag. On arriving at the taxi, however, we found that the place I had reserved in the front seat was occupied by another man.

'Excuse me, mister,' Seydou said to the man. 'My friend here was the first person to buy a ticket for the taxi and he has reserved this place.' The man gave Seydou a blank look and continued sitting where he was. 'Excuse me, mister,' Seydou said again. 'I ask you politely to let my friend here sit in this seat he reserved.'

Still the man ignored him. And so again, even though I had by now indicated to Seydou that I was quite willing to sit somewhere else, Seydou said, 'Mister, I say this place is reserved. It is not right for you to stay sitting there.' The man mumbled something irritably under his breath and turned around to say something to a large and wealthy-looking businessman who was sitting in the seat behind him.

'What are you causing trouble for, anyway?' the businessman said sharply. 'Who are you, this person's slave? You carry his bag for him, you do his dirty work for him. I thought the days of slavery were over.'

The word 'slave' had a dramatic effect on Seydou. He suddenly became quite demented with rage and screamed back at the man, 'A slave, a slave! You, you fat slob, it is you who are the slave, the slave of money. You, look at you, look at your age, you should know better by now than to behave like this, but you don't because you are a slave of greed,' and he continued to abuse him in this way.

The businessman, at first a little taken aback, just chuckled with his friends in the taxi, but soon he was angry and sneered back at Seydou. He got out of the car, heaving his bulk off the seat, and attempted to grab hold of him. But there were a great many people crowding around now, laughing and enjoying this spectacle, and they kept the two apart.

'Come here, you urchin, I'll teach you a lesson your father should have taught you,' the fat man shouted, as Seydou continued to abuse him.

Meanwhile, the taxi was hastily being prepared for departure. When all was ready, and after I had completely failed to make any impression on Seydou to calm down, I was told to get into the taxi, the fat man was pushed back into his seat, and we departed, the two antagonists still shouting at each other so I never had the chance to say goodbye to Seydou. This scene seemed to me too sad. Seydou always insisted on being helpful to everyone as he had been taught as a boy and as his religion dictated. But this was not such an easy thing to do here on the coast. Things were different here because of the presence of so many tourists and help could so easily be seen as subservience, so when Seydou was called a slave it hurt him because he knew this. Everybody had laughed at his outburst and now I could see him going off with his hurt and confusion and shame.

Had I done wrong, I thought to myself, to befriend Seydou and use him in the way I had so often done? Just before we got back to the taxi I had given him some money in payment for all the help he had given me. He had accepted the money and perhaps it was this recognition of the fact that his helpfulness was not so pure after all, at least not pure enough for him, that had triggered his outburst.

This was the coast of Gambia, a place, by means of a cheap aeroplane ticket, dangerously close to the bare facts of an entirely different culture, a place that is confused and different from the lands I was now following Mungo Park to in the interior of West Africa.

II

Upcountry

MUNGO PARK SAILED gently up the Gambia river and I sped along the adjacent road towards Georgetown. Because of the argument that Seydou had had with the fat businessman who had called him a slave on my departure from Serecunda, the atmosphere in the taxi was tense, not to say unfriendly. The passengers fell into a morose silence and the man next to me on the front seat, the same man who had started the whole incident by taking my reserved place, slept for the better part of the journey, swaying like a pendulum between the window on which he hit his head each time and my lap into which he would have subsided had I not elbowed him back towards the window.

At first the countryside was lush and fertile, as at the coast: a tangle of trees and creepers and palms of many types, interspersed with patches of tall, yellow grasses or impenetrable bushes. There were flowers and flowering trees such as the red silk cotton tree, the tallow and sausage tree, and the symphonia. In the air there were butterflies and bees and many birds, one kind of which, the great red bishop, was of such a startling, almost fluorescent, red you could hardly believe it was not man-made: it perched like a Christmas decoration on top of tall stalks of dry grass.

We passed many villages beside the road. They consisted mostly of traditional round mud huts with thatch, but occasionally there was a modern rectangular house with a corrugated iron roof that glinted in the sunlight. In the middle of each village would be a tall tree such as a baobab or a red silk cotton tree under which old men sat. Beside the villages would be small plantations of bananas and in them a few pawpaw trees with clutches of their succulent fruits hanging from their tatty heads.

Also in each village was a pump above which was a metal sign that told you it had been installed by the Government of Kuwait. Women worked at the levers of some of these pumps and others

33

carried buckets of water back to their houses. At a little distance from the villages there were clearings in the bush in which were planted crops of millet, cassava or groundnuts, and sometimes one caught sight of herds of cattle making their slow, methodical way through the countryside with young men with sticks in their hands at their heels. In and around the villages were goats and pigs and chickens, and sometimes groups of schoolchildren carrying satchels appeared on the road from invisible pathways in the tall grasses that grew beside it, or, as we approached, disappeared down them like magic. Sometimes when we passed groups of these children the boys danced little jigs, thrusting their hips at us. But because we were never very far from the river, which here was still salty and tidal, we occasionally came across mangrove swamps and had to skirt them or cross them by means of causeways. They were dull and drab-looking, the mangrove swamps, the mud banks revealed at half-tide with the coarse, tangled bushes standing high above them on long, black roots like spiders' legs. In one of these mangrove swamps we crossed the Bintang creek, further down which was the town of Bintang, an old Portuguese trading settlement which Mungo Park had visited on his way upriver.

It was late at night by the time I arrived in Georgetown, having exchanged my taxi for a bus that afternoon. The town was dark and silent, tall trees shading it from the moonlight. A policeman with whom I walked the short distance from the ferry which brought passengers to MacCarthy Island led me to the commissioner's guesthouse where he told me I would be able to stay. We passed along wide avenues and across open spaces that were like pools of darkness into which you stepped blindly. The buildings were well spread out, large and old, and only the occasional light was visible, watery and yellow-looking in the hot, humid air; dogs bayed in the distance. There were no people except for the nightwatchman and his wife whom we saw at the commissioner's residence and with whom I waited fifteen minutes whilst the policeman kindly went in search of the guardian of the guesthouse.

The nightwatchman was old. He had stripped off most of his clothes because of the heat, revealing his thin, leathery torso. He sat on an iron bedstead, occasionally raising a straw fan in his hand to wave away the swarms of mosquitoes that hummed about him; when I arrived he gave the straw fan to me. Sitting next to the nightwatchman was his wife, as old and leathery as himself. The two of them sat staring at the dark, silent building before them, spasmodically saying things to each other and sometimes breaking into laughter. Then the old woman, her eyes watering from mirth, crinkled up her face to reveal her toothless gums, and the old man, with heaving chest, raised his hand up and down on his knee like a puppet.

★

Georgetown, after the old colonial capital of Bathurst, had once been the most important British settlement in the Gambia. Throughout the early nineteenth century the British had increased their influence further and further up the Gambia river, trading with the many small, local kingdoms. Then, in 1823, shortly after a protectorate was declared over the area of British influence, a fort called Fort George was built on MacCarthy Island. Gradually the settlement had grown into an important administrative and trading centre and in it a mission school was established. This school evolved into the famous chiefs' school, a boarding school exclusively for the sons of Gambian chiefs. Today this school has become the Armitage High School, the only secondary boarding school in the Gambia.

The Gambia became a full crown colony in 1888 and then, after seventy-seven years of colonial rule, gained its independence in 1965. Since then Georgetown has gradually slipped into its age of retirement. It has the Armitage High School and it is still an administrative centre, but these are about the only two distinctions left to it. Today, the river in whose stream it sits has been made virtually redundant by the construction of the through-Gambia road. The traffic of river trade upon which the town once thrived now speeds along this road, bypassing MacCarthy Island to which there is no bridge. Its wharfs and warehouses, and many of its trading shops, are closed and empty; the old colonial buildings are gradually decaying, the corrugated iron roofs brown from rust, the deep verandahs unswept and broken in places, and the large cool rooms empty but for the odd steel desk and a bored civil servant. In fact the town is as peaceful as a town can be, drawing on the harmony and simplicity of what is little more than village life, housed in the elegance of colonialism, untroubled by the press and haste of a more modern Africa.

I met a young man called Soso in Georgetown. I had been sitting on the river bank one evening, watching people washing themselves and their clothes. Or rather I had been sitting in one of the few places that was clear of vegetation when a group of men came to wash there. Every evening many people came down to the river to wash. The women would go to one place and the men to another and they would all unabashedly strip naked then cover themselves with soap suds and meticulously scrub every part of their anatomies before dunking themselves in the water.

The sun was beginning to set and an old man paddling a small dugout boat had just passed in front of me when Soso appeared at my side. He introduced himself and said that he had been looking for me because he was the brother of a friend of Seydou's whose address Seydou had given me.

'Seeing as my brother is not here at the moment,' Soso said to me, 'I will be your friend instead because I know that he would wish me to do that.' He sat down beside me and began to talk to me with great earnestness.

'I am a journalist,' he said. 'I used to work for the government, but they did not like me so now I have become a journalist.'

'For the local newspaper?'

'No, no, I have no work.'

'It must be hard to get a job, I suppose,' I said.

'Ha,' Soso went on, 'you know nothing. You foreigners know nothing. But I will tell you.' And lowering his voice, he crouched down as if this would make him less noticeable. 'They are bad and corrupt, oh, so corrupt. I can tell you so much ... but only because you are a foreigner. You I can trust. There are so many spies.' There was a long silence during which we both looked at the river.

'Yes,' he continued thinly at last, 'they are all corrupt from the ministers down. Everybody is corrupt and scared. No one can say anything or he would lose his job. Yes, lose his job or even go to prison, and bad things can happen to a person in prison here.'

Soso explained that the villages around here had used to get two crops of rice a year, one grown in the wet season and one grown in the dry season, irrigated by pumps. 'It was the Europeans who gave the villagers those pumps, but now all the pumps have broken and the money to fix them has been taken by the very men who are supposed to maintain them. Now the villagers only get one crop a year. Oh, so corrupt.'

Soso continued talking in this fashion, speaking with an urgency that belied the tranquillity of our surroundings. He told me many stories, becoming more and more excited until he would suddenly laugh as though embarrassed.

'The people are powerless. There is talk of democracy, but what a joke. We Africans cannot know democracy. We only know fear and intimidation by men who are corrupt. They keep us like slaves and we cannot understand why you foreigners keep supporting them with your money. Look, look at this,' he said, rooting around in his pocket and taking out an old newspaper cutting. It was the story of a representative of an African country answering questions in the United Nations about loans. 'We know why the African nations are always coming here to ask for loans,' an American delegate said to the representative, 'because all of their presidents are corrupt.' In answer the representative cleverly replied, 'Not all African presidents are corrupt, and not all corrupt presidents are African.'

'You see,' said Soso, excitedly, when I had read this, 'the foreigners know the truth, but still they go on supporting our evil regimes. This I cannot understand.'

Here Soso finished and simply got up and left. He had performed what he thought was a duty. He wished to express his and his people's grievances to the outside world, and I was a representative of it. As he walked off his step seemed a little lighter as though he was relieved of a burden. I never saw Soso again because the following morning I crossed the river to a very different set-up.

★

It was full moon upstream and quiet in the camp except for the sound of the electricity generator coming from Georgetown across the river. 'It'll break down soon,' the German sailor called Peter, sitting opposite me, predicted as the sound fluctuated, and sure enough, within half an hour, it had stopped.

'Ah, well,' he exclaimed, 'you don't need electricity on a moon-lit night like tonight.'

We sat slapping mosquitoes, some of which burst into smears of our own blood. 'Painting the walls,' Peter said and then went over to the fridge to get two more cans of beer. We poured the beer into our glasses and as we drank them Peter slipped into nostalgia about his cutter: 'A fine, handsome craft built in 1904, a real sea-going vessel she was, not built for speed and only speed, not like these modern yachts which have no need to face a real sea, always forecasting the weather the way they can nowadays and dashing into the nearest port at the first sign of a storm. During the war she was used up near Scapa Flow,' he continued, 'to make special deliveries. Now she is sitting rotting in a creek down near Banjul. But I'll fix her up again, and when I've finished my work here I'll travel again and then before I'm too old I'll sell her in England in her birthplace at Lyme Regis. There's an old shipbuilder there who remembers her.'

Once Peter began to talk, like one of the old tall ships under full sail, he did not easily stop. He talked of his travels with his dog and boat when he had been a young man, about how once when he was down and out and penniless he had gone into a bar and a sailor had said that he looked as if he needed some money and so gave him a hundred pesetas. He had gone upstairs, paid for a shower, some soap and a towel, later in the evening met a pretty girl and the next day found a job fixing up somebody's boat. 'Fate is a strange thing,' he remarked. The mosquitoes were bothering him and he hunted them around the oil lamp on the table between us. We talked of Africans. 'They cannot organize, be responsible,' he said, 'they only sit around soaking up my money.' He was trying to run a tourist camp and was frustrated because it was difficult to import Europe to Africa. 'The Gambians are a lazy people, and the

38

funny thing is, I have been here so long I too have become lazy. It's the heat.' He chuckled.

Later on we went in his launch across the river to Georgetown because it was Saturday night and there was a dance. But first we went to the only bar in town and drank a few more beers in the company of the Armitage High School Headmaster and a few of the teachers who frequented the place. By the time we went back to the camp the moon had set and there was the rose of dawn on the horizon. The river had a blanket of mist on its surface that was rising in trails and wisps to hang from the trees and forests on the river banks that were already awake.

I passed a number of days staying at Peter's camp when I left Georgetown. It was on the other side of the river, on the north bank, near a village. The camp was constructed along traditional village lines: it had many thatched, round mud huts and a tall grass wall encircling it. Peter had taken great pains to build it and had done a good job because he was a boat-builder and knew much about carpentry. In a way it was as if he had not left the sea. He had just moored himself temporarily, even if it was for many years, at its side in a place where it penetrated inland. The camp was organized efficiently and tidily, like the deck of a ship. Behind it was forest and before it was the river, Peter's lifeline to the sea, and on the river was moored the launch in which he gave tours to the tourists who came to his camp.

The first two days at the camp had been very peaceful, Peter and I and Peter's staff having it all to ourselves. Peter had a second-in-command, called Boaleng, to whom he left much of the organization of the camp and so, when on the third day some tourists arrived, it had been up to Boaleng to welcome them and install them in the huts. Boaleng was a helpful and cheerful person so it was not long before the tourists were relaxed and standing beside the river sighing, taking deep breaths of its air and remarking that this after all was where paradise was to be found. That evening, whilst Peter took the tourists to Georgetown to see some traditional dancing that he had organized, I sat talking to Boaleng, or rather I sat listening to him tell me all his problems. He was Ghanaian and, as Ghanaians tend to be, he was a very intense character. Everything in his life was dire and dramatic and he sat close to me, hunched up over an oil lamp, talking to me as if we were fellow conspirators. 'I have had many problems with juju,' he said. 'All through my life people have used bad juju against me because they are jealous of me. One has to be so careful because, you know, the world is full of bad people.

'I left my home in Ghana many, many years ago. One time I had a job on a fishing boat in Ivory Coast and one night when I was alone in the engine room, all of a sudden, the engines turned off. Nobody was there to turn them off, they just went off of their own accord. I was left in total darkness. And then, suddenly, a plank flew off the wall and hit my leg. My leg was badly wounded and soon it began to grow. It grew and grew until it was this thick': he indicated something the size of a tree stump. 'Oh, the pain,' Boaleng cried. 'It was terrible, and because my leg was so big I, of course, lost my job.'

'But why were people so jealous of you?'

'Why, indeed,' Boaleng replied. 'Because I was such a good worker, of course. They hated me because I worked so hard.' And he told me another similar story, but this time it was his thumb which, having been pierced by a fish bone, lost him his job. 'My thumb,' he said, 'fell off. It went bad with the juju poison and fell off. This one here,' he said, showing me his left thumb, 'is a brand new one. It took four months to grow.'

Boaleng had ended up coming to the Gambia to look for work but was promptly thrown in jail for having no official travel papers and no money to give to the police. When he was later released he had sought out Peter whom he had heard of. He asked him for a job and Peter, having paid for his permit to stay in the country, employed him at the camp.

'Peter is my saviour,' Boaleng said with passion. 'I will serve him well, so well. I will not steal from him and I will stay with him for ever, even though it is so hard. These Gambians are ignorant people and give me so much trouble. Oh yes, they try to use their magic against me as well. They are thieves and they know that I know all about their thieving. But they do not scare me. No, they do not scare me.' But hunched in the glow of the oil lamp, Boaleng had a furtive air about him. The yellow glow revealed him to the darkness, to the pressing African night and the fears it holds for the stranger. His face glowed with sweat but whether it was the sweat of his fears or of the hot night only he knew.

On my fourth day at Peter's camp I had my first opportunity to see something of the Gambia river from the deck of a boat. Peter took the tourists who had arrived the day before on a day cruise on his launch and I went with them.

We set off early in the morning, heading downstream. The river was fresh and pale blue at this hour, the greenery on either side of it dwarfed by the wide expanse of sky that had not yet shrunk with the rising of the sun. In no time at all the camp and Georgetown had disappeared with the curve of the river as it swung to the south, to the tapering end of MacCarthy Island, after which it joined its other half and swelled to a kilometre wide. Floating down the middle of the stream, other than the thumping of the launch motor, there was silence and peace. This was a private, secluded place far from any roads or towns or even villages: the river was a little-frequented highway into a world of thick riverine forest; there were no fishing boats and no barges and the villages were out of sight, far back from the banks of the river on land that could be more easily cultivated, as if they too knew that the river, here at least, was the domain of nature.

As we drew nearer to the river banks they grew: grew and came to life. The vegetation hung heavy and chaotic over the water: a desperate struggle of the old and the new, the rotting and the fresh, for sunlight and a taste of the river. There were tall and ancient trees hung with mosses and lichen, a press of secondary growth clamouring at their trunks. Black meshes of root and thorny bush clawed at the muddy river banks and, stretching out before them, hovering only a few inches above the water's surface, were mangroves with their odd, selected shoots dipped into the water like straws. Palms thrust their heads above bushes and smaller trees; trunks and branches as big as trunks, fallen and rotting, sometimes lay quite far out into the river's current with eddies of water swirling about their tips and barrages of flotsam collecting against their sides. And over

41

everything, save the palms, grew creepers: strangling, suffocating, knotting their muscle about the living and dying forest.

This was primary forest, as yet untouched by the axe. It droned to the noise of its insect life and it clamoured to the song of its birds. For long stretches of it the small, round nests of weaver-birds hung from every available branch or twig that kept them over the water and so out of the reach of landbound predators: the swarms of busy yellow birds hovered about them or clung to them weaving in new pieces of grass with such care and dexterity it was tragic to see the number that had fallen and floated off with the current. Perched atop high trees were buzzards, and swaying far above the forest on thermals of air were a few black-and-white vultures. In one of the dank creeks we gingerly ventured into, parting the canopy of branches overhead, I saw some of the great red bishop birds, their startling colours breaking the monotony of heavy greens. In the trees we saw troops of black-and-white colobus monkeys launching themselves from tree to tree as though they were trying to fly, and there were troops of smaller, chattering monkeys that grew frantic with excitement at our approach.

We lunched at midday far downstream opposite a small island that was a nesting colony for black-headed herons and great white egrets. These two tall, long-necked fishing birds covered every inch of the island with themselves and their large, messy nests. They were edgy and aggressive at our proximity. They thrust out their necks, fluttered their wings and cackled and screeched their warnings. The day by now was burning hot; the sky small, sucked into the orb of the sun; the forest formless and shapeless with no contrasting shades, closed in upon itself like a book; and the river glittered cruelly like steel or broken glass. And so it was, in this torpid primeval world, that we dined on the shaded deck of the launch in great style: a small pocket of absurd incongruity, sipping cool beers and nibbling at an array of delicious meats and salads.

The motor back upstream was much slower due to the contrary current. In the middle of the afternoon we stopped at the small riverside port of Kuntour where the tourists were supposed to meet their minibus and their bags to go back to the coast. But there was no minibus and a long wait did not help it appear.

Because of this delay we motored back home with the dying day. The river again became friendly with the reflected colours of the sky, now flushed with the declining sun. The river banks spilt their shadows across the water and again revealed their deep and secretive insides. There were turtles in the river who dove at our sides and as the evening set flocks of great white egrets flew down the river towards their nesting island. They flew in loose and wavering lines, sometimes barely inches above the surface of the water. They held their long necks cocked back and they trailed their long legs behind.

You would see a whole line of them approaching, swaying and rippling on the surface of the river, then rising as they neared the launch, passing large and clear overhead only to shrink again until they were just a shimmering ribbon of white, then just broken and drifting movement, and then nothing.

The tourists' minibus had somehow been lost. There was talk of an argument that the driver had had with a ferryman and there were unspoken thoughts about the value of all the tourists' luggage, let alone the minibus itself, and the fact that Senegal was only 20 or so kilometres away.

When we arrived back at the camp the tourists looked confused. They needed showers and changes of clothes. Their sunburns were in need of creams. Pills had to be taken. Where were their toothpastes and toilet rolls, their books and diaries, their fly sprays and perfumes? Most of them wore only shorts and T-shirts and the mosquitoes were beginning to descend.

They stood around at first, looking awkward and lost, laughing nervously but saying nothing about the true nature of the situation. 'If you have to get marooned, this is not a bad place for it,' one man remarked weakly. 'We're not marooned, silly,' his wife replied. 'The driver's probably just gone to visit his girlfriend.' Everyone laughed. Soon the night came and so did a storm. It came with a great rush of wind, then thunder and lightning and the downpour. Everybody gathered in the big round bar house, huddled, cosy and close around oil lamps.

Now the tourists were happy. There was an air of camaraderie. They could and would cope and the storm was thrilling and strong. In each flash of lightning the river could be seen as though in daylight, its brown, troubled surface hopping and hissing with millions of particles of water, and swelling like a sea.

An hour after the rain stopped a boat arrived from Georgetown with the tourists' bags. The minibus was apparently stuck in mud somewhere further upcountry, its gear box now ruined by the driver's efforts to dislodge it. The bags had been transferred to a taxi and taken to Georgetown. The tourists could not suppress their relief and, as the mosquitoes once again descended with a new and fierce vigour, we escaped under the mosquito nets on our beds.

All the following day the tourists had to wait. In the afternoon the minibus was towed into camp by a tractor. The driver looked tired and nervous, but he need not have been because the tourists displayed towards him the same goodwill and gentleness they had shown throughout the trip. They crowded around him sympathizing and cheering him up. It was not until the following morning that their guide eventually took the decision to hire alternative transport and in the early hours the tourists left, all looking much stronger and more confident for the adventure they had had, and not upset that their itinerary was now in disarray.

The following day I, too, left the camp to walk to the village of Karantaba Tenda which was beside the old site of Pisania, and a monument to Mungo Park some 20 kilometres upriver.

★

Karantaba literally means 'the tree under which the Koran is learnt'. This refers to the central place to be found in many villages, generally in the shade of some big tree, where young boys attend Koranic school conducted by a holy man, or marabout, or one of the mosque elders to learn Arabic and study the holy Koran, the Islamic bible.

Being a wharf town, Karantaba Tenda was somewhat different from the rest of the villages in the neighbourhood as it was cosmopolitan and had the structure of an old riverside trading post. Guineans and Senegalese as well as Gambians of the Mandingo and Wolof tribes lived here, and there were old warehouses and many merchants' stores and a small pier. Of course today, as with all the old wharf towns, there was little trade in which to indulge and so the warehouses were mostly disused and many of the merchants had left. In the groundnut harvesting season, however, there was still a small amount of trade because barges stopped off here on the way down to Banjul. Karantaba Tenda also had the advantage of holding the area's weekly market, so there still remained the slight air of a town about it.

It had been the cook at Peter's camp who happened to be the son of the headman, or Alkaid, of Karantaba Tenda who had found a guide to take me there. The guide was a boy about fifteen years old who called himself James. He was an intelligent lad who, one could see, had higher ambitions than being a guide. He was from Georgetown and the direction he wanted to go in was not east to the villages but west to the coast and the big towns. He was reluctant to accept this employment and I was reluctant to employ him but, having difficulty in finding a guide at all, I had no choice, so I offered him a wage that was persuasive.

The walk had been hard and had taken most of the day. My rucksack was too heavy and the day was very hot, but I had stepped ahead, inspired by the thought that I was now truly on the heels of Mungo Park, often leaving James trailing far behind.

For much of the time we were alone on small paths and tracks and it was not until late in the day that we again met the river which had been on a deep southern loop before coming north again towards Karantaba Tenda. But even here the river was not accessible. I was over-heated and sweaty and ready for a swim, but the path ran behind the wall of impenetrable vegetation that hugged the bank and did not break until it reached the town. Along this path at one point we had come face to face with a crocodile. It had immediately dived for the river, being terrified of humans, as the few crocodiles and hippopotamuses who remain on the river have become after their history of persecution.

On arrival in Karantaba Tenda I found and introduced myself to the Alkaid. An Alkaid, Mungo Park states in his book, is a chief magistrate whose office is hereditary, and whose business is to preserve order, to levy duties on travellers, and to preside at all conferences in the exercising of local jurisdiction and the administration of justice. Today the role of the Alkaid, although of less importance due to the creation of a nation with its own laws and officials, is much the same. He is the village headman and he is empowered by law to collect the village taxes and to judge small, local disputes. The way in which these disputes are judged is by calling together the village elders and holding what is known as a 'palaver', from the old Portuguese *palavra*, where each side of the case is heard and a judgment reached. Any important criminal case has to go to the district court that comes to the villages on market day. The palavers, or courts, Park says, relied in his day much upon the laws of *Alsharia* that are contained in the Koran. This gave rise to Muslims making it their business to be professional advocates of that law. And, Park continues, 'in the forensic qualifications of procrastination and cavil, and the arts of confounding and perplexing a cause, these advocates are not always surpassed by the ablest pleaders in Europe'.

The Alkaid of Karantaba Tenda was old, not that his wits had lessened with his age. He was a small man with a round, mobile face and wore a long gown and a pair of yellow moroccan slippers. He lived in a large compound or family homestead with four wives and fifteen children, although they were not all present at that time. When I had told him about my acquaintance with his son, the cook back at Peter's camp, he had to think a minute in order to place him. 'Ah yes, that one,' he said, eventually, 'he left long ago. Yes, that one was a clever one, I knew he would go far.'

The compound consisted of two long earthen buildings split into many small rooms, each with a doorway on to the central yard and another out back to a washing area. There was a well and one large wicker chair that was like the Alkaid's throne and upon which he insisted I sat.

Everything in the compound was dirty and in a bad state of repair. Some of the rooms had partially fallen in and the walls around it were constructed from old pieces of corrugated iron and odds and ends of rotting wood. Children and women came and went and sat by cooking pots, and I was introduced to a man dressed in only the rags of trousers who was the Alkaid's eldest son, the next in line for his title. He was very friendly and told me that this day was a happy one for him, not only because I had come, but also because his wife had given birth to a son a few hours before, a sheep of his had given birth to a lamb and only the day before yesterday his horse had produced a foal.

I passed three days staying with the Alkaid, who not only insisted that I make use of his wicker chair but also gave up his large iron bed for me to sleep in. Each morning I would sit for a while with him in his compound and we would make polite and flattering remarks to each other. He would tell me bits and pieces about Mungo Park because, as the Alkaid of the nearest village to Pisania, he saw himself as an authority on the subject. Generally he got Park mixed up with the European traders who had been here at that time and told me stories of him collecting ivory and mediating in various disputes between local tribes. When he found out that I had Park's book with me he became defensive and said, not understanding that the book had actually been written *by* Park, that many incorrect things had been written about him but it was only he, the Alkaid, who knew the real truth.

'You see,' he said to me, 'we have a big tradition of history, us Gambians. We may not write it all down like you Europeans but our history is here.' He tapped his head. 'For example,' he continued, 'near to here is a large, old tree. When Mungo Park came back to the Gambia a second time he got some of the local people to dig under that tree. They had to dig for most of the day until the hole was very deep, and then they found a large jar. But before they could open the jar Mungo Park took it away from them and put it on his boat which was on the river nearby. Nobody knew what was in that jar but our history relates the time that Mungo Park hid that jar under the tree on his first trip to the Gambia.

'And you know what was in that jar?' he asked. 'Gold and diamonds were in that jar, and this is something you won't find in that book of yours. The history of Mungo Park is very interesting. I have much I can tell you about it, yes, very much,' but he did not go on to tell me. History was a possession, a closely guarded heirloom passed down from centuries ago. In it facts became fables and those fables became truths. It was not something to be so easily given away.

We would sit in his yard discussing matters in this fashion, watching his family going about their daily chores of washing, cleaning and cooking. There was one child, a boy of about three years old, who was badly emaciated. The child spent most of his time wailing feebly and wandering aimlessly about the yard. His head, with its deep, dark eyes, looked big on his thin, naked body. He would sometimes just stand still for long periods, snivelling and looking curiously and expectantly about him, mucus running freely from his nose and faeces running down his legs. The Alkaid was gentle with him and often hugged and patted him and sat him on his lap as if it was this and not a doctor that the child needed: there were a great many children in the family, a great many in the village and there were not the means to give them all the care they needed, so it was only the strong ones that survived.

At midday a large platter of rice, fish and vegetables was produced with a thick and delicious peanut sauce. In the afternoons I would go swimming off the end of the pier in the company of many small boys, or try to take a siesta, but the swarms of flies made this difficult. And when night came I would go again and sit with the Alkaid outside his compound in the company of his wives and daughters who would be shelling groundnuts for the next day's peanut sauce. On my first morning in Karantaba I went to visit Pisania.

★

Pisania was only a short distance away from Karantaba Tenda. It was in a lonely spot, not directly near any place of habitation or cultivation. Only boys took herds of goats there to browse on the thick but dry vegetation that grew thereabouts. I met two of these herd boys on the way and got them to lead me to Mungo Park's monument which was difficult to locate in the bush. When we arrived they stood looking curiously at me as I stood looking curiously at the small and unimpressive cement obelisk, solitary and incongruous, in a clearing by the river. On a metal plaque on its base were written the words, 'Near to this spot Mungo Park set out on the 2nd December 1795 and the 4th May 1805 on his travels to explore the course of the Niger'. A few feet from the obelisk was a rectangle of stones in the sand, said to be the foundations of one of the buildings of old Pisania.

During the five months that Mungo Park passed at Pisania he stayed with an English trader called Dr Laidley. He employed himself industriously during that time in observing and meticulously recording anything that he thought might be of interest to his employees, the African Association, and he learnt Mandingo, a language that was widely spoken in the lands he was to visit. And then, at the end of July, he went through what was locally known as 'seasoning': he had a large dose of fever.

Almost all Europeans who came to West Africa went through this seasoning, either dying from it, which the majority did, or acquiring a partial immunity to what today we know as yellow fever and malaria but what in Park's day, a hundred years before quinine was discovered, was attributed to the night dews and foul airs of the land, a hypothesis from which the Italian word *malaria* stems. Park survived the fever and his long convalescence was much relieved by the company of Dr Laidley whose conversation, he says, 'beguiled the tedious hours during that gloomy season, when the rain falls in torrents; when suffocating heats oppress by day, and when night is spent by the terrified traveller in listening to the croaking of frogs (of which the numbers are beyond imagination), the shrill cry of the jackal, and the deep howling of the hyena'.

Pisania was in the domains of the Kingdom of Niani, the king of which country had good relations with Dr Laidley and aided him in his business which was mostly devoted to the trading of gold, ivory and slaves. Mungo Park was often to sympathize with the pitiful condition of slaves as during his journey he saw in only too close detail their sufferings. On the last leg of his journey, when returning to the Gambia, he in fact travelled in the company of a caravan of slaves who were being taken to the coast for sale.

During this journey, although Park himself was suffering a great deal from weakness and fever and from having to walk in bare feet, he describes with much feeling the fate of a female slave called Nealee who could not keep up with the caravan on account of the pains in her legs that had resulted from her having spent so much time in irons. She was whipped and made a pathetic attempt to escape, falling down in the grass nearby from weakness. Then one morning, all the slaves having spent the previous night in irons because they had that evening 'snapped their fingers', which Park says was a sure sign of desperation, 'poor Nealee' had become so stiff she could neither walk nor stand. She was tied to an ass only to be thrown off and so, no way being found to carry her forward, the general cry of the caravan was now '*Kang-tegi, kang-tegi,*' 'Cut her throat, cut her throat.'

Park, not wanting to see this done, walked ahead only to have a slave come up to him a short time later with Nealee's garment on the end of his bow. He asked the slave, no doubt in indignation, whether he had been given the garment as a reward for cutting her throat. But the slave replied that her throat had not been cut: she had instead been left beside the road where, Park says, she soon probably perished and was devoured by wild beasts.

Park estimates that at that time slaves were in the proportion of three to one to free men in Africa. Not that they all had the same status. For example, Park explains, those who were slaves from birth, having been born of enslaved mothers, enjoyed much protection under the law and a master could neither mistreat his slave nor sell him to a stranger, unless he called a 'palaver' and proved that the conduct of the slave merited this. The most unfortunate type of slave, however, the kind which had no right at all and was more often taken to the coast for sale, was the one who had become enslaved in one of four different ways. These were by being either captured during a war; or, as was sometimes the case during a time of famine, by a person selling himself; or through insolvency, for a person who went bankrupt forfeited his person to his creditor; or, lastly, by being found guilty of murder, adultery or witchcraft.

Park parted company from Dr Laidley on 3 December 1795. For his journey to the Niger, Dr Laidley had provided him with an interpreter called Johnson and one of his personal servants: 'a sprightly youth' called Demba, who, in order to induce his good behaviour, had been promised his freedom on his return should Park report favourably on his services. His baggage was meagre, in fact positively skeletal in comparison to the vast baggage trains later explorers were to employ. It consisted merely of provisions for two days, some trade goods with which to buy new supplies, changes of clothes, an umbrella, geographical equipment, two fowling pieces and two pairs of pistols. Park was going to make do by using his initiative and surviving on what the land had to offer.

'I had now before me,' Park writes, 'a boundless forest, and a country, the inhabitants of which were strangers to civilised life, and to most of whom a white man was an object of curiosity or plunder ... and I reflected that I had parted from the last European I might probably behold, and had quitted perhaps forever the comforts of Christian society.' Mounted on a small and sturdy horse, Park was launching himself into the unknown as surely as when the first astronauts rocketed into space. But Park was endowed with the confidence of youth and the durability and pragmatism of a Scottish upbringing, and it was these things that brought him back to the Gambia two years and seven months later, having survived sufferings and dangers that would have destroyed a lesser man.

The first ten days of Park's journey took him approximately 150 kilometres across the kingdoms of Walli and Woolli. In those ten days he had some indication of the problems he was to face in the later parts of his journey. In both kingdoms he had to pay duty or tax, at first not too willingly, claiming that he was not a trader, but then quickly giving in as he was thereafter to do and which was eventually to cost him everything he had. In Medina, capital of Woolli, a town containing eight hundred to a thousand houses but today merely a small village, he met the king: a 'venerable old man' with whom, through custom, he was advised not to shake hands, and who gave him permission to travel through his land, adding that he would offer up prayers for his safety. This was something the king thought necessary as the only other white man he had ever seen was Park's predecessor, the African Association's Major Houghton, who, the king informed him, had been killed on his journey, as he said Park would undoubtedly be if he followed after him.

In the company of a guide provided by this king, Park continued over what is today the Senegalese border and it is at Tambacunda, near the border of the Woolli and Bondou kingdoms, and today a large Senegalese town of the same name, that I shall leave Mungo Park whilst I remain in Karantaba Tenda awaiting market day.

★

People did not arrive early for market day in Karantaba Tenda, but then many of them had far to come. In the morning, although it was quiet at first, there was an atmosphere of expectation like that before a festival. People were busy at their homes dressing themselves in their best clothes and preparing the wares they were going to sell.

Today was like a holiday, a day in which the usual routine was broken. Many people came to the village. Relations and friends who had not seen each other for a long time met up. Families reunited and family matters were sorted out. Business plans and contracts were discussed, stories were told or caught up on and old debts collected or revenged. There were arguments and even fights. Many palavers over disputes and difficult tribal or civil problems were held; cases were judged in the travelling district court. There were many things going on in the village that day besides buying and selling, and by mid-morning old men were already gathering to plan how to cope with a certain problem or what to say to a certain person when the correct time arrived; women were discussing how to introduce young marriageable couples, persuade difficult fathers-in-law and settle a good bridal price; merchants were sucking their teeth over a deal with a big groundnut trader who they knew was coming today; and young men were wondering whether pretty Tulu from Sami Medina would be here or whether they could ask a friend if they could borrow their bicycle to go to Georgetown to see a man about a job on the coast.

It was in the market area near to the main street where all the traders' shops were to be found that early risers set up their stalls. These were the people who had arrived the night before and were mostly young men, often Senegalese, with an assortment of all that came from the factories of the far industrialized Orient such as scents, mirrors, combs, padlocks, Biros, creams, ointments and pills. But it was not long before others began to arrive. They came on donkeys and carts, by bicycle and foot, horse and ass, and some in battered old bush taxis. But the market did not grow to its full vibrancy until midday when two boatloads of people arrived from the town of Bansang, downriver.

Now the market began to puff and plump itself out. On every available patch of ground down the sides of the roads and path-ways and under canopies of thatch were stalls, some big like the two permanent steel containers filled with sacks of flour and rice, and some just girls sitting in front of handfuls of tomatoes. There were parcels of the kola nuts that the old men chew as a stimulant wrapped up in banana leaves, and large packages of coarse, black tobacco wrapped up in the same. There were plastic shoes, packages of tea and slabs of desert salt. There was a whole corner of women selling the bitter tomatoes that are so popular in the Gambia and can be found in any meal. There were straw baskets smelling fresh and wholesome, woven hats and fans, leather and decorated bicycle seats; there were earthy-smelling home-made soaps and imported soaps scented with roses, foods and pungent spices and high-smelling pieces of meat. There were horses and goats and sheep for sale. There were eating shacks with huge pots of rice and fish and there was a baker with a bathtub filled with his dough.

In between all these were processions of people with every kind of face: ugly, beautiful, black, brown and white, and every kind of dress from rigorously smart and clean mamas to virtually naked fools and madmen playing their private, gibbering games, as were the many children dashing in and out of the crowds. At lunchtime I ate a meal with the Alkaid's son, in the company of some young men who came from the village of Yoma, the home of a famous reggae star called Demba Conta, to whom everybody seemed to be a brother.

As the heat rose in the afternoon, so did the tempo. Everybody was sweating and running high on adrenalin. They were shouting and cursing and buying and bargaining in a frenzy. Tea was on the make and cigarettes consumed at a great pace. Everybody worked hard because even a tiny profit could buy a cake of soap or a packet of tea and make the day worthwhile. And then when the sun began to sink the market quietened down. Out came the dishes of roasted meat and fried plantains, to be consumed by the exhausted marketeers.

Gradually people began to depart with as much merchandise as they had arrived with, but hopefully of a different sort. I was also ready to depart, having said goodbye to two people with whom I was not on such good terms as I had been before the day had started. One was the Alkaid, who felt so guilty about charging me for my stay in his house (because he charged me far too much) that he became surly and bad-tempered. And the other, my guide James, who had waited for market day to find his transport back to Georgetown. He had taken the opportunity the day before to inform me that the villagers were very untrustworthy and lowly characters. He had said that I should keep a close eye on my money. I had indeed found that some of it was missing. It was not the villagers I suspected though, for James had appeared with a brand-new radio which he showed me with great pride *before* I had paid him his wages.

With my head ringing from the market, my body tired from the heat, and my spirits dampened by the unfortunate condition of the Alkaid and by James's new radio, I left Karantaba Tenda for a wild and wandering detour that took me far to the south, beside the sea; and it was some weeks before I returned, via sea trip and aeroplane flight and train ride, to meet up again with Mungo Park, still waiting in Tambacunda in Senegal, 150 kilometres north-west of where I now stood.

III

Into Mali

TAMBACUNDA APPROACHED SLOWLY. It jolted and came closer: a cement water tower standing high above a low town; then a row of tin shacks and huts heaped together like garbage beside the railway tracks. We passed a railway crossing clanking and flashing red lights, holding up a jam of cars and mopeds with bicycles in between them and pedestrians gathering at their sides: they watched the train pass as they eased down the carriages. Soon the station, with its large sign, drew in front of the window and stopped. Now there was much noise and commotion as a market appeared on people's heads below the windows and embarking and disembarking passengers bottle-necked at the carriage doors.

It was late afternoon. Nine hours had passed since leaving Dakar, capital of Senegal, and at least another nine were expected before we crossed the border into Mali. The heat was stifling and swarming with flies that came in the windows.

It had been a monotonous nine hours, the countryside outside the windows an uninterrupted scrubland with few villages. There had been large burnt areas where the ashes billowed out from under the train and came in the windows so that everybody had spots on their faces and looked comical. Sometimes the fires were still burning when we passed. Then a slam of heat would come through the windows.

During the journey my mind wandered back to the last few weeks, picking over the events that had brought me to the railway station in Dakar. I found the movement of the train therapeutic and conducive to thought. There had been little to disturb me after the departure and after I had recovered from the excitement of it, the air of hysteria amongst the crowds of people waiting to board the train because it was important to get a good seat, or a seat at all, as the journey to Bamako in Mali, where the majority of people were going, was over thirty-six hours long.

57

Soldiers had appeared, yelling 'Lines. Get into lines, you rabble. Anyone not in a line is in for some trouble.' Then they started hitting people with sticks and butting them with rifles to get them queuing correctly at the platform gate. They were brutal, the soldiers, and only added to the sense of hysteria. When everybody had boarded the train, they turned their attention to the street sellers who had come down the railway track to hawk their wares to the passengers before the train departed. They hit them as well and chased them away but the street sellers kept coming back, ducking under the train and running through the carriages to avoid them.

All that had happened to me since I left Karantaba Tenda that market day now seemed already very distant, already a part of my greater past. Things had happened to me but they had now left me, run off me like water. I had no scars or souvenirs, only memories, and to forget those would be as if they had not happened.

I had gone to the small ex-Portuguese colony of Guinea-Bissau, a tiny country tucked in amongst the dense forests of the West African coast. I had not been intending on going there the day that I left the Gambia. But whilst I had been waiting in a town in eastern Senegal for a bus to Tambacunda and my rendezvous with Mungo Park, I had struck up a conversation with two men also waiting for a bus. They had said that they were going to Guinea-Bissau. Having always wanted to visit that country, when their bus arrived, before mine did, I had got on it. It was that simple.

Guinea-Bissau is not an easy country to visit. There are few roads connecting it to its neighbouring countries, and even fewer vehicles using those roads. I had waited for two days in the town of Kolda in the south of Senegal before finding two other people with whom to share the price of a bush taxi to take us there. The border, a small muddy village in a forest, was manned by angry, shouting soldiers who, in essence, held you under arrest for the time you were within their power and they had possession of your passport. I had no visa, no common language with the Creole- and Portuguese-speaking inhabitants, and no local currency could be obtained as it was a Sunday.

But with time all these things were put to rights, and in the town of Bafata beside the steamy and slack Rio Geba, Guinea-Bissau's main river, I was introduced to the country by a friendly Senegalese man who was staying in the same lodging house as myself. 'Don't worry,' he said to me, 'once you get to know the country it's not a bad place. The people like parties too much. And the women, ah, the women. There are five of them to each man, since so many men died so recently in the bloody war of independence, and they are as beautiful as you will find any-where. But beware, the food is very bad and these people,' he added disdainfully, 'know cats by the name *lapins de la maison* and they eat them.'

Indeed Guinea-Bissau was a strange country and often felt as though it was not a part of Africa. One saw women dressed in black, knitting on chairs outside doorways hung with lace, and string-vested men taking siestas on verandahs, and chubby chil-dren throwing stones at packs of miserable dogs who could have been in some Brazilian *favela*. They were fair-skinned with manes of waxen black hair.

From Bafata I took a bus to the capital, Bissau, placed on the wide, blue estuary of the Rio Geba. This was a much larger town than I had imagined it would be. Spreading out from the old and rusty colonial centre with its Mediterranean avenues and iron balustrades were miles of suburbs, some poor, little better than shanties, and some surprisingly middle-class.

At first, at mid-afternoon, the town seemed lifeless. As I marched the empty and baking streets looking for a hotel, pass-ing only a few street boys with shoe-polish boxes and packets of black-market cigarettes on corners, I found only one place in which I could buy a drink to quench my thirst: a pavement bar in which a group of tough-looking Cubans stood drinking beer out of large mayonnaise jars. 'Fill my jar,' one of them barked at the barman. 'So I can drink and forget the many years I must stay in this hole.' This was a country with Marxist ideals and these Cubans had been posted here by their Government to help fulfil those ideals. But as evening set in, the town unfurled and I saw, through the stirring doorway curtains, shops and bars and restaurants. Behind the grand if faded and crumbling façade of the town there was indeed life, not vibrant, but ticking over as fast as the oppressive heat would permit.

I had passed only two days in Bissau before I caught a ferry across the Rio Geba estuary to the town of Boloma, capital of the Bissagos Islands, an archipelago that lies just off the broken and swampy coast. Boloma had been one of the first Portuguese settlements on the West African coast, a pretty, provincial place that had fallen into disrepair since the departure of the Portuguese fifteen years ago. There were grand, ornamented buildings with wide sweeps of steps leading up to their tall, iron doors. There were little gardens and whitewashed villas, and a smart hotel. But everything was overgrown, untended. Bushes grew from the sides of buildings. The hotel roof had caved in, and the streets of tall and healthy grass were grazed over by sheep.

In order to give Boloma some kind of distinction, the Minister for Development had insisted on street lighting. A squad of Portuguese workers had been drafted in and for a month chopped down trees and put up many tall lampposts in their stead. These lampposts now lined every street and even strung out into the forests for short distances. Occasionally, at times when there was some fuel for the town's electricity generator, and perhaps when some important minister was visiting the town, these lamps would be turned on. Then, as they flickered into life, bathing the well-turfed streets and wandering sheep in a brilliant orange light, the town's few residents would rush out of their homes, clapping and praising the President for his development project. They would sing the national anthem but then soon the fuse would blow and the lamps would go out and the town would be sucked back into the void from whence it had sprung.

I ended up staying with a French Canadian agronomist who had been sent to Boloma to encourage the villagers to grow more food and grow it with new methods that he could teach them. He was called Robert and was lonely because his wife was off in Dakar having a baby. His apartment was two storeys up and overlooked the bay where a tide came in to flood the mangrove swamps and which, when it seeped back, almost out of view, left one and a half kilometres of mud on which the tiny forms of men could be seen digging for oysters. Robert took me to see the forests of cashew and jack trees and his experimental plots of rice paddy. He also introduced me to the Bissagos villagers with whom he was working. 'These people are traditionally fishermen,' he said. 'But they do not like to work too much. Each of their homesteads has a personal distillery behind it, and in each village you will generally find one or two bodies lying drunk in the dust.'

When I had arrived back in Bissau a week later I had had to wait there six days in order to take an aeroplane to Dakar from where I could make my way to Mali.

That aeroplane turned out to be a small, two-propeller craft. It was delayed for a long time because the departure of an Aeroflot flight bound for Cuba had also been delayed and there was only room for one plane at a time in the embarkation park in front of the airport terminal. All the passengers stood around on the tarmac outside watching the Russian jet. There were only a few of us: one robust old politician who wore the darkest of sunglasses to hide a set of shifty, shrunken eyes; a group of chatty Danes forever rushing to be first in queues that never materialized; a handsome young Senegalese couple in the most modern dress; a large and merry Lebanese woman; one vastly overweight man who, when we boarded the plane, had to have two seats to accommodate his bulk; an American woman clutching a Bible; and a nervous German businessman who was only prevented at the last moment from boarding the jet and going to Cuba instead of Dakar. When that plane did eventually depart we all stood watching it turn towards the runway, none of us giving a thought to the fact that the rear of the jet engines were swivelling around towards us. Before the huge blast of hot air hit me I had noticed the people to my right falling to the tarmac and turning their backs. The jets cut a swathe through us in this fashion, dropping us all ridiculously to the ground.

From high in the air the forests of Guinea-Bissau, southern Senegal and the Gambia seemed virgin and uninhabited, no detail of those countries penetrating the haze except the great glittering waterways of the Casamanse and Gambia rivers. In Dakar I caught the train to Mali, passing on the way Tambacunda and my rendezvous with Mungo Park who had been nowhere near Bafata or Bissau or Boloma in Guinea-Bissau. His goal was the Niger, to get there by the most direct route.

★

Ever since I had visited Mali five years before I had wanted to return, even as I do now. I had become attached to the place. I am not sure why. Here there is none of the classical beauty to be found in the countries of eastern and southern Africa. There are not the vast expanses of lush grazing lands roamed over by herds of elephant, zebra and antelope. There are no great mountains here, no Kilimanjaro or Mountains of the Moon. The Rift Valley that slices through Kenya and Tanzania, with its abrupt changes of nature and startling views, and the great lakes of Victoria, Tanganyika and Malawi have no comparison of grandeur and beauty in Mali. There is even no seaboard in this land-locked country, no coral coasts as in East Africa with its spice islands and Arab ports and medinas (native quarters). And of the profuse tropicality of Central Africa and seaboard West Africa with their grand, primary forests and heavy rainfalls there is no hint.

No, Mali is essentially an arid land, a harsh and unforgiving world of scrub and sand whose inhabitants have to fight hard for their livelihoods. Here the climate can be counted as one of the most abysmal in the world with its hot, dry and dust-laden winds, its many months of staggering, life-sapping heat and its brief rainy season that in most of the country only allows a hasty and sparse cultivation and in some of it does not even allow that. To the north, in the large bulge nearly the size of France that stretches above the ancient town of Timbuktu, there is desert, the Sahara. Here there are only a few wandering nomads, and the workers and prisoners who toil in the old salt mines of Taoudenni.

Then there is the Sahel, that thin band of country stretching along the southern border of the entire Sahara from the coast of Senegal to Ethiopia: that dry and drought-stricken area which is becoming less like savannah and more like the Sahara that seeps its way southwards day by day. Here the black Bantu peoples meet the fairer peoples of the Sahara with their conflicting cultures and beliefs, conflicts that in so many of the countries that straddle this area have led to wars and still do up to this day.

'Sahel' is an Arabic word meaning 'shore', as indeed it is a shore to the great sea of the Sahara. Here, traditionally, live wandering pastoralists with their large herds of cattle and groups of sedentary peoples settled in villages. And then there is the south of the country bordering the more tropical coastal countries of Guinea and the Ivory Coast. Here the climate is gentler and more humid. But even here the forests are of poor quality; there is no abundance of fertile land and there are no great natural resources for Mali to exploit.

The only gift that Mali has is the Niger river, over 4,000 kilometres long. It forms a huge arc through the heart of West Africa for, having travelled in a northerly direction from its source in the mountains of western Guinea, it finds itself at length faced with the Sahara; as if fearing a desert large enough to extinguish even so mighty a river, the Niger then veers away to the east before plummeting southwards through Niger and Nigeria to seek its eventual release into the sea. It is the Niger's curious route which caused so much confusion to geographers and explorers alike, and led them to conjecture that the river had its termination in such diverse places as the Sahara, the Nile in Egypt, and the Zaire river. Although the Europeans had been for long sailing past its outlet into the Gulf of Guinea they did not recognize it, for the Niger meets the sea through a huge delta of mangrove swamps, seeping into it by means of thousands of small streams and rivers.

In the dry savannahs of Mali the Niger brings much relief. It is here that the river meanders and loses force, breaks up into hundreds of streams and small lakes forming an inland delta. This inland delta is Mali's jewel. When it rains in the mountains of western Guinea and the Niger swells, the delta and large areas around it are flooded. As the floods subside crops can be planted and pastures spring up to feed livestock. There is a diverse wildlife and a fishing industry. And up and down the Niger, and threading the ways of the delta, a fleet of river boats indulge in a busy trade between river ports and market towns. The Niger is Mali's coast.

It is in this area of the middle Niger, just south of the Sahara Desert, that some of the greatest empires to have existed in black Africa developed. Mali, perhaps more than any other country of black Africa, is rich in history. For almost a thousand years a succession of empires ruled over much of it, at times extending their influence well beyond its borders to encompass a larger part of the western Sudan. They had a sophistication and wealth that is all the more surprising for the fact that they remained largely unsuspected by Europe throughout their time. In them developed complex systems of government and law. The first empire, the Ghana Empire, which the eighth-century Arab writer Al-Fazari called 'the land of gold', was said to field an army of 200,000 warriors and have a capital city of 15,000 inhabitants.

When the famous Moroccan traveller, Ibn Batuta, visited Africa in the fourteenth century during the time of the second empire, the Mali Empire, he could praise it for its good government. 'There is complete security in this country,' he wrote. 'Neither traveller nor inhabitant in it has anything to fear from robbers or men of violence.' At the height of its splendour the Mali Empire was so wealthy that its king, Mansa Kanka Musa, when on his famous pilgrimage to Mecca, devalued the gold market in Cairo by 10 per cent simply by lavish gifts of the vast quantities he had brought with him across the Sahara.

The third of the empires, that of Sonhay, attained a degree of sophistication that matched many of the kingdoms in medieval Europe. It had an organized civil service and a professional standing army. It was during the time of these empires that such famous cities as Timbuktu and Djenne grew up to become important centres of learning and craft to which scholars from North Africa and even the Middle East would travel to study.

What allowed the empires to develop was the trans-Sahara trade. They were well positioned to act as middlemen and grew wealthy from the taxes they could impose on it. In the early days the trade was conducted by the Berbers of North Africa who traded principally in ivory and gold, which was plentiful in West Africa, exchanged for salt which they mined in the Sahara and for which the West Africans had such a craving that at one time they exchanged it with gold on an equal weight basis. When the Arabs invaded North Africa in the eighth century, they took over the trade and developed it further. And with the increase in trade and the growing influence of Islam, the West Africans of the middle Niger now began to flourish. Their cities grew rich and powerful, and gradually they extended their influence until kingdoms became empires, and those empires became part of a wider network of international trade consisting of North Africa, western Asia and southern Europe where some monarchs would strike their coins in gold that came from West Africa.

The Mali Empire, after which the country of Mali is named, was founded by the famous god-hero Sundiata. The son of a king of a Malinke kingdom, he was born a cripple but later cured by a miracle. When Sundiata's home came under the tyranny of a powerful Fulani ruler called Sumanguru – the Fulani were a distinctive people, sprung of different stock from the others of West Africa – Sundiata, who had been driven into exile by his elder brother, was called back to save his people. With an army at his back, Sundiata set out on a course of conquest that at last brought him to confront Sumanguru. In the thick of battle, the story goes, Sundiata uttered a great shout in the face of Sumanguru's warriors, who at once ran to get behind Sumanguru. The latter, in his turn, uttered a great shout in the face of Sundiata's warriors, who all fled to get behind Sundiata. Sumanguru's witchcraft, however, proved weaker than that of Sundiata and he was struck by an arrow made from the spur of a white cock which was fatal to his power. Sundiata now went on to lay the foundations of the Mali Empire.

The power of the Mali Empire began to wane in the late fourteenth century, having overextended itself, and was finally broken by the state of Sonhay which, by 1464, had entirely eclipsed the Mali Empire and created one of its own. This was the last of the great empires and it was brought to an end by a Moroccan invasion from across the Sahara at the end of the sixteenth century. It is doubtful, though, whether the Sonhay Empire would have lasted much longer as by now the European maritime nations were beginning to break the monopoly of trans-Sahara trade on which the empires had been dependent, by trading directly with the West Africans via the coast.

That time five years ago when I had come to Mali I knew nothing of its history. I knew only that which I saw. But this did not matter. In the same way that one can see and feel the wisdom in the eyes of an old man without having to know his story, I had felt the history of Mali from the most potent of its few resources, its people. The country was like a well and the water that was drawn up from that well tasted sweet and pure, for it had come from a great depth. It was to taste that water again that I had been so inexorably drawn back. This time, though, I knew more about the country. I now knew how deep that well was. I now knew that this country had not always been the poor and comparatively backward place it is today with its broken economy, its crumbling infrastructure and its dying, drought-stricken land.

Sitting on the train from Tambacunda I looked into people's faces, searching for a history in the glint of their eyes.

★

Not long after we left Tambacunda it grew dark. The soldiers who accompanied the train now converged on the bar in the carriage at the front. Later they came back, noisy, red-eyed and aggressive. They began harassing some of the passengers, demanding to look in their bags and hauling off people who did not have adequate identification with them.

When they asked the young man sitting next to me for his, he said, 'It was stolen in Dakar. But I . . .'

'No identification,' one of them shouted, interrupting him. 'That is a joke. What's to be done with a person who has no identification? He hardly exists, does he?' The soldier turned to his comrades, who laughed.

'But I . . . I went to the police and they gave me this,' the young man stuttered, producing a dirty piece of paper. The soldier ignored his piece of paper, though, and barked, 'You're in big trouble. Get up and come with me.' He pushed him up the carriage as though he was a criminal. Later the young man returned. Nothing had happened to him except some bullying because the soldiers were not serious but only bored and in need of some entertainment.

It was four in the morning by the time we reached the Senegal border. Here there was a long stop as everybody had to go through customs and immigration. Again the soldiers came through the carriages looking at all our bags and papers. Now they were more serious and the passengers sat nervously hoping that it would not be them that the soldiers would find 'irregular'.

But it is never hard for soldiers to pronounce somebody 'irregular'. The next man who was picked on in my carriage was ejected from the train, split from the party of people he was going to Bamako to do business with. At the Malian frontier we all had to leave our seats and walk to a house at a little distance which had a weak light-bulb shining on its verandah. Here immigration officials stood looking down at the sea of people below them. Those people were called up to the verandah one by one where the immigration men looked at their papers, choosing, as if by whim, whether to show aggression or charm to them. They were like actors on a stage who had absolute control over the emotions of their audience.

Mungo Park had taken eighteen days to travel the distance from Tambacunda to the Malian town of Kayes, 100 kilometres over the border. In that time he traversed the two small kingdoms of Bondou and Kajaaga. In Bondou he commented on the number of schools he saw where people were learning the text of the Koran in Arabic, as they still do today. He was impressed by this desire for education and would have been even more impressed had he known that 60 per cent of Bondou were literate in Arabic, a higher rate of literacy than in England at the same time. And in Fattecunda, the capital of Bondou, he had an amusing audience with some of the women of the king's court. They insisted on the artificiality of his white skin and his prominent nose, saying that the first had been produced when he was an infant by his being dipped in milk, and the second by being pinched every day until it had acquired its present 'unsightly and unnatural conformation'. When Park, in return, flattered the ladies on their beauty, they only replied that 'honey mouth' was not appreciated in Bondou. But they did send him a jar of honey and some fish that night.

Kajaaga, to where Park travelled next, was inhabited by Soninke people or, as the French call them, Serakolets. This kingdom was preparing for war with its easterly neighbour, the kingdom of Khasso. Here Park did not fare so well as he had done in Bondou. On Christmas Day, when he was resting in the town of Joag, he suddenly found himself surrounded by twenty horsemen with muskets in their hands. The men accused him of entering the king's land without paying duty. All his possessions and even his companions, he was informed, were therefore for-feit and he must come with the men to the king. But Park avoided this by offering the horsemen some gifts which, luckily, they accepted. They also took an interest in his baggage, however, relieving him of exactly half of what he had brought into the kingdom.

The following day, not wishing to produce any article which might also be stolen, Park and his group went without food. Then, in the evening, as was to happen so often in his journey, Park's predicament was relieved by a woman: as he sat dejectedly on the ground an old slave pressed a handful of groundnuts on him. Park remarks that 'experience had taught her that hunger was painful, and her own distress made her commiserate those of others'.

At that time there was a man called Demba Sego, nephew of the king of Khasso, in Kajaaga on a mission to improve relations between the two kingdoms. Hearing of Park's presence in Kajaaga he came to see him and offered him his protection and guidance on the journey to Khasso, to where Park had next to go.

And so, in the company of this Demba Sego, Park arrived at the village of Kayee on the Senegal river, today's town of Kayes where I disembarked from the train.

★

Kayes was like something that has been left out in the sun too long. It was dry and parched, its colours bleached and dull. Most of the town was constructed from mud bricks, now worn away by the wind and rain. Many poor villagers trek to Kayes in search of work, but there is little money to be found in the town, so most of them live there like peasants; the streets are lined with unemployed youths, and those people with a job and a wage have many mouths to feed.

And Kayes has a very bad climate. Reputed to be, in the long dry season, one of the hottest towns in the world, it is a difficult and unhealthy place in which to live. For much of the year the air is laced with a fine dust, the dry season is known as 'the period of no air', water is scarce, disease prevalent, and food from the surrounding countryside, is basic and meagre.

Kayes came into being as a result of the railway line the French had built from Dakar to Bamako on the Niger river. It was one of the principal anchors on this line which, after Kayes, entered an area that had not yet been pacified by the French, the heroic, fighting empire of Samori Toure who was one of the most successful opponents of French colonization still holding sway over much of it. The town began as an administrative stronghold and trading centre and in time grew to be the capital of the second region of Mali. Today, though, this distinction has little merit. The capital city of Bamako, some 500 kilometres down the railway line, is eclipsing such provincial towns as Kayes. It is to Bamako these days that all men of influence, power and wealth must go, for Mali is a military dictatorship and in such places wealth and power are a nucleus. They must huddle close to the President and the heart of political matters or they will be seen as a threat. The regions must, ideally, be powerless, poor and, therefore, obedient. Kayes these days has little more real function than that of continued existence and that existence is not an easy one to continue.

There are two Kayes; Kayes N'di and Kayesba. Kayes N'di, or 'little Kayes' is on the opposite bank of the Senegal river from the main town of Kayesba, or 'big Kayes'. This is a rambling suburb of villages. Between the two is a long stone bridge that when the river is dry and low hops from one rocky outcrop to another, when it is higher becomes a ford and when the river is in full spate disappears from view almost entirely. The water of the river is, for much of the year, yellow and sickly-looking, as is the dust- and heat-laden sky, and on it floats the suds of the hundreds of washerwomen who line its banks.

Over the bridge there comes a continuous procession of traffic. First thing in the morning out go the convoys of donkey-and-cart wood collectors; peasants to their fields with hoes and bottles of water; straw collectors; the motorbikes of officials and army personnel, doubled or even trebled up, and bush taxis laden to their axles. And across the bridge throughout the day comes the produce of the countryside in the arms and on the heads of tough and gnarled village men and women. In the evening cattle are driven across the bridge to the slaughterhouse in Kayesba to be butchered for tomorrow's market. These great white beasts of the Fulani people with their long scimitar horns have ropes attached to fore and back legs and young men attached to those ropes. Wild-eyed, nervous and frisky, they edge along the bridge, their pounding, muscular power crippled by a pull on the ropes.

On the waterfront, near the bridge, are the old colonial buildings built from stone. These days they house administration: the department of water and forests, the bureaux of rural development, the employment and the fisheries office. In them sit bored civil servants with little to do, and a crowd of petitioners waits at the doors only to discover that nothing can be done. Near here is the post office and then beyond the post office the downtown area of merchants' shops beside the busy market-place.

I had a friend in the downtown area with whom I would sometimes go and sit in the mornings. He was a street-side watchmender.

'Hey, stranger,' he called to me the first time he saw me passing, 'come here, come and pass some time with me. Don't be shy, we like strangers in this town.' And he moved over on his bench to give me room to sit next to him.

Jean, as was my friend's name, had the sort of face that inspired confidence. He had charm mixed with the air of an overgrown street boy. He conducted his work on a small wooden desk which had tall wire-mesh sides and a small window in the front: a cage to deter unwelcome hands. He was perpetually cheerful and always had an audience of street people watching him work.

'You see how they gather round,' he said to me once. 'They know a true expert when they see one.' And indeed he was the ultimate craftsman and worked always with great speed and dexterity. Customers would be coming all the time dropping off watches that generally needed only the tiniest amount of work. Jean could be working on five or six at a time, his hands creating a sort of dance: firm and confident in their actions, but delicate in their results. Nothing could confound him. He had learnt through trial and error what could and what could not be done. He had none of the sophisticated electronic and mechanical tools a watchmaker would desire. But tiny electrical circuits and hair balance mechanisms could be fiddled with by Jean as he chatted to friends, took money, gave change and smoked a cigarette, with all the time goats and trucks and dust swirling past a few feet from his desk.

In the downtown area is also the town's one cinema. Here Saturday means war film; Sunday, karate; Monday, gangster and Tuesday, Hindu. I went to this cinema one Tuesday with a girl I knew. As it was Tuesday the film was a Hindu one, and, as in most Hindu films, the plot was simple. The evil characters, dressed in black, represented the rich and cruel class, and the heroes, dressed in bright sequined white, fought evil on behalf of the poor. The singing and dancing and fast karate fights were a source of much entertainment for the audience but once the hero had killed the leading representative of evil, the crowd got up and left even though the film was not yet over. All through the film the girl I went with whispered to me, telling me about the characters and letting me know right from the start every detail of the plot. 'That was the seventh time I have seen this film,' she said with pride when we left.

After the downtown area one comes to the indefinite residential areas called quarters, such as Plateaux, Khasso, named after the old kingdom of Khasso, and one called 'the smiling quarter'. The streets in the quarters are of uneven bare earth and all look the same, the tin-roofed, mud-brick houses uniformly run down. The scattered children, the limping dogs, the abandoned machinery and piles of refuse, the old men sitting on logs on corners, and the deep pits from which the earth has been excavated to make bricks do not look significantly different from quarter to quarter, let alone from street to street.

The army barracks is on the long station road, near the centre of town. One looks straight ahead when passing the barrack gates for fear of rousing interest in the soldiers who guard it and who are, like all soldiers, unpredictable quantities. Everyone in Kayes professes to dislike soldiers, but then most people have at least one relation who is a soldier and may at one time have thought of becoming one themselves, because soldiers, after all, earn a wage.

Travelling up this station road towards the outskirts of town one passes first the moped mechanics – oiled, rag-in-hand men beneath trees with skeletal mopeds, littered tools and gatherings of idlers and advisers – then the shunting yards which cross the road, and then, opposite the railway station in two identical, tall red-brick colonial buildings, the police headquarters and the station hotel in which the Saturday night disco is held. The arrival of trains at the station means busy times for Kayes. The baggage-cart boys, the taxi drivers, the street sellers and parts of the market all converge and find perhaps their only custom of the day.

These are the bones of Kayes, a town slipping into oblivion on the perimeter of the world.

★

I met a man called Michel the night I arrived in Kayes. That day, the President of Mali had come to the town on an official visit, an occurrence that caused many a tremble and shiver as he sped about in tinted-glass convoys. With him the President had brought enough security men and officials to occupy every room in every hotel or lodging house in town, as the persevering taxi driver I employed was to discover. I ended up at the *maison de jeunesse*, a State-run place where rooms could be had cheaply. Late as it was, a group of men were playing cards at the gate. Being told that there was no place for me to stay here either, I was invited to sit down and partake of some tea the men were brewing. Michel was the largest, most impressive figure in the group. He wore a long blue gown hemmed with golden stitching and had a thick black beard, a generous belly and an attitude of age and wisdom quite above what his actual age could have been. When the game of cards was finished he simply said, 'You will come and stay with me,' and, picking up my bag, walked away into the night with me on his heels.

Michel lived in the Khasso quarter. This was a slightly up-market one near to the military barracks. In it men with wages were to be found, and it also housed the expatriate Ghanaian community, the majority of whom were women who also earned a wage by servicing the military and other moneyed men.

Michel was a man of comparative wealth and therefore of some distinction. He worked for one of the many Western aid projects in Mali and they paid good and, more importantly, guaranteed wages. He was instinctively authoritarian and the Western projects needed people like him. He lived in a large compound, divided into two, with many relations and family dependants. In fact there were so many that, being the principal money earner of the family, Michel could not, having fed all the mouths, afford a higher standard of living than most people in town.

His two compounds were basic: hole-in-the-ground toilets; buildings of crumbling earth and curled corrugated iron containing small windowless rooms which were bare of anything but trunks of possessions and mattresses; one tap of running water, and cooking on open log fires. He did, though, whilst I was there, buy a black-and-white television set and, syphoning off some of the town's scanty supply of electricity from somewhere further down the street, he set it up each evening in the bigger of the two compounds. This became a focal point for all the children of the street who came and sat in front of it each evening, bathed in its blue light, giggling, fidgety and uncomprehending of the monotonous ministerial and presidential monologues that seemed to be the principal feature. Michel presided over this nightly occurrence, standing behind the rows of children with his arms folded on his chest and a wry grin on his face, the meaning of which he kept secret to himself.

The room I was given was in the smaller of the two compounds. This one was in a worse state of repair than the first: the wall between it and the street having partially fallen down, it was exposed to every passer-by. Directly outside my room was a large ram that bleated incessantly because it was pegged down in a corner until the day, no matter how distant, of its slaughter. Also tied up in the compound was a young puppy, restrained from wandering until a later age when it would not get itself lost. And sharing the fate of these last two, there was a small monkey tied up in the ruins of a building at the side. This miserable creature was there for no other reason than entertainment for poking, teasing children.

Many people came and went, mostly young relations in from the countryside with small bags and radios who would pass a couple of nights sleeping on the verandah outside the rooms. Of the more permanent guests, there was Michel's mother, an ancient lady who lived in a world of her own and who smiled nervously at me whenever she saw me and brought me an oil lamp each evening. There was a young blacksmith's apprentice who left each morning before dawn and did not reappear until late in the night. The woman in the room next to mine had no husband or money and when her daughter got ill and coughed continually for five days and nights the blacksmith's apprentice asked if I would give her money for some medicine. And there was Fatima, a healthy and hearty lady of unfailing good spirits who took it upon herself to teach me Bambarra, the prevalent language in Mali.

'*I ni sagoma*,' she would greet me each morning, and I would have to reply, '*Nba, I ni sagoma.*' '*Here sira*,' she would continue the greetings. '*Here doran*,' I would reply, and throughout the day, whenever she saw me, she would make a point of teaching me new phrases such as '*Dugu tigi be min?*' ('Where is the village chief?') or '*M'ba fè dominikè*' ('I want to eat'). Fatima, and a friend of hers who had a small night-time eating table on the street beside the compound where you could buy beans and salad, were, they informed me, unmarried. 'We both had children, though,' Fatima said, 'and I even had two of the tiniest babies die.' She laughed out loud at this as though fate was a mischievous but not unloved child itself.

Another inhabitant of the compound was a young marabout called Mohammed. 'Marabout' is a title of broad usage in Mali, sometimes merely referring to a person who can read Arabic, but at others, as with Mohammed, signifying someone who has devoted his life to a study of the Koran. These people employ themselves in teaching, prayer and advising those who believe marabouts can do such things as divine the future. Many parents send their children at a young age to live with and study under a marabout. In fact in the towns of Mali one sees many of these young boys going around begging for money and food, for the students of marabouts are often required to beg for their livelihoods, depending upon the charity which the Koran instructs Muslims to give away. The students, if they devote themselves successfully to their studies, graduate from their Koranic school and can go on to become marabouts themselves. Mohammed had reached this stage and, even though he was a country person quite unfamiliar with modern town life, he was held in great respect. He was gentle and peaceful and lived on an old iron bedstead in the middle of the compound. Even though he and I had virtually not a word of a common language, we became friends and would share meals and sit together in the early evenings.

Life in Michel's two compounds mostly took place outside, the rooms used only for storing things and for sleeping in during the cold season. The men would absent themselves in the morning to go to work or to try to find work but in any case to get out of the way of the women. The women then had all their tasks, hard tasks which accounted for their calloused hands, their muscular arms and the fact that they aged very quickly.

The most time-consuming task and the most strenuous was the pounding of millet or maize or sometimes rice and wheat in large wooden mortars to create flour. The women stood around the mortar, two or three at a time, and, throwing heavy three- or four-foot pestles in the air, clapped their hands before catching them on the way down, then, with a tight and powerful ripple through their bodies, hammered the pestles into the grain. They worked in rota, throwing up, clapping and pounding in turn, switching hands, shifting hips and shuffling feet as though they were performing a dance. The thump, thump ... thump ... thump, thump ... thump in the mornings and evenings was like a heartbeat, reverberating throughout the town.

Then there was the cleaning of rice of the small stones merchants mixed with it in order to make it weigh more; the creation of the staple food, couscous, by working dampened millet flour on wicker platters to form tiny congealed lumps. The women toiled over bowls of washing, working in the suds. They sat and shelled groundnuts. They swept the compounds, backs bent nearly double, one hand on hip and the other clasping a small reed brush. And then there were the children who, although mostly self-sufficient, needed a degree of looking after; the shopping in the market; the collecting of wood and water; the mending and ironing of clothes – the list was nearly as long as the list of things for which money was asked of the men when they returned. The women had it hard but if you gave them pity the backlash was even harder, for they had the greatest of pride born out of their bearing, their dresses of starched and colourful batiks that could have passed for ball gowns, their imaginative hairdos of intricate plaits and weaves, their oiled skins and their loyalty to their work. And they, it is said, are endowed with a resilience of nature denied to their male counterparts.

The afternoons were a time of peace. By then it was generally too hot for much exertion. After the separate parts of the family, eating communally from their separate bowls of rice and vegetables that Michel's money had provided, had finished, tea would be made, radios turned on and the men would lie on mats. The women in Michel's compound gathered at this time of day to plait each other's hair, sitting one behind the other, weaving in the long synthetic strands.

As a result of so many people living so close together under hard and meagre conditions, there was often much tension and conflict. Sometimes these were unspoken atmospheres that could almost suffocate. At others, they broke out: the screams and shouts of two women having a go at each other about that medicine that went missing or the bucket that 'is mine but in your house'; the bickering of family jealousies; the anger and hurt at husbands who are always absent and keep their money to themselves. In Michel's compound a problem arose that created a rift for many days. Michel's younger brother had got into trouble with the police. He was a light-spirited boy, quite different from Michel, and the women of the compounds loved him for his sense of fun and his sympathetic nature. But he was always getting into trouble and whenever Michel gave him money to start a business he would spend it. He had fallen in with a group of marijuana-smokers and had been caught by the police for possessing the stuff a number of times, a serious crime in Mali. On these occasions Michel had always bailed him out, but this time he was not going to.

'I've had enough of that boy,' he explained. 'Let him pay the penalty. I wash my hands of him.'

The family was divided. 'Ah, Michel is too hard, too cruel,' some of them said. 'To leave a brother in that gaol where you share your food with the rats and lie on the floor like a cur of a dog. It's too bad.'

Michel stood firm for many days, but in the end he did bail

his brother out, unable to take the bad atmosphere in the compound, and perhaps his conscience as well.

Michel was essentially head of the family, his father having died and his elder brother proving a layabout who did not work or even look for work. This was a position of much responsibility and Michel took it seriously. He was stern and intimidating when at home and his smallest statement was an order quickly carried out. He found his home a place of pressure, the demands on his pocket for food and medicine and the hundred other things a strain. He felt suffocated by the domesticity of the compounds and so he spent much of his time out. I would sometimes accompany him on his evening sojourns.

On our first night out together Michel said, 'Tonight we shall go and visit all my girlfriends and I shall break all my appointments with them.' He drove a moped and I sat on the back. The first of the girlfriends had a small stall beside the station road from which she sold roasted meat. She was a pretty girl with a gold ring in her nose and a long silky dress. She rushed up to Michel when we pulled up nearby with genuine delight in her eyes. 'You are now the only one I love': Michel dismissed her with this and on we sped.

The second was a large, powerful woman on whose head sat a pile of expensive-looking material that matched her dress. Michel joked and teased with her and at one time she told a story at which he roared with laughter. 'She has been telling me,' Michel explained, for she was speaking Bambarra, 'how in some recent local elections we had here she was in charge of some ballot boxes. Everybody came and put their vote into either the big, black box marked "Yes", or the one marked "No". When all was finished a fat and important lady came and, taking the box marked "No", emptied its entire contents into the one marked "Yes".' Again Michel roared with laughter.

Once he had managed to extricate himself from this somewhat forceful girlfriend we went to meet his third girlfriend. 'This one,' Michel said, 'is very intelligent and good at making conversation.' We found her at home in a large compound at the far end of town. She was with her sister who was dancing to Zairoise music under a tree. She was young and bright and sat listening attentively to Michel as he told a long story about his experiences in the peep shows and sex parlours of Paris, which town he had once visited.

'What an interesting life you have led,' she said coyly. 'I wonder why you come to visit someone as dull as myself.'

But Michel only laughed and said to me, 'I told you this one was a clever one, did I not?'

Michel liked to drink and so some evenings we would go to a bar. Being a country in which the majority of people are Muslims there are, other than in Bamako, the capital, few and sometimes no public bars in Mali. In Kayes there was only one public bar, at the station hotel. Instead people set up private, secluded bars. These were always down side streets, out back of some inconspicuous-looking house. Many people liked to drink in Mali. Islam in this country was tolerant. Those who did not drink did not think themselves superior to those who did, but those who did still liked to do their drinking privately, out of public view.

Alcohol being expensive, it was only those who had money who could afford to drink. Customers, therefore, were mostly policemen, businessmen, people of the professional class like teachers and civil servants. To walk into a bar, though, one would not have thought this. There you would often find much uproar. Everybody as they drank would soon become everybody's friend, then soon had cause to argue with that friend. 'What do you mean, I can't afford to buy a round of drinks? I am a man of means.' Or 'I am friends with that fool. You sit there and insinuate that . . .'

Soon, everybody else would join in on sides of the argument. The argument would break down and become a discussion. Long and interesting theories would be aired, agreements made and new and fantastic angles to the theory found. Then everybody would be friends again and a new round would be ordered, nobody asked if they wanted another: to buy a drink for somebody was a privilege for the buyer, to refuse was an insult. Sometimes the rounds would build up to a row of bottles sitting before you, even before the man asleep in the corner. Great warmth and camaraderie were to be had in the back-street bars of Kayes. A man to whom you said, 'Your eyes are as red as your socks and your teeth as yellow as mine' might turn out to be a captain of police and he would in return buy you a new bottle.

I remember one particular evening sitting with a circle of drinkers which included a policeman of high rank, a ministerial chauffeur, a teacher and an undertaker and his apprentice. The undertaker, a small, grey-looking man, was telling a story about a girl who died with her arms sticking out, because she had epilepsy. 'Ah, you should have seen them,' he said, 'they stuck straight out like the draw-bars of a donkey cart. What could we do? How could we fit them into a coffin? We'd push them down but they'd jump straight back up again.'

'That is not possible,' broke in the teacher. 'How can a dead person's arms jump about like that? I cannot accept that. Quite impossible.'

'No, no, I assure you it's not,' the undertaker replied. 'Once a body has rigor mortis there is little you can do to alter its position. I have seen people buried in a sitting position. I have seen people buried in all sorts of strange positions. You see, if you imagine that for example a body is a lump of dough, now when that lump of dough is put into the oven it will set in whatever shape it is formed into. Now if you . . .' At this point the undertaker's apprentice, a cheery young man who had been standing nearby annoying the barman by spilling beer on the floor, laughed so hard that he had to leave the room. 'If you were to attempt to reshape the dough,' the undertaker continued, ignoring the behaviour of his apprentice, 'you would find . . .'

'Rubbish. This is total rubbish,' interrupted the ministerial chauffeur who had been trying to conduct a conversation with the high-ranking policeman about the speed at which a Mercedes could go in reverse, but had lost the policeman's attention to the undertaker. 'Absolute rubbish,' he reaffirmed, and then continued to discuss cars once more with the high-ranking policeman.

The drinkers swayed between the two discussions, the undertaker and chauffeur vying with each other for their attention, one of them often left to discuss his subject on his own.

'What did you do with the girl in the end?' Michel asked the undertaker at length.

'We had to break her arms,' he replied, 'it was the only way.' This closed the subject.

'Boy,' the undertaker called to the barman who visibly flinched, 'another round of beers.'

But the bars were not always as jovial places as this. There were the times when everybody sat on their own, bent forwards like dolls, clumsy and uncoordinated as they reached for their bottles. Then there would be silence, any attempts at conversation or conviviality quickly killed by inarticulate and aggressive argument.

One of the bars Michel and I went to was far on the outskirts of town beside some railway sidings. One night when we came out of it we saw that a goods train had pulled up. There were clusters of men unloading sacks from the back of some of the wagons and, it being cold that night, they were wrapped up in scarves and turbans giving them a somewhat furtive look. They loaded the sacks on to small hand-carts which they pushed away at a quick pace. A little further up the siding, however, they were brought to a halt by a tall dark figure in a greatcoat. He shone a strong torch into their faces and barked some words at them. Then, as the men pushed their carts slowly past him, he turned and followed them, jabbing the last man on the shoulder as if to hurry him up. A short distance away there was a pick-up truck parked on a road. Michel and I, who had been following these proceedings at a distance, saw the men load their sacks into the back of this pick-up. Once this was done the pick-up sped off in a cloud of dust leaving the men standing silently and dejectedly beside their now empty carts.

'You see now how this country of ours is,' Michel said to me. 'The police steal from the smugglers. Dog eats dog.'

That night there was a full moon rushing behind veils of clouds, throwing darkness, then again its chill blue light.

★

I had two other particular friends in Kayes. They were two brothers called Ousman and Amadou who ran a small shop on the station road. They were both intelligent and well educated, but, like so many of the other young men in Kayes, they had found no proper jobs and so after a few years living in Bamako had come back to their home town. Their father had died and they now looked after their mother and their many young brothers and sisters.

Life for Ousman and Amadou was very simple. They slept late into the mornings, then ate a meal with their family before opening their shop at around one o'clock in the afternoon. The shop was not much bigger than a large cupboard. It was neat and clean and consisted of the most common items required by households such as cigarettes, torch batteries, sugar, tea, mosquito coils, bread, candles, cooking oil and soap. They did reasonably well, being on the busy station road, and remained at the shop until three or four o'clock in the morning. These were good business hours, at least during the long, hot season, as the temperatures were then so high the inhabitants of Kayes did not go to bed until the early hours of the morning when there was a brief, if barely noticeable, reduction in the heat. There was a small bench outside the shop where the brothers sat with their many friends who would drop by and sometimes, late in the night, I would go and sit with them, waiting for the long hours of night to pass.

'Ah, Mi–st–er Peter,' Amadou, the younger of the brothers, greeted me cheerfully and enthusiastically one night. 'We have been sitting here wondering if Mr Peter was going to come and talk with us tonight. You see we sit here on the bench all our lives because we have very boring lives and are very happy when someone comes to see us.'

He laughed and got up to give me a place on the bench. 'My brother here wishes to discuss some very big matters with you. He is a very serious person you know, v–e–r–y serious, and he wishes to sort out many problems that the world has.'

'Yes, Mr Peter,' Ousman, who was the more earnest of the two, said. 'Tell me, is it correct that a white man cannot marry a black woman in your country? This is something I have heard.' Then he went on to ask me questions about my opinions on such matters as the unification of Germany and the downfall of Communism.

'Ah yes, that's a very good answer,' he always replied. 'We

Africans cannot know about these things properly, you see, because we never leave our countries and have not seen these things like the Berlin Wall and the Red Square. We have not seen with our own eyes, we only hear on the radio the big happenings of the world and that is like eating food without being able to taste it, is it not?'

'Tell me,' he said, 'I've heard about a man called Dracula. Now is this person a real person? I mean, does he go around sucking people's blood like they say? This is something I've wanted to know for a long time.' And when I told Ousman that it was a fable and not supposed to be true he only half believed me because it was the sort of story he liked to believe.

Ousman and Amadou had by now accepted their jobless fate and no longer had any ambition beyond their shop. They remained perpetually cheerful, but the frustration of being well educated but unable to make any use of their education could be seen in their restlessness and the deep lines etched into their foreheads. Both of them loved their country and regarded it as the best in the world. 'We are a real country,' Amadou told me. 'We are not like some others of the old French colonies who try so hard to be like the French. No, we threw the French out. We are proud of ourselves here.'

But Ousman once said to me: 'Sometimes, we rue the day of our independence. We hailed our President into power and he has deceived us and cares nothing for his people. This country is run by the gun. But we do not think about this because we are impotent to do anything. We laugh instead.'

And they did laugh, laugh and chat. They and all the many other young men who passed their lives sitting on street corners and outside small shops were never not chatting. They were experts at keeping the conversation going. All those hours and days and years passed in chatting.

In Mali it was as if everybody was a brother or sister to everybody else. There were no strangers and individuals were only individual in the framework of a larger conformity. There was little privacy and loners were regarded as strange. The bonds of humanity were strengthened by hardship and a shared upbringing. And so the process of chatting was as easy as breathing.

Thoughts were almost tantamount to words, and silence almost tantamount to madness and death.

Towards the end of my stay in Kayes I bought myself a moped. I had been wondering how I was going to follow Mungo Park from Kayes to the Niger river because this part of his journey covers over 1,000 kilometres of deeply rural countryside where for most of the time there would be just tracks and footpaths leading from one small village to the next. It had come to me one morning that I might do it on a moped. There is a type of French moped that, the parts having been imported from France, is constructed in Bamako and is very popular in Mali. Although it is a basic machine, it would not only give me the chance of reaching the places Mungo Park went to on his horse, but it would also allow me to do so in a fashion I liked: slowly, open to the elements of the countryside and accessible to its peoples.

And so, having been informed that I would have no difficulty in selling one later on when I had no more use for it, I bought one of these French mopeds and the following day left Kayes. I drove across the bridge over the Senegal river, passed quickly through Kayes N'di, and soon found myself in the bush with only the image of Mungo Park and his companions treading the same route as company.

IV

To the North

I DEPARTED FROM Kayes in the afternoon. A village called Tisi Gonsoye was only about 20 kilometres away, and I had noticed that Mungo Park had stopped at a village he called Teesee, only a day's walk from the Senegal river. According to my map, the two were in a similar position.

My moped, being brand new, was spotless and I was proud of it. The silver chrome and blue paintwork shone brilliantly in the sunlight. On the back was strapped my rucksack. I had a bottle of drinking water and a full tank of petrol; enough, I estimated, to take me 200 kilometres, a distance in which it would be hard not to find some small town or even village with at least a drum or can of petrol. This type of moped had a weak engine, however. It was not particularly well adapted to overland driving or, for that matter, to highway driving. It could not, I was to discover, travel much faster than 20 kilometres an hour over the sort of roads I was to use for the next two months. But it was good-looking and tough, and ticked over as simply and unfailingly as a sewing machine. I was happy and felt secure perched atop it.

Having crossed the bridge and passed through Kayes N'di, I took a track towards the village of Dag Dag. In no time at all any indication of the proximity of Kayes disappeared. There was no cultivation or habitation, only small, stumpy trees and bushes and the odd, solitary baobab. I did, though, after a short while, come face to face with a convoy of donkey-and-cart wood collectors coming back from whatever distant place they had to go to these days to find any wood. The young men, plodding wearily beside their donkeys, pulling them along by their ears, waved cheerily to me as I passed.

This was a flat, uninspiring landscape, the Sahel, an area of small, coarse trees and bushes, dry as tinder for much of the year, and often burnt to a cinder. It was poor land, land that had once been able to support kingdoms and empires, but which today has been devastated by the great drought of the 1970s and early 1980s. The drought has killed the cattle of its pastoralists and, year after year, desiccated the earth from which its villagers attempt to reap crops. And once begun the desiccation of a land such as this is almost irreversible. Once villagers, for whom wood is essential for the construction of their houses and cooking, have cut down the trees; once their goats, which must eat, have destroyed the secondary vegetation; once herds of cattle and sheep, which must graze, have overgrazed the remaining good pastures; and once rainfall, which is affected by the deforestation of lands, be they here or further afield, becomes only a fraction of what it once was, a chain reaction is started where the land progressively loses its ability to hinder the wind that strips the surface of the unbound earth and carries sand and desiccation in its grasp. This was indeed poor country, some of the poorest anywhere to be found, but I was prepared to find there much other than poverty.

When I arrived in Dag Dag a man directed me down a footpath to Tisi Gonsoye but, as directions tend to be, his were not very comprehensive: it was not long before the footpath branched into two or sometimes three separate directions, and I had to guess as to which I should take. Soon the paths I had chosen petered out and I found myself driving through rough, virgin terrain. I wove my way onwards between bushes and trees until I suddenly saw that I had a puncture. No matter, I thought to myself, I shall fix it with the puncture repair kit I bought in Kayes. But, I quickly realized, I did not have a spanner with which to remove the wheel. This did not so much indicate the inefficiency of my preparations for the journey as my meagre knowledge of matters mechanical, for one does not, I later realized, need to remove the wheel of a moped in order to mend a puncture. Unaware of this, however, I had no choice but to continue driving on the punctured tyre.

By now it was getting dark and I started to get concerned: my moped was becoming increasingly difficult to drive, swaying drunkenly from side to side as it was; it would be even more difficult to push over the broken terrain; and it appeared that I was lost and I knew that I would not be able to follow my tracks back to Dag Dag in the dark. Would I have to pass my very first night out from Kayes sleeping in the bush? I had no food and only the company of the stars and the wild beasts which, one quickly realizes when one is marooned in the dark bush, are all about one: creeping up from behind, there, that shadow that is darker than it should be. It is true Mungo Park had passed many a night sleeping alone with the beasts in the bush, on one occasion even having to spend the night up a tree to avoid being eaten by lions, but I did not feel that it was necessary to mimic him in this respect. As luck would have it, though, just as the last stains of day were disappearing from the horizon, I saw in the distance the outline of some palm trees. Knowing that palm trees did not grow wild in these parts, I guessed there might be people thereabouts and steering that way I was delighted to discover that not only was there a village, but it was Tisi Gonsoye.

Pushing my bike now, I walked into the village and, meeting a young man, asked him to steer me to the house of the village Imam. An Imam is the leader of a mosque, the one who gives the call to prayers. Normally in a village one should ask for the house of the village chief as, by tradition, he is responsible for feeding and lodging strangers. But I had been given the name of the Imam of Tisi Gonsoye by an old woman I had met in Kayes who was his cousin. The young man obligingly led me through the, by now, almost dark ways of the village. The air smelt of dust and cow dung and the mud walls of the houses between which I passed were warm from the day's sun and pressed close together.

The Imam of Tisi Gonsoye was old and as devout and wise-looking as you would expect. He wore a long, dirty white gown and a skullcap on his head and welcomed me into his home as though I was expected, and then, when I mentioned the name of his cousin in Kayes, I became an honoured guest.

The Imam's compound was large and well constructed. The doorway was an arch big enough to take a man mounted on a horse and decorated round the sides with simple but pleasing designs. Inside there was a long sandy yard with a row of rooms down either side. Both the buildings containing these rooms looked neat and well finished. They were covered with a plaster of cow dung and fine sand that looked like cement. All walls, window frames and floors were smoothed over with this stuff.

Inside, the rooms were cool and spacious, the only objects being perhaps a bamboo bed, some trunks of possessions, and a pile of drying corn cobs. At the far end of the yard was a horse and some goats tied to pegs and at the near end circles of blackened stones with cooking pots on them. Outside the two rows of rooms were verandahs, on the thatched roofs of which were bundles of straw and hoes and other tools. Out the back of each of the rooms were enclosed toiletry areas, which were clean and practical with a hole in the ground for the toilet and a small wooden stool for sitting on when taking a wash.

In fact the whole place was well organized, with large clay water jars in many places, a tall and shady tree in the middle of the yard and, backed up against one of the buildings, a raised dais with a carpet on it. On top of the carpet were two deckchairs made from bamboo and it was to one of these deckchairs that I was directed to sit next to the Imam who occupied the other.

It was not long before the news of my arrival spread round the village and many people came to the Imam's house to greet me. They were mostly the village elders and they sat on the dais talking with the Imam, few of them able to communicate with me in French. There were some people who could, though.

'Why is it that you have come to our village?' one of them said to me.

'I am making a long journey,' I replied. 'I am following the route of an ancient explorer called Mungo Park who passed by here on his way to the Niger, long before the French came to Mali.'

This did not draw much response as nobody had heard of Mungo Park and nobody understood the concept of following in someone's footsteps just for the sake of it.

'Do you follow this man because he is an ancestor of yours?' the man asked me.

'No,' I replied. 'I do it only because I wish to.'

The man discussed this for a while with his friends. Then he said, 'So you are a historian making research.' This was the conclusion people were often to draw when I told them of my journey and I would generally let it go at that, and they, even if they were still a little confused, would also let it go at that. I was there, that was the only really important thing. And they were happy I was there, and let me have my peace.

Peace was something that poured out of the very substance of the home of the Imam of Tisi Gonsoye. It was in the women stirring pots and stoking fires, making supper at the end of the yard. It was in the stirring and shifting of the goats and the horse at the other end. It was in the old men sitting beside me, not asking me questions, but talking gently amongst themselves or just sitting in silence. It was in the tall, dark night and the gentle, wavering noise of the many small boys who sat under the thatch of one of the houses, chanting the Koran. These were the pupils of the Imam's Koranic school, the children of villagers sent to him to be educated in the traditional way. They had wooden boards with verses of the Koran written on them. They had to learn to recognize the scriptures of the Koran and recite them, even if they did not know their meaning. The more someone knew, the more religious merit he had. These boys all chanted the verses they had written on their boards for that day, each one chanting a different verse so that the conflicting sounds of their small voices created a sort of melody, bits of it rising as a boy tried to keep track of his piece, but the whole drifting sweetly on the night air.

That night a mattress was laid out on one of the verandahs for me with a blanket and a mosquito net over it. When I lay down to sleep, having been well fed and having had a good wash from a bucket of water that had been specially warmed up for me, I felt as comfortable and relaxed as I would have been back in my own bed in my own home. Here was the heart of it, I thought to myself. This is the security, the bedrock from which all those cities and peoples come: the village. Just as I was thinking this, a shriek came from the room behind me, then another and then the shouts of a woman. Soon there were more shrieks and the sounds of someone being hit, then hysterical wailing. Voices came from other rooms, shouting from one to the other. Soon the whole compound was filled with shouts and screams and the sounds of hitting continued behind me. After a while it died down to just whispered voices and snivelling, and then soon to silence and peace again.

The next morning I was encouraged to eat a huge breakfast. I sat in one of the rooms with the Imam, making the best I could of the many different dishes of food that were produced. There was milk, with millet flour and sugar added, maize porridge, the remains of a chicken that I had been fed the night before, and some couscous.

As we ate this meal the day became hot outside and flies swarmed about us. By the time I left the room the compound was bathed in that sharp, raw sunlight of mid-morning that seems in rural areas to be all the stronger and sends one scurrying from one patch of shade to another.

The Imam took me to the *bentang* after our breakfast. Mungo Park describes a *bentang* as answering the purpose of a public hall or town house. It is a platform of wooden logs constructed three or so feet from the ground, generally sheltered by some large tree near the centre of a village. It is here that public affairs like palavers and celebrations are conducted. It is also, Park says, where the lazy and indolent meet to smoke pipes and hear the news of the day. It is, in fact, an important part of a village where one will generally find some old men gathered. These days the old men do not smoke pipes, but instead chew kola nuts, those large and bitter red or white nuts that act as a mild stimulant. They are popular in Mali and the giving of them as a gift is a sign of friendship and respect, so they are a good thing for a stranger to carry around. Arriving at the *bentang* the first thing I did, having shaken hands with and greeted the men gathered there, was to give some of these nuts to the chief of the village.

At the *bentang* a small, sturdy man dressed in a tattered shirt and shorts introduced himself to me. He was called Lamine. He carried himself with poise and had a fine, handsome face and a bright smile.

'You are staying here for a long time?'

'No,' I replied, 'I shall probably be leaving today.'

'Today,' he said. 'That's not possible. No, no, not at all possible. You must stay tonight, and tomorrow, and tomorrow night, in fact you must stay as long as you wish. You can stay for a month, or a year even, and nobody will mind. Because, you know, that is our tradition. You will find that in the villages people are very hospitable. Never is a stranger turned away. Whatever we have is yours for as long as you wish to use it. Certainly you must stay at least tonight.'

And so I did and that morning I went with Lamine to his fields where he had some work to do.

With an axe over his shoulder and walking in bare feet Lamine led me out of the village along a small track. 'I left this village many years ago,' he told me as we walked, 'when I was a teenager. All the young men do that these days. Our villages are too poor and we, the young men, must go out into the world to earn some money.' Lamine had gone to the Ivory Coast to do business and then, after seven years of this, had taken a passage on a ship bound for Portugal.

'Portugal was a good country; the people were very friendly. Unfortunately,' he continued, 'I had only spent two days there before the police caught me because I had no visa. They put me on another boat back to Ivory Coast. Now I am back in the village and I shall not leave again. I am married now and I shall have many children. Children are like crops. Without them a village soon dies.'

The fields of Tisi Gonsoye were about 5 kilometres away, around a large dry river bed. There were many fields of millet here, a few palm trees and some plots of vegetables. Women were watering the vegetables from nearby wells and boys were cutting grass and loading it on to carts. Lamine had harvested his field of millet the day before. The tall, dry stalks stood broken and tangled in the field and the heads, heavy with grain, had been put into piles. Lamine now, with my aid, stacked the heads in a neat, circular formation. Once this was done he picked up his axe and with a few deft and vital strokes cut a number of thorny branches of a bush nearby and laid them round the stack of millet heads to prevent any stray or wild animals from eating them whilst they dried.

We got a lift back to Tisi Gonsoye that afternoon in a small donkey-drawn cart driven by two young boys. On the way back Lamine pointed to some low hills in the distance.

'There,' he said, 'there are gold and diamonds. Frenchmen came and looked for them but could not find them, but we know they are there. Maybe one day the Frenchmen will come back, and then they will find them and the village will be rich because it owns those hills.'

The two boys who drove the cart wore hats made from tightly woven sisal. They were well-made hats and neat, almost like Spanish flamenco hats but even shallower, like two round platters. The boys wore them at such a jaunty angle that the backs of their heads were completely exposed and their eyes were hidden far under the rims. The hats had a touch of artistry and sophistication about them that was otherwise lacking in the practicality of the village.

I had planned my journey across Mali as close as possible to the route Mungo Park took. Following Park, if I could, village by village, the journey would start from water, the Senegal river, and end up once again on water, the Niger. Park's primary objective on leaving Kayes had been the town of Segou on the Niger. It was then capital of the Bambarra kingdom of Segou. Here Park could set about an exploration of the true course of the river, perhaps with the help of the powerful ruler of Segou.

The distance between Kayes on the Senegal river and Segou on the Niger is approximately 575 kilometres. Park's route, however, and so the route I was to take, covers over 1,000 kilometres. He had to make a large detour to the north in order to avoid a war which was pending between the kingdoms of Kaarta and Segou which lay on his route. In fact, Park could hardly have chosen a worse time to travel across this part of Africa. Ever since the break-up of the old empires which had brought a degree of security and stability to this area, and when the Moroccan influence imposed after the Moroccan invasion of Sonhay had disintegrated, there had been much confusion and turmoil.

As Mungo Park travelled, he saw preparations for many wars and conflicts: the fleeing of towns; the stocking up on provisions for a siege; the coming and going of messengers and emissaries. But, like a tidal wave devouring towns, villages and people's lives, the wars always broke out a few steps behind him. He did not see the razed villages and burnt crops. He did not witness the thousands of men, women and children being put to the sword or sold into slavery. He managed to avoid becoming directly embroiled in the troubles of these times, but his detour to the north was to bring him a fate perhaps much worse.

During his journey from Kayes to Segou, Mungo Park depended much upon the goodwill of the rulers of the many kingdoms through which he had to pass. A man of his 'uncommon appearance' could not pass unnoticed, and because of the goods he carried with which to buy provisions, he was rich. The official laws of the countries he passed, Park says, afforded him no protection so he needed to solicit protection from the kings, and those kings, on the whole, did their best to aid him. It was the ambitious sons and relatives of kings who were to trouble him and relieve him of much of his wealth. But, 'Let us suppose,' Park writes, 'a black Hindustan to have found his way into the centre of England, with a box of jewels at his back, and that the laws of the kingdom afforded him no security; in such a case the wonder would be, not that the stranger was robbed of any part of his riches, but that any part was left to a second depredator.' And the first of these depredators was not far away in the person of Demba Sego, the young man who had offered to guide Park across the Senegal river and into the kingdom of Khasso.

On the way over the Senegal river in a small boat, 'the king's nephew', as Park described the scene, 'thought this a proper time to have a peep into a tin box of mine that stood in the forepart of the canoe; and stretching out his hand for it, he unfortunately destroyed the equilibrium, and overset the canoe.' Having successfully saved the baggage, crossed the river and arrived in Demba's nearby home town of Teesee, today's Tisi Gonsoye, Demba then twice borrowed Park's horse, the first time to pursue an eloping slave, and the second, causing Park to be delayed for nine days, to travel to the north to settle a dispute that had arisen with some Moors. Then, on the day of Park's eventual departure, Demba, with a number of people, came to him claiming that he had been sent by his father, who was chief of the town, for a present. After refusing the present Park offered, Demba and his companions set upon Park's baggage, relieving him of exactly half of the half of it that Park had salvaged from his last robbery in Kajaaga, including, Park notes, the tin box that had so interested the young man on the way over the Senegal river.

But Park, on the whole, had found that the people of Teesee

were kind and generous towards him and in his time there he had witnessed a number of interesting things. One of these was the trial of a holy man. This 'old gallant' was being tried for the crime of seducing the bride of a young friend of his. That young friend had come to him asking for some charms to protect him in the forthcoming war with Kajaaga. The holy man had told him that to make the charms more potent he must not indulge in nuptial intercourse with his bride for six weeks. The holy man, who was in the habit of saying his evening prayers outside the door of the bride's house, then secretively seduced the girl. Having been found guilty of this act at his trial, he was sentenced to be sold into slavery or to find two slaves for his redemption. The young man, though, 'was unwilling to see his friend so severely punished and desired rather to have him publicly flogged and this was immediately carried out, the roars of the holy man at the forty strokes, save one, resounding in the woods'.

I spent only two days in Tisi Gonsoye, and most of that time I passed in the company of Lamine. He had now given up his ambitions to go to Europe, or indeed beyond the village. He looked after his field, and his family were happy with that. And when he was too old to grow his millet, Lamine would join the old men who sat all day on the *bentang*.

Long after I left Mali, nearly a year after I had visited Tisi Gonsoye, I received a letter from Lamine. In it he said:

All the village salutes you and are very happy to receive your letter. Do not forget us and remember that time when we went to my field of millet and travelled back to the village in a donkey and cart which we called the 'African taxi'. This year was not good because the rains were bad and the millet was bad, and the maize and the groundnuts, everything was bad, but we, who do not forget you, always have courage.

★

I left Tisi Gonsoye for the town of Koniakary, the old capital of the kingdom of Khasso to which Mungo Park had gone to meet the king. At first I passed through an open, gentle landscape of tall, yellow grasses with low hills and escarpments in the distance. But soon I found myself rising up on to the top of one of the escarpments and here I discovered a desolate scene. Here fire had destroyed all, leaving only charred growth and a black, ash-covered surface of rock. The nakedness of the place in conjunction with the heat of the sun created the atmosphere of an inferno; one felt exposed and insignificant amidst such a barren wilderness.

The burning of the dry grasses that produces this kind of terrain was, in Mungo Park's day, a purposeful action which, Park says, 'was soon followed by fresh verdure, thereby rendering the country more healthy'. Today this practice is illegal. The pastoralists who still come to these regions need the dry grass as fodder for their animals, and the burning kills the smaller and newer trees and bushes, therefore giving the winds and sands more opportunity to desiccate the land. It is still sometimes practised, though, but more often the fires are accidental and huge areas of the Sahel are burnt out like this place I was now driving through.

Somewhere on this escarpment I met two men riding bicycles, coursing down the incline of the land at a precarious speed. Their bicycles were large and black, as solid as scaffolding, with thick tyres patched with colourful pieces of material, no brakes, no footrests on the pedals, and large wooden boxes strapped to the backs. I was at that time a little lost, so I asked the men the way to the village of Medina, through which I had to pass on my way to Koniakary. But they could not tell me which tracks led that way. They were on their long way home from Kayes, and all tracks to them, it seemed, led that way. When, however, later on, I arrived in a village called Kouniandji, a tiny, one or two family place tucked into an overgrown valley, some women and children pointed me down the track to Medina.

Medina appeared as a forest of perfectly conical thatched roofs gone grey with age. I made my way through the maze of round, brown huts and by the time I pulled up to the *bentang*, I had a trail of children running behind and beside me. The noise of my machine had alerted the women in the compounds who came to the fences to have a look. The old men on the *bentang* stopped their talking and held still, caught, as it were, in their posture of day-long sloth, with, for a moment, a dumbfounded look on their faces. These arrivals in small, remote villages where the appearance of any mechanized means of transport was an occurrence of rarity and note, let alone one with a European on it, were met with a certain degree of excitement and surprise. I could not with ease slip into a village, inconspicuous and ready to immediately depart.

I pulled up my moped, put it on its stand, and went and shook hands with the old men, then the young men, and then all the little grubby hands thrust at me with a mixture of nervousness and pride. The old men broke from their dumbfounded freeze.

'*I ni sagoma?*' I greeted them, wishing them a good morning.

'*Nba, I ni sagoma*,' they responded in the traditional way.

'Did you have a peaceful night?'

'Peace only,' they replied.

'How are you?' I continued.

'Fine.'

'What about the wife?'

'Fine.'

'And the children?' And on we went with the long, ritualistic greetings that are such an important part of life and that Fatima in Kayes had rehearsed me in. Once I had completed this I became more human and comprehensible to the old men, at which point they invited me to sit beside them on the *bentang* and shifted over to make me a place. Once sitting, more greetings and wishes of well-being for family, home and friends commenced to wind around to my mission, as my voyage came to be known.

Then I produced my copy of Mungo Park's book and my map and tried to explain. The book was of immense interest to the men and they leafed through its pages and marvelled at its size. It was an impressive book, well put together, with pictures and hundreds of pages in it. Books, or indeed writing of any sort, were, amongst the older men, rarely seen and special. They knew only the writings of the Koran and those words were divine. When, for example, Mungo Park had one time written the Lord's Prayer on a board for someone, that person had washed off the ink and drunk it as a charm.

But my map had no meaning for these people. They looked

at it, holding it perhaps upside down. They saw no connection between it and their land. Their land was a living thing and their knowledge of it came from the stories, past and present, that had occurred in it. It was where they took their goats to graze, that place where their ancestors had once lived. It had themes and plots and they could not comprehend that these could be put down on a piece of paper. My maps were very detailed and so my knowledge of their lands amazed them and made them laugh with incredulity. How could I, a stranger, know the names and directions of things they had learnt from their fathers and grandfathers?

Once all this had been performed, the village chief, or Dugu tigi, invited me to partake of some hospitality in his compound opposite the *bentang*. Here I was seated in a chair and immediately an old and withered woman, bent nearly double, came up to me and, cackling with mirth, began to dance around me mumbling the words of a song. Everybody in the yard laughed, so I did too, and soon the old woman shook my hand and went off. Then I was given water and milk with maize flour in it to drink. An old man had problems with his eyes and I was asked if I could help, so I put some eye drops in them with most of the village gathered round to watch. And then soon I was off, thanking my hosts, shaking all hands again, and gradually dropping off my trail of running children as I sped along the track that led to Marena, another place through which I had to pass in order to reach Koniakary, and which had in Mungo Park's day been called Jumbo.

Marena was situated in the wide valley of the Kolibine river where there were small villages and a considerable amount of cultivation. This had been the home town of one of Mungo Park's travelling companions, a blacksmith called Tami. On Tami's return home after an absence of more than four years, two of his brothers in the company of a singing man and a procession of dancing townsfolk came a short distance to meet him. Then, when he entered his town, Tami was received by his relatives, and especially his old and blind mother, in, Park says, the strongest and most expressive manner of emotion. His mother stroked his hands, arms and face with great care, and on observing this tender meeting Park was moved to state that he was now 'fully convinced, that whatever difference there is between the Negro and European in the conformation of the nose and the colour of the skin, there is none in the genuine sympathies and characteristic feelings of our common nature'.

Park passed two days in feasting and merriment in Marena. The people there were, as were almost all the people he met, amazed by him for they had never seen a white man before. 'A few women and children,' he writes, 'expressed great uneasiness at being so near a man of such uncommon appearance ... and when by accident I happened to move myself, or look at the young children, their mothers would scamper off with them with the greatest precipitation.'

I was also often to come across people who were amazed by my appearance. Generally these were people who, even if they had seen a white man before, had never seen one at close quarters, perhaps hunkered down with them around a bowl of food. In the remote villages, however, the young children often had never seen a white man at all and when I happened, by chance, to look at them, and catch their eye, they would melt into terrified sobs as though I were the very devil himself.

Marena was, these days, a small traditional town: a maze of thin passageways wending through a medina of brown mud buildings. There were many merchants' shops and *bentangs* and an atmosphere of activity and urbanity. Here a group of merchants insisted that I eat a large bowl of rice, not allowing me to move until it was all finished. On the far side of the town a thin young man picked up my moped and, with apparently little difficulty, carried it, laden as it was with petrol, water and my bag, across the Kolibine river which still had a small quantity of water lying stagnant in its bed.

★

I arrived in Koniakary just before sunset. The capital of the old kingdom of Khasso, Koniakary once had been the seat of kings. It is built in the lee of an abrupt and solitary mountain on a wide and fertile plain. The mountain is like one huge block of rock. Its crown falls away to slopes clogged with vegetation which then fall to sheer, dark cliffs. Sitting small and round at its foot, the town still looks regal. The mountain is like a monument to it and the plains of crops and glittering waterways that surround it are a wealth fit for kings. In Mungo Park's day Khasso had been a kingdom of some considerable population. The king, Park says, could raise an army of 4,000 fighting men by the mere sound of his war drum.

I drove first to the market-place in the middle of Koniakary where a tailor advised me to go to the post office where I might find some lodgings for the night. The telegraph wires would, he said, take me there. They led to the outskirts of town to a large, rectangular building which had two green window shutters propped open at its front. By a side door there was a woman washing clothes in a bucket and a man in a track suit with a knife and a long gun in his hands. I exchanged greetings with the man and asked, 'Is this the post office?'

'Yes,' the man replied.

'I was informed that I might be able to find lodgings here for the night.'

He did not reply.

'I was told,' I continued, 'that the post office chief sometimes puts up travellers.'

'I am the post office chief,' the man said, shortly. 'I am going hunting tonight, but you can sleep in there if you like.' He indicated a back room of the post office, through the open door of which I could see two large green safes. Then he stalked off with his gun, not to reappear for the rest of the night. I passed the evening in the company of his wife and some friends of hers and then, later on, when I went to lie down on a mat in the room with two safes, I listened to the celebrations of a marriage or baptism that was taking place somewhere in the town: the beat of a drum, rising and falling in tempo, the shrieks of women and the shots of guns which conjured up an image of dancing and revelry about a roaring fire.

Early the following morning I went for a walk around the town. Unlike Marena, this was not a town of solid, well-constructed buildings with streets and an atmosphere of urbanity. It was like a huge village: a sprawl of peasantry surrounding a nucleus of the stone shops of merchants and a large square mosque. Each part of it was a village, each village a complex of compounds.

Each compound was surrounded by sticks planted in the sand for a fence. The ways between them were the streets, deep in sand and refuse. It was a haphazard, cluttered and confusing place rooted in agricultural life. Its roofs were a sea of thatch and every part of it crawled and hummed with activity like an ants' nest. Around its perimeter the earth had been worn bare for a distance. Then beyond this were the wells from which continuous lines of women came and went with buckets of water on their heads. Then past the wells began the crops of millet. At this hour hundreds of goats and sheep were being chased out of the many pathways that led out of the town by small boys who collected them into herds before taking them to browse for the day in the bush.

The post office chief was present when I returned to the post office that morning. He was a 'functionary', as civil servants were known. These functionaries could be found throughout rural areas, sometimes in the smallest of villages. They might be agricultural advisers, pest control officers, teachers or administration officials, among other things. Their jobs were hard as they were generally posted far from their homes, sometimes without their families. They represented the modern nation of Mali with its new hierarchy of authority. The local people did not always appreciate these commanding, educated strangers. Also their jobs were sometimes very boring or even pointless, and their wages often did not materialize for months on end. The post office chief in Koniakary was not a very happy man, or a very friendly one at first. He had shot two jackals when hunting the night before. 'Will you eat this meat?' he asked me aggressively, as if expecting me to refuse. 'It's all we have anyway.'

That day, being Sunday, there was no work at the post office and so the day was devoted to the preparation and eating of a big lunch. The post office chief was surly and ignored me. But once the meal was produced in a large bowl, and everybody had sat down around it on small stools, he cheered up a little, as indeed did everyone at the prospect of satisfying their hunger.

'I shot at three other jackals in the night,' the post office chief told me. 'I saw their red eyes in the dark but they were too far away to hit. Push that boy out of your way,' he said, more friendly now, referring to his young son who had squeezed himself between my knees and the bowl of food.

We passed the hot part of the afternoon sitting under a tree outside the front of the post office, making tea and listening to a football match on the radio. Cameroon were playing Algeria for a qualifying place in the 1990 World Cup. Being south of the Sahara everybody was on the side of Cameroon and it was they, amidst the hysterical screeching of the commentator as he came and went with the airwaves, who won.

Later that afternoon I went to climb the mountain next to the town. The post office chief who thought this a very odd thing to want to do said to me, 'If you wish to climb the mountain you must first go to the small village at its foot and ask permission of the "Bedanise". This mountain,' he added, 'is no ordinary mountain. It is magical and anybody who climbs it without the permission of the elders of that village will never come down again.'

When I got to the village which had authority over the mountain, I met the village elders at the *bentang* and, when I had paid some money to the village chief, a guide was provided for me. Then I and my guide were taken into a room where prayers were said over us and we had to spit on our hands and rub them on our faces. 'You can now climb the mountain in safety,' the village chief said. 'You have the blessing and protection of the "Bedanise".'

My guide was an old man, gnarled and heavily wrinkled, but he was fit and strong. With a knife and a stick in his hands he set off up a small, steep path with a speed that soon left the village and the plain of Koniakary falling away beneath us. At each of the rests we took, the last many hundreds of feet above the village, when we turned round to see the view, there were new and ever more distant horizons. The whole land around us began to take shape like a map: the hills opposite, curving round to the east to cradle the plain; a gravel road running west to Kayes, lying flush to the undulations of the terrain, tapering to a condensation of haze and distance; Koniakary, round and brown upon its bare patch of earth; and then the plain laid out like a mat below us with its quilted crops and the small Kourigou river cutting through it, in many places dry, but with odd pools and small flood plains of water glinting in the sunlight. This stream then lost itself in a wild and hilly land far to the east. Here rock and boulder and broken hillside merged with thick, brown vegetation, the distance that way looking forbidding and inaccessible. That was the way I would go when I left Koniakary.

Here on the mountainside all this was still a part of us, but once we had climbed over the lip of the mountain we entered the hidden world of the mountain top. The horizons were lost. By now both of us were sweating from our exertions but we did not stop. We pushed our way through the tangled vegetation on the broken, boulder-strewn flat that encircled the steep summit. Slowly we made our way round the flat and when I enquired why we did not climb to the top of the summit, I was told to listen. At first I could hear nothing, but as we progressed I noticed a steady, low hum. Once we had reached the far side the hum became louder until it filled the air and I recognized it as the sound of bees. The noise of them grew and grew until it became menacing, like a warning. It was all about us and soon the flats around which we were walking became thinner, drawing us ever closer to the summit and the sound of the bees. Our way was clogged with broken gullies and thick, tearing bushes. We struggled through, my guide working fast to break a path, and the bees droned ever louder.

We did not stay on the mountain for long. My guide seemed keen to leave as soon as possible. He was silent and earnest in his attempts to regain the path back down the mountain. Soon we found it and left the domain of the bees, and as we disappeared over the lip of the mountain to the view of the other world, a flock of black, ugly birds in a tree nearby cackled at our backs as though they were laughing. In no time at all, it seemed, we were amongst the huts and yards of the village, two of the tiny ants that scurried around its white paths.

When I arrived back at the post office in Koniakary late that evening and mentioned the bees of the mountain to the post office chief, he exclaimed, 'Ah, the sacred bees. You have heard them. You are a lucky one to have come back alive. Never would you get me to go up there, never.'

Before I left Koniakary I went to see an old man who was a direct descendant of the royal line of Koniakary. It had been the post office chief who, on hearing something of the object of my journey, had mentioned that living nearby was a descendant of Demba Sego Dialla, the king Mungo Park had met. Just near the post office there were the ruins of a large fort that had been built by El Hadj Umar, a religious leader who, inspired by a divine vision, had set out on a holy war and conquered much of what is modern-day Mali sixty or so years after Park's visit. The fort was only a tall and crumbling outer wall today, inside of which was a large field of millet and one small mud house. The fort had come into the possession of the royal family of Koniakary after the downfall of Hadj Umar and now their descendant lived in a shack, reduced to poverty and insignificance.

The old man was called Demba Sego, as was Park's young guide two hundred years ago. He was, by his own account, ninety years old, born in 1900. I found him lying on a mat in the mud house. He was frail and misty-eyed but his mind was sharp and he could speak some French. I sat beside him and listened to many stories of the history of his family, but I was unable to follow them well as he whispered in a thin, wavering voice. He was proud of his ancestry and he knew of Mungo Park – 'the white man who sailed down the Niger to his death'.

After a while the old man grew tired and so I left him to the care of his daughters and granddaughters. He was the only person I met in Mali who had any direct connection with Mungo Park, the only link between the living young Scot and myself.

★

Mungo Park, on departing from Koniakary, travelled to Guemou, capital of the neighbouring kingdom of Kaarta. In doing this he first followed the valley of the Korougou river, and so when I left Koniakary I did so as well.

The cultivated plain of Koniakary quickly gave way to thick bush before I came to the village of Tinti. In Tinti I was pointed down a track and told to drive slowly. 'This is the real bush,' a man said to me, 'full of hyena and even lion.' And having rounded a hill, I soon found myself having to part bushes and fight my way through undergrowth. For a long stretch there was no sign of man, except the path that was having difficulty in holding its own. Then I came to a bend of the Korougou river, here wide and almost dry. The two banks on either side of it were too steep to drive the moped down and up, but finding no other place to cross I was forced to carry it. Down was quite easy, across the river also easy, but up the far bank I had the greatest of difficulty. I was glad nobody was around at that moment because the sight of me trying to inch my moped up an almost sheer mud slide, scrabbling against the loose earth with knees, hands and toes, heaving, swearing, sweating and shouting like a demon would have been cause for much entertainment.

Having composed myself after this, I drove into a hilly and broken landscape, the Korougou valley twisting through it like a snake through tall grass. For a long time there was still no sign of man's presence, but then I came upon a small village and, soon after this, having once again crossed the Korougou river, I had to negotiate my way down a path which became increasingly rocky and so increasingly difficult to drive or even push my moped along. It was not until mid afternoon, by which time I was doubting whether I would be able to follow Mungo Park much further along the Korougou valley, that the path suddenly improved, and not long after this I came to the village of Fakama.

Fakama was a poor, scrappy village of Soninke people. The land around it was almost devoid of fertility and the valley in which it sat trapped the heat in a vice. Like a piece of old, torn material found enmeshed in a gorse bush, the village was ensnared in the rocky valley and the barbed vegetation that pressed in close all round it. The only blessing was the Korougou river a short distance away, here quite wide, although for nine months of the year as dry as a bone.

At the *bentang* I found the old men. They lay at all angles on the wooden platform, their dirty, torn garments pulled close about them against the strong wind. One of them was making rope by binding strips of tree bark together. This man spoke some French. 'I'm an *ancien combattant*, an *ancien combattant*,' he said to me. 'I fought in the Second World War for the French. They came here and took away young men to build their towns and join their army. They came and took me, so I'm an *ancien combattant*.'

He was also, it turned out, the Dugu tigi, or village chief, and I now entered into a long and complex conversation with the people on the *bentang* about the possibilities of continuing my journey along the Korougou valley.

'It is impossible,' the Dugu tigi kept repeating. But a young man who was sitting nearby who could also speak French said that it was possible. Yet another said something about a path to the north.

'You'll have to return to Koniakary,' the *ancien combattant* said.

'Where did you say you wanted to go?' another asked.

'He wants to go to Koniakary,' someone replied.

'No, he wants to go north. Or was it east?'

When it became apparent that I was not about to get on my moped then and there and go in any direction, the young man who could speak some French invited me to come and have some food. We left the old men still hotly discussing in which direction they thought I wanted to go.

The young man's name was Samba and he was, he explained, a Bambarran, as opposed to Soninke like everyone else. This, it became apparent, formed a bond between us: we were brothers of displacement. 'I've been in this village for four years,' Samba said, 'but now I want to leave. How much is a ticket to France?'

Samba had a somewhat dishevelled appearance. He carried himself with a hang-dog stoop, wore a pair of trousers frayed off below the knees and sported a large 'afro' of unruly hair which was unconventional in a country where everybody shaved their hair close to the scalp. He was the village blacksmith, and he now took me to a house from on top of the roof of which he produced a small bowl of *to*, a stiff porridge of millet.

'The Soninke only eat millet,' Samba said, handing this to me. 'Millet is their life.'

I passed the remainder of the afternoon with Samba in his workshop. This was a small shed made from grass mats. The strong wind tugged at its frayed edges and the blowing sand hissed against its sides. Inside, the ground was deep in sand and littered like a junk yard with pieces of metal and wood, and

107

scraps of paper and old tea leaves lay about. There was a block of metal which served as an anvil and two goatskin bellows with their metal ends planted into the earth to reappear in a small pit where some old charcoal lay. Replenishing the charcoal, Samba squatted down to pump the bellows and, once the coals were hot, he put a small teapot on them.

Samba was regarded by the youth of Fakama as worldly wise. The many young people who now joined us in the shed listened attentively to him as he spoke about the advantages of life in France. 'There,' he said, looking to me for confirmation, 'there are many good jobs and lots of money to be made. And if you marry a French woman her father will give you a house and a car. You can live like a king in France.'

I stayed only one night in Fakama. Despite its poverty it was a cheerful village. For seven months of the year it had to face heat so staggering that even the goats did not leave the shade of the village in the daytime. Then there would be nothing to eat except *to* and the wells would dry up one by one until there was only water enough for cooking and drinking: the harshness and the barrenness of the elements ruled village life and to make the most of what they had was the code of the villagers' existence.

The evening in Fakama, as in villages throughout Mali, was a busy time. Everybody employed themselves in some industrious way, making the most of that brief spell of time between the dying of the heat and the coming of darkness. The scene was one of intense domesticity revolving round the preparation of the evening meal and the shutting up or pegging down of the livestock for the night, the two occupations taking place in the space of each other's chaos. The women and their apprentice daughters pounded the grain and chopped wood for the cooking fires. Calabashes of millet flour or couscous lay about amidst others containing groundnuts or beans. Meanwhile all the small boys devoted their attention to capturing lambs to be pegged down for the night. Round and round the compound they chased them, diving for their hind legs, in and out of the women and their work, across mats where men were saying prayers, in and out of houses. Those lambs that were not at that moment being chased gave their attention to the bowls of food lying around, grabbing mouthfuls, and were beaten back by volleys of stones. Herds of sheep and goats were driven to enclosures and the chicken shooed to cardboard boxes to be shut up for the night.

The women soon had large pots of water on the fires over which would be placed other pots with perforations in their bases in which couscous could be steamed. Gradually all the family members converged on the compound, some washing themselves, some saying prayers and some making tea, but everybody from the eldest to the youngest occupying themselves usefully until the food was prepared. Then the women and young children took a bowl of the food to one part of the compound and the men huddled round another. By now it was dark and so the eating was done blindly. Everybody was expert at eating with their hands, capable of scooping up the hottest or the most liquid food with their fingers and delivering it to their mouths without a drop falling to the ground. That night I ate three dishes of couscous with a delicious bean sauce in the three different compounds to which I was taken by Samba to meet people.

Once everybody had eaten they dispersed, the women and girls together, the men to stay sitting on the mats in the compounds, and the youths off to socialize in different parts of the village, everybody chatting idly in the darkness with only the odd flash of a torch, until tired enough to sleep. I slept on a mat under a mosquito net with Samba who kicked all night long.

The following morning I left Fakama. The previous evening I had been able to determine from the villagers that it would be impossible for me to continue along the Korougou valley. The path was impassable to a moped, I was told. The alternatives were to retrace my steps to Koniakary or to take a small path that climbed into the hills to the north before descending towards the town of Lambatara on the road that connected Kayes to Nioro du Sahel, a large town to the north. For a while this road travelled adjacent to the Korougou valley and from it I would be able to rejoin Mungo Park's route a little further on. I decided to take this path and it was arranged that my friend Samba and the village chief's son would accompany me as my moped needed to be carried a considerable part of the 20-kilometre route.

The journey was indeed not an easy one. As soon as we had crossed the Korougou river, waving goodbye to a group of those endlessly hard-working women drawing water from a well in its bed, we rose up into a thickly vegetated, boulder-strewn land-scape. At times I thought we would not be able to manage the moped up the steep rock paths that squeezed between, and sometimes went over, the boulders.

In the small village of Diakone, a few kilometres from Lambat-ara, I said goodbye to my companions, Samba and the village chief's son. Then they were off at a quick pace, leaving behind the wide valley with its road to another world, back to their small and inaccessible valley and their village.

★

The wind was blowing fiercely when I arrived in Lambatara. The wind and the sand that flew in its grasp were eclipsing the importance of mankind, and Lambatara seemed hardly to exist. In the town there seemed to be no people, just empty, dust-besieged streets, but in a merchant's shop I found a small, warm knot of humanity. Here the merchant gave me a handful of boiled sweets, and a tailor working on the verandah with whom I sat for an hour or so made me some coffee.

After Lambatara the gravel road which went north to Nioro du Sahel deteriorated rapidly, the broken, rocky country steering it through gullies and up round hillsides, and in many places replacing its surface with something like the bed of a river. After 30 kilometres a string of mud huts beside the road represented the only sign of man I had come across.

After this the country became flat and burnt out with tiny, twirling dust devils, spinning ash into the air. At one point I came across a Fulani family. There is much mystery about the origins of these people. They are different stock from all other West Africans. They have fairer skins, prominent profiles and soft, silky hair. They have, for much of their history, been a wandering people, not unlike the gipsies of Europe, and can be found now in countries all the way across the savannahs of West Africa. Traditionally they are pastoralists, semi-nomadic keepers of large herds of cattle. But they have also been the rulers of kingdoms and, at times, especially devoted Islamic scholars.

This family I now met were poor people. Perhaps they, like so many of their race, had lost all their cattle in the recent droughts. There was a string of donkeys with pots, pans, blankets and other domestic equipment strapped around them, on the backs of which, nestled amidst all these things, were women and young children. The women had bright, flashing eyes underlined with mascara, and fine noses. They wore black shawls and the gold which represented their husband's wealth shone from their ears. That husband walked behind them on bare feet with a stick over his shoulder, and behind him came the sons herding sheep and goats. The women looked in amazement at me as I passed, and the husband did also, remembering only at the last minute to raise his hand in greeting.

I passed that night in a small town called Sandare staying with a group of functionaries who were housed a little apart from the town in a row of dilapidated rooms. They were young men, all of them, and the discussion round the fire that night was about their wages which had not been paid for six months. 'We are in such debt to the town merchants,' they said. 'How will we ever pay them back? Last week we heard on the radio that our wages are soon to be paid. But they are only going to pay us three months, meaning that we lose three months' worth.'

'Ah, they have big appetites, the big men in Bamako,' one of them said. 'They eat up all the money, leaving none for anybody else.'

'What do we need money for?' another exclaimed. 'Look at all this sand around us. We can eat that, can we not?'

After Sandare I took a thin, sandy track which passed through an area that was thick with tall, yellow grass: there had been no fires here. Along this track I met a few Soninke men mounted on horses and at one time I passed a Land-rover, the first vehicle I had seen, other than in the town of Koniakary, since leaving Kayes. Apart from these I was left with the birds and lizards who scattered as I slewed through the sand.

In the village of Lakamane I was given lunch by the wife of a functionary who lived there and was a friend of the functionaries I had stayed with in Sandare but was away at that time. Whilst I was eating the rice provided by this kind woman, a man came and sat beside me and asked me to give him the food. He was an odd, wild-looking man and refused when I invited him to share it with me. He set his hot eyes upon me and questioned me deeply about my journey. 'Why do you travel alone . . . ? What is it you are looking for in Mali . . . ? Have you got permission to do this journey?' he asked. His French was good but he never listened to an answer. He just went on asking questions ever more fiercely. He seemed an intelligent man but when the woman who was feeding me returned from inside the house where she had been busying herself, she shooed him away as though he were one of the sheep who continually besiege the cooking areas of houses. 'That man is a fool,' she indicated, by tapping her head, and one of her sons who spoke some school French said, 'He was a teacher, in a faraway town, but he gave up teaching and came home to farm instead. Then one day he beat up his wife so badly she left him and he has been mad ever since. His problem drove him crazy,' the boy said.

Guemou, the old capital of Kaarta, was only 30 kilometres northwest of Lakamane and so I reached it before the sun had set. It was, as Mungo Park also states on his first view of the town, situated in the middle of an open plain, the country for two miles or so around 'being cleared of wood by the consumption of that article for fuel and building'. In Park's day the town, being the capital of Kaarta, would have been of considerable size. Its many inhabitants were so amazed at the appearance of Park they surrounded him to such an extent that he was not able to dismount from his horse and then, when he was shown into a large hut, the mob of people took it in turns to enter and ask him questions, in this manner, Park says, filling and emptying the hut thirteen separate times.

On meeting the king, Desse Koulibali, or as Park calls him, Daisy, Park was impressed by the number of attendants he had and the general order that prevailed amongst them: the fighting men sitting to the right of the king, the women and children to the left, and the king, distinguished from his subjects only by a mound of earth with a mat on it upon which he sat, in the middle.

The kingdom of Kaarta and its neighbour Segou had an historic enmity and the causes for the war which was about to take place between them stemmed from this. When a few bullocks belonging to a frontier town of Segou were stolen by a party of Moors and then sold to a town chief in Kaarta, Monsong, the king of Segou, availed himself of this incident to declare hostilities.

He sent a pair of iron sandals to Daisy with the message that until such a time as he had worn out the sandals in his flight, he should never be secure from the arrows of Segou. Daisy then made an eccentric proclamation that those of his subjects who chose to leave his domains and remain neutral in the forthcoming war would be welcome to return afterwards. But those, he said, who took an active part against Kaarta had 'broken the keys of their huts'. Sadly a great number of people availed themselves of the indulgent clause and retired from Kaarta and so when the Bambarran army of Segou advanced on Guemou, Daisy was forced to abandon his capital without firing a shot and take refuge in some hilly country to the west. Monsong then ordered a part of his army to overrun the kingdom; this was executed with such speed that within a few days 'the whole kingdom was a scene of desolation'.

These days Guemou was little more than a village and in it, at first, I had difficulty in locating anybody with whom I could communicate. A few old women I met smiled pleasantly at me and nodded when I asked, *'Dugu tigi be min?'* – 'Where is the village chief?' – but did not seem to comprehend. At the *bentang* I found an old man fast asleep. Having disturbed his slumber I did not have any more success with him than I had had with the women. He simply gazed at me through the blue haze of cataracts in his eyes as though I were an apparition in his recently disturbed dreams. After five minutes, though, the apparition not having disappeared, he went off, to return a few minutes later with another old man, the Dugu tigi.

It was not until the following day that I was to discover why this village was so empty of people. There was a marriage festival taking place in a nearby village and almost all the inhabitants had gone there, leaving only the oldest men and women behind. I passed one night there in the company of a 'slave', sleeping on a mat which the Dugu tigi, on meeting me, had pulled out from a nearby hut and unceremoniously deposited on the sand in the middle of the village, and which, I concluded, must have belonged to the 'slave' because he slept next to me on the ground.

The 'slave' spoke some French and, even though slavery in its true and original form no longer existed in Mali, he was a self-professed member of this caste. He came from a family that

113

had once been owned by the nobles of the village and so still had an inferior status. 'I'm an old black slave,' he said to me. 'These men are my masters and I work very hard.' He was a tough and simple man dressed in rags and had learnt his French, he told me, when, in 1952, he had worked for a team of French cartographers who had come to the region to draw up the map I was now using.

He gave me a handful of peanuts to eat and shared his bowl of *to* with me and we passed a quiet night disturbed only by a flea-ridden dog which attempted to lie down beside us. 'Away with you, you devil,' the 'slave' yelled at the miserable beast when he saw it, and jumping up delivered a kick to its ribs which sent it yelping into the night.

The following morning, before I departed, I talked to a group of old men on the *bentang*. With the help of the French-speaking 'slave', they informed me that the king of Kaarta in Park's day, Daisy, was remembered primarily as the man who deserted his capital on the advance of the Bambarran army without even the pretence of resistance. The 'slave', amidst much mirth, translated as such: 'The old rogue fled with such haste he did not even have time to spit at Segou.'

★

Mali is divided into seven administrative regions. Each region is divided into *cercles*, each of which is further divided into *arrondissements*. The head village of the *arrondissement* I was now in was a large village called Simbi, and it was to Simbi that I went from Guemou.

The road north from Guemou was sandy and in more open countryside than I had been used to. I was now approaching the fringes of an extended Sahara, and what fire, goats and the axes of the villagers had not done to clear the vegetation for the way of the sand, droughts had.

Simbi was the town Guemou should have been. Here was a well-constructed medina: a weave of sandy passages between sturdy earthen walls which enclosed large and well-organized compounds; open areas with shady trees and *bentangs* in them; and a tiny market-place with a meat seller and a merchant's shop.

Although Simbi was really only a village it felt like a town, and one could at first get quite lost in its ways and end up in open areas that one was never sure were a part of the public street or someone's yard. On the outskirts of the village, to the east, was an area of modern cement houses where the administrative staff from the military commandant down to the teachers lived and worked.

To the west of the village were two large ponds covered in lilies and inhabited by thousands of frogs. These ponds were all that remained of the rains which, when they came, collected into small rivers which then gradually evaporated to a string of ponds, and then, later into the dry season, to nothing at all. Women came to do their washing in the ponds and, here in Simbi, orchards of guava trees had been planted next to them. The orchards were divided into separate enclosures by walls of matted grass and in each enclosure, in the shade of the trees, were vegetable plots. At that time of year, the guava trees were fruiting. The fruits hung heavy from the boughs and people were collecting them into panniers. They would then be cycled overnight to Nioro du Sahel some distance to the north ready to be sold fresh in the next day's market there.

On this side of the village there were also many kraals for cattle and goats and some encampments of the Fulani with their small, tatty tents and strings of sad-looking donkeys.

When I arrived in Simbi I met an old man at a *bentang* who, being another *ancien combattant*, spoke French. He invited me to his home to drink some tea and there I ended up staying for two nights.

My host was called Mohammed. He was a tall, thin man who had an air of sprightly youth and a constant companion who never left his side: his grandson. His wife looked much older than he and was also tall and thin. I met her on only one occasion when a woman came over to me and, taking me by the hand, led me to her. She was, apparently, scared of white men and the presentation of myself to her was cause for a considerable amount of amusement for the women and children of Mohammed's large family. The old lady was waiting in a small hut and when I was led in she hopped from one foot to another as if the ground was too hot, and shook my hand, trying her very best to smile and squint the fear from her watery eyes. Mohammed was as indignant at the laughter of his family as at the behaviour of his wife. 'What do they think they are doing?' he grumbled. 'Is this the way to behave with a guest?'

Simbi's crops of millet were not quite ready to be harvested and so other than the job of scaring away the birds there was not much to be done. Each morning Mohammed's eldest son would go off early to the fields mounted on a large black bull, controlling it by a piece of string attached to a ring in one of its nostrils. But the group of young men who lived in Mohammed's compound who attended the secondary school, it being the harvest season and so a holiday, had nothing to do all day except to think of ways of leaving the place. I went with them sometimes to their rooms and there they would ply me with questions.

'How much is an aeroplane ticket to France?' was one of the first.

'Very expensive,' I replied.

'Yes, but how much exactly?'

'Oh, perhaps a thousand American dollars,' I said. This came as quite a shock, so the conversation shifted.

'How much do wives cost in your country?'

'They cost nothing,' I replied. 'In fact, it is the family of the girl who pays for the marriage.'

'Aha!' one of them exclaimed in delight. 'In that case I will have at least ten wives. Here bridal prices are so high, I could not afford to have even one. But tell me,' he continued, 'do you hit your wives very much in your country?' And so the questions continued.

These young men were getting an education and their ambitions were fired. There was no money in the villages. The crops this year which had been badly damaged by locusts would hardly even produce enough to eat, let alone enough to sell for money. They had their eyes on the big towns like Nioro du Sahel. But then there was no money there either. There were in fact two Nioro boys in Simbi at that time come in search of money. They were watch menders and they had been sitting in Simbi's small market for two months hoping to make some money, passing their time listening to their radios.

Almost every male of a reasonable age in the village had a

radio, as indeed they do throughout Mali. On acquiring some money this would be one of the first things a young man would buy. Indeed some people, even if they did not have a pair of shoes to wear, might have a large and modern tape recorder. Music is the spice of life in Mali. It is an essential, and people sacrifice a lot to buy a tape recorder or radio. It is rare that one is out of earshot of music. It is, for the villagers, one of their few luxuries and diversions. There can be found drama, poetry, history, sadness and joy. The most popular music is that played by traditional troubadours or *griots*. This is simple, unadorned music, sung by famous *griot* families to the accompaniment of flutes, balaphones and *koras*. They sing the histories of Mali or praises to the men who pay them to sing, and their songs hang in the village air as readily and fittingly as the dust. They taste of the same atmosphere of simplicity, beauty and hardship that is the matter of village life.

Mohammed, my host, one afternoon told me a story about the *griot* caste. 'One day long ago,' he said, 'a village chief went for a walk with his best friend. Before long they found that they were lost in the bush. They were lost for a long time, so long, in fact, that they began to suffer from hunger. "Sit down here and wait for me," said the village chief. "I will go and find some food." He then went and hid behind a nearby tree where he cut a piece of flesh from his thigh with his knife. Once he had built a small fire and cooked the flesh he returned to his friend and gave it to him to eat. "Where did you get this meat?" his friend asked him, once he had finished eating, but just as he said this he saw the blood flowing from the chief's leg. So great was his gratitude to the chief for what he had done that he said, "I am your servant, and my children and their descendants shall also be your servants." And when they returned to their village the friend composed a song to celebrate the chief's great deed.

'It is in this way that the caste of the *griots* came to be,' Mohammed said. 'They are our storytellers, the guardians of our histories and the praisers of our heroes.'

The other music that is much listened to in the villages is the modern jazzy music from the big cities of West Africa, those swinging rhythms to which one cannot but dance. And then there is the music of the West, most commonly reggae, which is, not

117

surprisingly, the spirit food of the many young men with their hearts set that way.

Mungo Park did not come to Simbi because in his day it did not exist. He travelled directly northwards from Guemou to the town of Jarra in the Moorish kingdom of Ludamar in order to avoid the army of Segou which was about to invade Kaarta. Jarra today is only a small village but it is near the modern town of Nioro du Sahel, the town to which I travelled from Simbi.

Coming to an infinite, baking plain of what by now was little more than desert I saw in the distance a tall water tower in what appeared to be a small forest of trees. Having driven across the baking plain I passed a police road block and quickly found myself immersed in Nioro du Sahel. I had come to the northern limit of my journey. Mungo Park very nearly came to the end of his.

V

On to the Niger

I T WAS MID February 1796. Mungo Park, with his two companions, young Demba his servant and Johnson his interpreter, was making good progress despite his detour to the north. By using tact and patience, giving gifts to village chiefs and kings alike and treating them with respect, he had come so far. Now, in the town of Jarra in the Moorish kingdom of Ludamar, although he knew the Moors had no great love for Christians, he hoped, by using these same things, he might travel unmolested across their land to the kingdom of Bambarra. He sent presents to the sovereign of Ludamar, a Moor named Ali, and when a slave of Ali's was sent to guide him, he departed from the town of Jarra towards the kingdom of Segou.

All seemed to be going well, and when a few days later Park reached the village of Samee he could flatter himself that all danger from the Moors was over. 'Fancy,' he says, 'had already placed me on the banks of the Niger, and presented to my imagination a thousand delightful scenes of my future progress. . . .' But this was not to be, for just then a group of Moors appeared to inform him that he must come with them, for the wife of Ali, the sovereign, who was called Fatima, wished to see a white man. He had become, to all intents and purposes, a captive.

Of the Moors Park writes: 'It is impossible to describe the behaviour of a people who study mischief as a science and exult in the miseries and misfortunes of their fellow creatures. It is sufficient to observe that the rudeness, ferocity and fanaticism which distinguish the Moors from the rest of mankind, found here a proper subject whereon to exercise their propensities.' The Moors were a desert-orientated people descended from the Berbers of North Africa and the Arabs, both of whom had invaded the Western Sahara and bred there. They were fierce and unruly and lived in nomadic clans tending livestock and from time to time descending southwards to raid the sedentary black Africans who inhabited the lands adjoining the Sahara. Park had much to fear from being their prisoner. He was a stranger, he was unprotected and he was a Christian. Each of these circumstances was, he notes, sufficient to drive every spark of humanity from a Moor. When these were all combined in a single person, and there was, to add to this, a suspicion that that person was a spy, Park's position was precarious.

He was taken first to Ali's camp where he was kept prisoner for two months awaiting the return of Queen Fatima who was away travelling in the Sahara. When he was first led before Ali, 'a man of the Arab caste with a sullen and indignant aspect', a hog was presented to him and he was ordered to kill and dress it. As pork was detested by the Moors on account of their religion, Park sensibly told Ali that he never ate such food. Not to be defeated in his humiliation of Park, however, Ali ordered the hog to be released in the hope that it would charge the Christian for whom it was presumed hogs must have a hatred. But the animal attacked indiscriminately until at last it sought refuge in the only shelter it could detect: under the couch upon which Ali himself was sitting.

Some of the Moors were for putting Park to immediate death. Others merely wished to have his eyes gouged out. But on the whole they just wished to torment and humiliate him. He was given a hut in which the hog was his 'disagreeable inmate'. People spat and hurled abuse at him. He was paraded like a circus animal before Ali's concubines. He was so badly fed he began to lose his vision and he was permanently thirsty, at one time so much so he thrust his head between those of some cows in order to get a drink from a trough. When he was ill with fever he was not allowed to lie down and when he once left his hut to lie in the shade of a tree he was accused of trying to escape and a gun was put to his head and the trigger twice pulled to fire it, the cartridge chambers, as it turned out, empty.

Park's captivity was during the hottest time of the year, so hot that the draughts of air that came through the cracks in his hut gave pain at the touch. He was also plagued by dysentery and fever but despite all this he managed to remain in control of himself and was never, as he thought was intended, provoked

122

into behaviour that might induce dire or even fatal retaliation. And he even retained a sense of humour. When a group of women came to him one day to let him know that they wished, by inspection, to find out if Christians were circumcised, Park told them that in his country it was not customary to give ocular demonstrations in such cases but, if all the ladies would retire except for the youngest and prettiest one, whom he pointed out, he would satisfy her curiosity. The women were amused by his jest and went away without fulfilling their objective and that night he was sent some meal and milk by the girl he had picked out.

When Park was at last taken some days to the north to meet Queen Fatima he fared little better. He did, however, find the Queen to be somewhat sympathetic towards him and in fact it was due to her that Park was eventually able to escape. Ali, the king, was to return to Jarra in order to collect some tribute money from some refugees who had come to Ludamar having fled the war in Kaarta. The Queen, on Park's request, asked Ali to take Park with him and it was during the absence of Ali and his men from Jarra for a few days that Park simply walked out of the town.

Park was now left with nothing but the clothes he stood in and his horse which Ali had allowed him to keep. He had no goods with which to buy provisions, the rainy season was approaching fast and, worst of all, he had no companions. Both Demba, his servant, and Johnson, his interpreter, had been captives of the Moors with him. To Park's horror, Demba, who throughout had shown unfailing loyalty to him, had been kept back in the desert by Ali as a personal slave, and Johnson, taking Park's notes with him, had left for the Gambia, not willing to follow Park further on his hazardous quest.

Park himself would not turn back to the Gambia having achieved none of the aims of his expedition, and so, alone and penniless, he struck out in the direction of the Niger. At first he avoided any contact with people, fearing he might again be captured by the Moors, but the hunger and thirst he experienced in the wilds were such that at one time they had him lying down upon the earth convinced he was about to die. 'Here then,' he writes, 'after a short but ineffectual struggle terminate all my hopes of being useful in my day and generation; here must the short span of my life come to an end.' But nature soon resumed its functions and he regained his senses, and a little later a rainstorm provided him with a drink which he obtained by laying his clothes on the ground and sucking the moisture from them.

From now on he tentatively approached villagers, exchanging his pocket handkerchief and his brass buttons for food for himself and his horse. Once he had arrived in the kingdom of Bambarra he could travel more openly, but being closer to Segou on a well-used route, the villages he passed often had no food to give to strangers, there being too many who came their way, so again he went hungry. Also, being reduced to such a destitute state as he was, walking barefoot, driving his emaciated horse before him, the villagers, he says, much ridiculed him. Then, on 21 July 1796, travelling now in the company of two men also heading for Segou, he had his first view of the Niger. 'Looking forwards,' Park writes, 'I saw with infinite pleasure the great object of my mission – the long-sought-for majestic Niger, glittering in the morning sun, as broad as the Thames at Westminster, and flowing slowly eastwards.' At last Park had solved at least one of the great mysteries of the Niger: in which direction it flowed.

Before him, on the opposite bank, lay the large, thriving city of Segou, with the king of Bambarra, Monsong, in residence, having only a short time before returned from the war with the kingdom of Kaarta. Park sent a message to Monsong asking for permission to enter Segou, and whilst he waited for a response he went to the nearby village of Kala to pass the night. In that village he was mortified to find the general fear of him was such that none of the villagers would admit him to their house, so he was obliged to sit all day with no food in the shade of a tree.

The night, when it drew close, threatened to be uncomfortable for a storm was brewing and the wild animals were numerous. At about sunset, though, as Park was preparing to pass the night in the branches of a tree for fear of lions, a woman returning from some fields observed his dejected state and with looks of great compassion took up his saddle and bridle and told him to follow her. In her hut she gave him some fish and told him he might pass the night there without apprehension. Then, in the company of the other women of the family, she commenced to spin cotton and as the women worked, they sang. They sang,

Park says, a sweet and plaintive song, the words of which were these: 'The winds roared and the rains fell. The poor white man, faint and weary, came and sat under our tree. He has no mother to bring him milk; no wife to give him corn – let us pity the white man; no mother has he....'

It is here, now, in this small village across the great Niger from Segou, that I shall let Park rest, awaiting news from Monsong, whilst I pay a visit to the town of Nioro du Sahel and then pick up his trail back in the kingdom of Ludamar, and follow him to this very spot where, not for the first time, the kindness of a woman relieved Park of his distress.

★

Nioro du Sahel was a town in which nobody pretended it was pleasant to live. 'What do you think of our town?' people would ask a stranger, and laugh at his attempts to be polite. For there was nothing commendable about the place. Everything that was bad about Kayes – the heat, the dust, the dilapidated buildings, the scarcity of water, food, electricity and hygiene – was worse here. The functionaries and soldiers posted here swore that they positively feared the hot season. The town was on the fringes of the Sahara and the large, dry river bed that ran beside it and that acted as an open sewer was only once flushed with water, during the brief rainy season. Then it would flood and the town would become a quagmire of mud and in some areas the houses would have to be rebuilt. For the rest of the year there was only heat and dust.

Nioro had grown out of a French administrative outpost. Now it was capital of a *cercle* and housed an army garrison and many streets of small-time merchants' shops. Seen from afar it looked as if it was hidden under a forest of trees, but in fact this was an illusion. The trees were small and well spaced. The town was not hidden under them, but its warren of buildings, squatting low and ramshackle in the bare sunlight, were the same brown as the earth from which they were made, and so, from afar, were unnoticeable.

Life in Nioro was harsh and unhealthy. Those who lived there were used to it and wrapped themselves in turbans and long gowns, insulating themselves from the climate. Those who were posted there were fatalistic about their fortune and tried to make the best of it. One of those was a man whose name I had been given in Kayes, Mr Agibou Traore.

Mr Agibou Traore worked for the National Transport Office in Nioro and, this being an important position, he was not hard to locate. I found him just leaving the bar situated in the small and segregated administrative part of town. He was youngish although already cultivating a middle-aged paunch. He had small, poppy eyes and an enthusiastic manner, and was dressed in a neat pair of nylon slacks and a buttondown shirt.

'Of course, of course, you must come and stay with me,' he said to me when I introduced myself to him. 'You have arrived on a very good day. I am organizing a little soirée this evening.' He then installed me in the bar from which he had just emerged and disappeared for a long time on my moped to make some arrangements for his 'soirée'.

It turned out that Mr Traore had not only, without hesitation, invited me to stay with him, but also to share his bed. He lodged in a compound consisting of ten small rooms surrounding a yard of baked earth in the middle of which was a well. Parts of the compound were still in the process of being built, which accounted for the large pit beside the entrance filled with wet mud and a small man, knee deep, slapping the mud into brick moulds. There were many people living in the compound, most of whom were women. Each of the women seemed to be the daughter of the last, from babies to teenagers and on upwards to a very old but alert lady who demanded some kola nuts from me the moment I arrived in an abrupt and forceful manner, and then, having received them, informed me that I was now a part of her family.

Mr Traore's room was at the end of the compound. It had no windows and inside there was a chaos of books and boxes of old clothes and sacks of millet and old trunks that gradually became invisible towards the dark corners of the room. Vast swarms of mosquitoes rose in a hysterical drone of noise each time you entered, and a family of rats lived in the holes in the walls, and these two things probably accounted for the fact that Mr Traore never remained in the room himself for more than a few minutes at a stretch. He pulled his mattress outside to sleep on at nights and the first night I joined him on it. But he was a restless sleeper and the mosquitoes were so bad outside that I was driven, the following night, into the room to sleep on a mat. There I could at least put the mosquitoes out of action by the deployment of a number of mosquito coils. This, though, would not do as far as Mr Traore was concerned.

'It is not right,' he proclaimed, 'that a guest sleeps on a mat whilst the host sleeps on a mattress. Tomorrow night you shall sleep in the room on my mattress and I will take the mat outside.'

'But Mr Traore,' I said. 'I do not wish you to have to sleep on the mat. After all it is your mattress. I have heard that there are rooms to spare at the rest house in the administrative sector of town. Maybe I . . .'

'Don't say it, don't say it,' cried Mr Traore in indignation. 'You are *my* guest. It is my honour to have you sleep on my mattress. Please do not even think of the guesthouse again.' And so for the rest of the week I passed in Nioro Mr Traore slept on the mat on the hard ground and I slept on his mattress.

Mr Traore, like all functionaries at that time, had not been paid any wages for six months and was broke.

'I do not eat,' he told me. 'I do not have the money for it. I drink water only. That is all I need.'

And indeed he rarely did eat, only grabbing the odd handful from the people who would invite him to partake of a bowl of rice they were about to consume, or being given kebabs by market women with whom he was friendly. But he did drink more than water. In fact, at any time when he was not working or visiting some of his friends, the most important of whom was a large and sumptuous woman who did not complain about the wife he had in Kayes and with whom he incessantly argued, he could be found in either of the two bars in town; and there he did not drink water. Quite how he acquired the money to drink in these bars was difficult to ascertain but debts were endemic for functionaries in these wageless times and as it was the functionaries who formed a large part of the bars' clientele, if credit were not forthcoming, they would have little trade.

One of the bars in Nioro was in the military garrison, a dark cavern of a place with slogans such as 'The might of the Mali army conquers all', and fading murals of tanks and marching soldiers on the walls. The other bar, a single room with greasy walls and a cement floor on which stood a selection of metal chairs and tables, was in the administrative sector of town, the only part of town, along with the garrison, to have centralized electricity, the rest of the town depending upon small, personal generators, but mostly going without.

Seeing as functionaries and soldiers tended to live lives somewhat separate from those of the town's inhabitants, these bars, and especially the one in the administrative sector, were meeting and socializing places for the functionaries and soldiers. In them generally there was an atmosphere of lethargy and boredom that was only erased when drunkenness took its place. Being, as it were, in the hands of a functionary, Mr Traore, most of my time in Nioro was passed in either of these two bars. Sometimes I would go with him to the straw hut beside the road to Bamako where he was employed to take road tax from the few vehicles leaving town, and sometimes I went with him to visit his girlfriend and listened to their arguments which Mr Traore would try to explain; and in the early evenings I would promenade with Mr Traore in the broken and dusty streets near his compound, greeting the many people who knew him as we wended our way amongst the potholes, piles of refuse and wandering herds of cattle with our hands behind our backs. But it was the bars of the functionaries and soldiers that I got to know best in Nioro.

That first night Mr Traore had been somewhat depressed as the soirée which he had devoted so much time and energy to organizing had been disallowed at the last moment by the commandant of Nioro on the grounds that it would be too noisy. We sat drinking outside the bar of the administrative sector on the patio where the soirée would have taken place. There were only two beverages available in the bar: beer and wine. The beer came in large litre bottles and the wine, which was imported to Mali in powder form and then had water added, was produced in the same bottles filled from a large plastic cask. The beer was good and the wine was strong, rough and chemical-tasting, but generally people would mix it with the beer to make it more palatable.

Late that evening, once Mr Traore's spirits had improved with a few samples of this mixture, and when we were about to leave, in staggered a skinny, wind-blown man. Everybody at the bar immediately leapt from their seats exclaiming, 'Ah, Mohammed, you have returned. Where have you been? How is your health?' and other greetings of the like, delighted at the appearance of this man. They shook his hand as he stood swaying, peering drunkenly at them all.

'This is a very famous man,' Mr Traore explained to me. 'He is a great man, a very big man and one of the most generous you will ever meet.'

The man was given a seat and everybody sat round him as though he was indeed a very famous and important person. 'This town is the best town in the world. And the thing which is so great about it is the generosity of its inhabitants,' the man said. 'Believe me, if you love mankind you will be generous. We all of us are flesh and blood. We are all humans. Brothers even, brothers of the flesh.' And on the man rambled, slurring his way through many subjects with the bar clientele listening to his every word as though no wiser ones could be heard.

'This man,' Mr Traore continued to explain to me, 'is one that everybody is scared of and respects for his generosity. His brother, who lives in Paris, once sent him much money with which to buy an aeroplane ticket to fly to France to join him, but this man, in his great generosity, gave all of it away. Greatly is he respected.'

And now this man, with all this talk about generosity going on, insisted upon buying everybody in the bar a drink. Unfortunately, however, he was just then a little short of cash. This was not a problem, though, for the barman, aware of his generous repu-tation, was naturally obliged to give him credit; and the drinks kept coming until everybody was slouched in their chairs with exhaustion, still trying to keep track of the man's incessant stream of often unconnected sentences.

The man who ran this bar was an unlikely person to find in such a situation in such a town. He was called Harumba and was a heavy bulk of a figure with a humped back and a long, bearded face with a scar down one side of it that disfigured one of his eyes. He was an unobtrusive man and his stoop and his dirty modern clothes made him look like a tramp. But in fact he was intelligent and well-educated and doubled his job as barman with his other occupation as a chemist for an organization which was researching minerals in the area of Nioro. He did not drink, but all the same passed all evening and most of the night sitting with the drinkers, listening attentively to their conversations.

One evening a man who had been going on about how he had been the first person in the bar to drink alcohol said, rather smugly, 'You see I went to a mission school you know, not an ordinary one.' As he continued with his subject, Harumba intervened: 'Excuse me, excuse me,' he repeated politely, to draw the attention of the speaker, 'I was very interested when you said that you had been to a mission school rather than an ordinary one, but what,' he continued as everybody tried to remember back to that part of the conversation, 'does that imply?'

At this the man was, at first, a little taken aback as everyone repeated, 'Yes, what does that imply?' But he soon saw the fairness of the question and continued his conversation in a fresh and clearer vein. Turning to me, Harumba said, 'I sit here all day and all night listening to the conversations of my clientele. And do you know why I like to do this? Because my clientele are not fools. There is much wisdom hidden in their talk.'

At one time I met a man from the country of Cameroon in the military bar. I was with Mr Traore and a policeman called Pierre. The conversation in the bar that day was about corruption, not a subject often aired in Mali, let alone in a military bar. But in Nioro all the soldiers and policemen I had met seemed relaxed and pleasant people and when the Cameroonian asked why it should be strange for a Malian to want to know about such things in his own country, nobody seemed particularly concerned and Pierre, who was a gentle man, much taken with his wine and beer, could only sit giggling.

The Cameroonian was a tough and self-sufficient-looking man. He wore smart, Western clothes and could speak both French and English. 'I am here in Mali for the purpose of hustling,' he said to me on introducing himself. 'I sell medicine, not modern medicine, but traditional medicine. The Malians are backward in this subject and so I do good business in the villages.' He had, in fact, he told me, just come back that day from a two-month tour of the villages. There he sold his medicine in the local markets and was treated well by the villagers, fed by them and lodged always in the village chief's house.

'Don't imagine,' he said to me when I informed him that I also had been treated well in the villages, 'that the good hospitality you receive is given just because you are a white man. I, a black man, get just the same. These Malians always give good hospitality to strangers. That is their custom. They are a very traditional and good people. In Mali the most important thing is the family. The family is very strong. If, for example, a young man was to leave his home for a long time, his family would use magic to draw him back again. And if a young man was to take as his first wife a girl not of his parents' choosing, a stranger, they might even kill him, with their magic.'

When the Cameroonian left the bar he gave me his hunting knife as a present and wrote a charm on its beautifully worked leather scabbard. 'One day,' he said, as he gave it to me, 'even though you are a white man, you might learn to believe in magic, and then this charm will work well for you. Keep it safe until that day.' This kind gesture, however, threw my host, Mr Traore, into a state of depression. 'I feel worthless,' he said to me. 'This man who hardly knows you gives you a present. But I, your host and friend, have nothing to give you because I am so broke.'

When I left Nioro it was not with reluctance, as it was not, everybody agreed, an easy place to be in. The lack of food, the heat and mosquito-fevered nights made me feel ill most of the time, but I was sad to leave Mr Traore who had so unequivocally taken me in and looked after me. As I left his compound the old lady to whom I had given some kola nuts on my arrival gave me a benediction. Taking my upturned hands in hers she muttered some prayers over them and spat on them, telling me to rub them down my face. In her old eyes I saw the true compassion of her religion and her best wishes and as I drove out of town into the bright, hot desert I felt sad at yet another farewell but also enthused at once again being on the road.

★

I departed from Nioro du Sahel in the afternoon. The sun had by then already sunk below those altitudes where it is only a small white disc barely discernible against the glare of the sky, and when all nature seems to cower in its light. And it was not long before the condensation of heat that is every afternoon gave way to the beauty and calmness that is every evening.

The countryside was open and soft, the gentle undulations of all the different shades of sand and thin grasses unhindered by bush or tree to the horizon. Far ahead of me were some large hills of red and greenish earth that gradually grew, then slipped away to the north. The light and the long shadows of the evening were beautiful and thrilled me as I sped towards the small town of Tourougoumbe 40 kilometres to the east, one of the places Mungo Park passed on his flight from the Moorish kingdom of Ludamar.

Tourougoumbe, like the many old caravan towns that had in centuries past grown up in the southern deserts, thriving on the north–south trans-Sahara trade, was positioned well to act as a middle-man in the different sort of north–south trade that took place today. Such things as cigarettes and rice that came from overseas through the ports of Mauritania, just to the north of Tourougoumbe, and salt that came from the deserts there, were exchanged for millet, kola nuts and cotton cloth from Mali. At the time I was in Tourougoumbe, however, almost all the stores of the Moorish merchants who profited from this trade, for the Moors today are great traders, were closed. There was a team of customs men visiting the town and as most of the merchandise that came from the north was contraband, there were intensive negotiations going on between the customs men and the merchants, and the stores could not be opened with safety until these were resolved.

Tourougoumbe, being a Moorish town, looked somewhat different from the towns and villages I had been visiting. Its aspect was something like an oasis. It was a collection of neat, oblong houses plastered with smooth, reddish earth with small wooden-shuttered windows in their sides and cooking fires in the yards out back. These buildings were placed upon the sandy plains like boxes and as they concentrated towards the centre of town, an intricate medina was formed. There were clusters of palm trees here and there and in the large, dry gully that ran beside the town were planted hundreds of tiny vegetable plots, shaded by more palm trees. The place was good-looking, sitting neat and tight on its golden sand with its weave of passage-ways and secluded courts and carved wooden doorways.

Tourougoumbe being small and quiet, the inhabitants were very interested in the arrival of a stranger such as myself. But the Moors, friendly and polite as they are these days, as opposed to in Park's day, are not of the temperament to overwhelm one with themselves, but are of a more dignified, reserved and proud nature. As a result, at first, my being in town was somewhat difficult, and my first venture into it, somewhat embarrassing.

I had found lodgings in a rest house which was usually reserved for functionaries on the outskirts of town. On my first morning I made my way from here to the centre of town down a small, sandy street. The street was quiet and peaceful with rows of idle, Arab-looking Moors sitting outside shops bulging with sacks of produce and rocks of desert salt and hoes and materials, and sugar and soap and in fact just about anything of use. They were dressed in loose, sky-blue robes and long black turbans, and occupied themselves chewing teeth-cleaning sticks and brewing small pots of tea, the favourite pastime of the Moors. As I walked every one of their quick, penetrating eyes was upon me and in every mind the same questions were being asked: Who is he? What does he want here with us?

And then, to my misfortune, I came across the town madman who was a squat, hairy figure dressed in the rags of clothes, and who for some unaccountable reason unfortunately spoke French. 'What is your name, white man,' he shouted at me. 'Is it John or Jack or maybe Mohammed like me? Tell me your name, Mr Bibble man, Mr Christian.' I could not avoid being drawn into conversation with him but soon, the conversation being quite pointless, I moved on only to have the madman follow me. Thereafter wherever I went I had him following a few steps behind me, laughing, dancing and generally making a fool of himself and a spectacle of me. The Moors sat impassively watching me and my madman pass and then, when I came to the end of a street and found myself in someone's courtyard, the inhabitants of that courtyard, who were a group of men talking earnestly to each other, looked at me in great surprise. My escort took this opportunity to once again involve me in conversation and, as I stood there trying to make sense of his questions, the men, in gruff and impatient tones, asked me those questions that everybody had been thinking. Having replied not very satisfactorily, for as usual Mungo Park was not a familiar name, I then had to run the gauntlet of those same streets of eyes I had already passed a number of times in my efforts to discover the way out of the centre of town. In the end, however, although the madman did station himself outside my room for a day or so, making it impossible to go anywhere without his presence, I made some acquaintances amongst the Moors by being invited into a shop to drink some tea, and then, thankfully, the madman abandoned me as no longer such a novelty.

I passed three days in Tourougoumbe and they were three wild, windswept days. In the nights I was besieged by termites which ate a hole in the top of my rucksack. In the mornings I was awakened before dawn by the muezzin calling the time for prayers and then, later, by the rustle of the herds of goats who were led out into the countryside past my door. By day sand besieged the town, whipping against the buildings and carrying high into the atmosphere to almost block out the sun. And in the evenings I went to eat at a small transporters' restaurant at the taxi park and drink tea with a friend I made there. He was a young man from Bamako who drove one of the ancient bush taxis that transported passengers between Tourougoumbe and Bamako. This was a gruelling trip with up to twenty-five people crammed into the back of a pick-up truck where they would have to sit, crushed at difficult angles on thin wooden benches lurching over broken roads, sand and wind assailing them for the duration of the twenty-four-hour journey. But there were few passengers in Tourougoumbe and my friend had been waiting here for ten days already. 'But this,' he said, 'is better than running the city routes in Bamako. Oh la la,' he exclaimed, 'there you might carry two thousand passengers in ten days, but you still would not make the money I do in one voyage to here and back.' This young man told me many interesting stories about such things as the fact that the famous American rock musician,

Jimi Hendrix, died shortly after he had asked his girlfriend to make him some spaghetti.

★

Cram cram seeds are burrs with vicious spikes. Those spikes are cruelly barbed and pierce the toughest skin or even the smoothest shoe leather at the slightest contact. In much of the Sahel, when at last the rains fall and the grasses grow tall, the blessing of this brief period of fertility has a flaw, and that flaw is the cram cram. The burrs hang heavy from the grasses, like clusters of flies about a fruit. The plains may look beautiful with their yellow, swaying grasses, but they are perilous to enter for the cram cram mercilessly attacks feet and legs, shoes and trousers, matting them until all flesh is inflamed and thumbs and fingers are spiked and bloody in the attempt to remove the cram cram.

When I left Tourougoumbe I took a path towards the village of Korera Kore, another place Mungo Park had passed on his flight southwards from the Moors, which traversed an area thick with cram cram. The path itself was deep in sand so I was obliged to take to the bush and there the cram cram leapt at me as I passed, crawling up my legs and even sticking to my moped's rubber tyres. That route was a bad one. Twice it punctured my tyres. Its deep sand had me at times crying out to the skies in frustration as I struggled and fell in my attempts to push and carry my bike in places where it was impossible to drive. It conspired, as it seemed, to send me down false tracks, and it forced me from its route into the merciless cram cram grass.

But in the villages I passed solace was at hand. In one, on a rocky hill where there was no water and where the women had to walk 5 kilometres to the nearest well, a man with a bald eye invited me into his home and the heart of his loving family to rest and be fed. That man, as it turned out, was a functionary, posted to this desolate village by an agricultural co-operative. He lived in his mud brick hut with his pregnant wife, two small children and a pile of books that were to him a source of great pride. I was given the books one after the other to look at and make comment as I saw fit. 'This one,' he would say eagerly, 'is about biochemistry, but,' he would add apologetically, as if it were something of which to be ashamed, 'the cover is lost and many of the pages are torn.'

In another village a young man helped fix one of my punctures that had just then begun to manifest itself. And in Korera Kore, which was a large village, being, like Simbi, the head of an *arrondissement*, where I arrived in the evening, I was welcomed by such a crowd of children, all jumping and shouting around my bike, there cannot have been a single person in the village who was not aware of my arrival.

Mr Traore in Nioro du Sahel had given me the name of someone here in Korera Kore. He was a young man called Niap and, as it turned out, he was yet another functionary. He was a co-ordinator for the 'National Corporation for the purchasing of Merchandise', but, as Korera Kore, which was a market village, had fallen on bad times, there was little or no merchandise to purchase. The crops that year had been bad and so there was no surplus to sell. But in fact what afflicted the village most was the absence of the Moors. Wherever there were Moors there was trade, but the Moors had ceased coming to Korera Kore a few years before and so now its market had slipped into insignificance.

Niap was a quiet, solitary person and lived in a small room by himself with magazine adverts and football teams plastered on his walls. I stayed three days with him but although I shared his bed with him at night, and perhaps because of a stutter he had which I noticed got much worse when he spoke to me in French, we did not communicate very much. He was highly dispirited by the boredom and pointlessness of his job and passed his days moping about not doing anything much at all. He had a friend called Hamala, however, who spoke English.

Hamala, a tall, good-looking man, had a neatly trimmed goatee beard and dark, penetrating eyes. He had spent seven years living in the southern African, English-speaking country of Zambia, which accounted for the fact that he spoke English. It also accounted for the fact that he was, at first, suspicious of me. In Zambia he had become involved in the business of gem and diamond trading, a business that in Africa is riddled with 'irregularities', and it was not until I had persuaded him that I was not a detective sent after him that he became more friendly.

Hamala, although happy to have come home to his village, was now eager to leave again, only he suffered from the problem that was endemic in the villages: he had no money and no way of making any. He had, he said, brought back a lot of money with him, but his long absence from home meant that he had had to give most of it away to his family. He was, by his own account, the grandson of a king of the Diawara people. 'I,' he said proudly, 'come from a noble family. But this means nothing these days. We nobles are now no better than slaves, slaves of the state. And those lucky ones who were taken away as slaves many years ago to America, they are now the nobles because they are rich.' He laughed at this. 'Truly, the roles have been reversed. Look at this man here,' he said, indicating a rough-looking character sitting next to the smith in whose workshop we were at that time drinking tea. 'He is a real slave, descended from a slave family, but he has more wealth than I. Oh, how the nobles have fallen! They are now lower than all the other castes, lower than the artisans, lower than the *griots*, lower even than the herdsmen and the slaves because today these castes mean next to nothing, for we are all free men, free to be the slaves of the state.'

One morning Hamala came to me with a letter he had received six months before, but, because it was written in English, he had not been able to find anyone to read it to him for he was himself illiterate. It was from a girl he had married in Zambia but had had to leave because of some 'problems' he had with the authorities there. Three-quarters of the letter was about how she had had difficulty in getting his address from her landlord to whom Hamala owed money, but the last quarter made up for all these practicalities for it spoke of nothing else but her love for him. 'Ah, that one,' Hamala said, on hearing this, 'she loves me too much, too, too much and she is so far away. Really I should like to see that one again but how can I ever get the money to leave this village?'

Hamala then asked me to write a letter for him to the girl. 'Tell her I shall try to come and see her,' he said, 'but also say how it is so hard. Say that I miss her and wish her parents well and tell her that all is night for me and the sun will not shine until I see her again. Tell her all that,' he said, speaking to the sky as if his words themselves would reach her and the actual composition of the letter was irrelevant.

In Korera Kore, at that time, people were practising hard for a competition that took place in Mali each year called *Le Concours National*. The first stage of this competition, which consisted of athletics, football and theatre, culminated in this part of the country in Nioro du Sahel during *La Semaine Locale*, at Christmas time. Every evening the football team and the athletes practised on the outskirts of the village. The athletes were all women who ran round and round the football pitch on bare feet, hitching up their skirts. The football team was of a good standard. One team wore shirts and the others did not. Some of them had shoes, others not, and the two wingers of one team split a pair between them for shooting at goal. They played hard and energetically and were not hindered by the sheep that wandered over their pitch or even by a man driving a donkey and cart laden with straw and closely followed by a train of goats, who did not think twice about taking the same route home as he did all year round, even if a football pitch was at that time in the way.

One evening I went to see the theatre rehearsals which took place just outside the village. A large crowd of excited children and youths had gathered to watch as well. The play being rehearsed was the story of a young man falling in love with a girl who was a she-devil and trying to obtain permission from the girl's father to marry her.

The story was set in a forest with a small stream running through it. The forest was represented by twenty young girls all dressed in a similar green-patterned material who stood swaying their arms above their heads like the branches of trees. They swayed and danced to the beat of a tomtom drum and, now and again, some of them would circle round to the back and come running lightly through the forest to represent the stream.

The young man spied the she-devil in the forest and immediately fell in love with her. Her beauty, he cried out, is purer than the forest stream; her spirit soars like an eagle. He decided to go to the girl's father to ask permission to marry her, but the father, a calculating old man with a gnarled walking stick, demanded such an extortionate price for her dowry that the young man had no hope of paying it. He ran to the forest throwing himself about in frustration, thunder rolled and the women of the forest stamped their feet and danced round the young man. Again and again the young man went to the father but each time the price of the dowry got higher and each time when he returned to the forest the she-devil would appear, running before him, tempting him with her beauty but always keeping just out of his reach. The audience laughed cruelly at his despair. 'Catch her. Throw her into the stream,' one person called. But in the end the young man's love was driven to such a pitch he threw himself into the stream instead and was drowned in the swirling arms of the women dancers.

★

The countryside through which I drove when I left the village of Korera Kore was once again back to the true Sahel. My journey now, from here almost all the way to Segou, was in a uniform landscape of dry, stumpy vegetation interspersed with patches of thin grasses and sand. It was a little-populated area with villages often 20 kilometres apart. There were no roads, only paths and small tracks leading from one village to the next. Fortune, I decided, must have been on my side during my journey here for it seemed that whenever I was at a loss as to which direction to go, perhaps standing beside my bike vainly studying my compass, somebody would always turn up to give me directions. Not once did I get badly lost although this was a distinct possibility on account of the myriad of bush paths criss-crossing each other, often quite confusing the track I was trying to follow, which ran far out into the bush to die in remote and waterless parts. Always, a boy with a herd of goats, or a man travelling with his family in a donkey-drawn cart, or some such people, would appear at just the right time.

This countryside was often burnt out, as sheltered and desolate as a battle's aftermath, and sometimes the trees were still smouldering because it was not long since the fire had passed. The paths and tracks I followed acted as fire-breaks so, where the land on one side of them would be completely burnt out, often the other was thick with dried grasses and bushes. For long periods, as I drove, there would be no sign of life except the odd squirrel which ran beside me for a while or coveys of sand partridge skimming the tops of trees. Very occasionally I saw tiny antelope, and there were supposed to be jackals and hyena hereabouts. But of the many lions of Mungo Park's day, and the other big game which once inhabited these parts, there was no sign, driven out by drought and the hunting of man.

But now and again I came across some humans, in these wilds always just passing through, hurrying from one village to the next: groups of Fulani women marching with calabashes of milk or bundles of firewood on their heads who, when I passed, called to me to stop and offered me drinks of their milk; trains of market-going donkey-carts transporting sacks of onions or piles of maize cobs or panniers of fruit which, if it was early in their journey, bounced along at a jaunty pace, the young men dangling their legs over the fronts, whipping and cursing their beasts, and shouting to each other from cart to cart, or if it was late, plodded along, the young men bowed forward in a stupor of lethargy. Occasionally I passed horsemen dressed in bright and colourful tunics sitting high and stiff on their mounts, stepping ahead at a controlled and leisurely pace. One time I passed a large, stern-faced posse of them trotting fast in a single tight bunch, all neighing horses and jingling harness. A little behind them was an old man drooped in his saddle fast asleep, but with one hand clasped firmly to his pommel.

There was the round, well-fed *patron* I met one morning, mounted on a donkey. His bulk quite dwarfed the donkey, the four legs of which appeared beneath the hanging white robes of the *patron* as though it was to him that they belonged. 'Good morning,' he called to me as I passed, 'and how are your spirits today?' For long stretches of time, however, there were no people at all, just myself and the uninhabited wilds. Then, suddenly, I would see ahead a clearing and the straggled remains of a millet field, the tall, dry stalks twisted all ways as though a storm had just passed. Then I knew that soon I would come to a village, often still a way off, but I would get a feeling of relief all the same, a subconscious sense of security, for here the wilds had been tamed, put into order by man.

Large areas around each village were cleared for the planting of crops. Herds of cattle and sheep roamed about and a myriad of tracks criss-crossed like webs. Nearby there might be groups of men singing hearty songs as they threshed piles of millet, hitting them with long bent sticks to separate the seed from the heads. Next to them women winnowed the seed, pouring it to the ground from calabashes from the lips of which trails of the husk and dust flew with the wind. And other women cleaned the seed of its accompanying sand in large round sieves, or at least, as one discovered at every meal, of some of the sand. Young boys supplied the threshers with new loads of millet heads, ferrying them in donkey-drawn carts shored up with dry cow hides from fields where young men with machetes sliced them off the stalks. Other young boys carried hay back to their homes, the huge piles of it on their heads falling in veils to their feet and leaving golden trails down the paths they trod.

Further down these paths were the village wells, and, if it was a village unfortunate enough not to be endowed with a pond, or the pond had already dried up, there might be teams of men lifting large rubber buckets of water from the wells and spilling them into long, wooden troughs over the bustling heads of thirsty cattle or goats. And, of course, there were always the women beating the paths to and from their homes to the wells, carrying cooking pots to be washed or buckets or sometimes huge steel basins of water on their heads, the great weights of which were only indicated by the trickles of sweat running down their bulging necks: little slops of water fell from the basins to land at their feet. And then suddenly there would be the village: a few surprised looks from the first people I'd meet; then I'd find the *bentang* and soon a crowd would gather and I would begin to explain myself.

In this way, hopping from village to village, I slowly made my way along Mungo Park's route towards Segou. The first village in which I passed a night was called Warourou. Here it was that Mungo Park, having struggled through the kingdom of Ludamar, had at last found himself arrived in the kingdom of Bambarra. Warourou had in Mungo Park's day been a town with a high wall surrounding it. Today it was only a small village and had no wall. Here I was taken to the village pond to see some crocodiles.

I was doubtful about there being crocodiles in such a dry area

141

but in fact not only were there quite a number of them, a couple of them were at least seven feet long. They lay motionless on the sandy banks of the pond, the only sign that they were alive being a slight contraction and expansion of their large white bellies and the odd flick of a yellow eye. Only a few yards away from them village women were washing clothes. The villagers, I was told, did not bother the crocodiles, and so the crocodiles did not bother the villagers for whom the presence of the crocodiles was regarded as a good omen, for crocodiles like and need water, so their presence signifies that water will be plentiful in years to come. When the pond dries up in the hot season the crocodiles, I was told, disappear down large holes to what must be subterranean caverns where there are reserves of water.

Warourou seemed a contented village. Here the young men were not asking me the price of tickets to France. They had had no education other than in the village Koranic school and were content to be farmers as their fathers were. Sadly, though, this was not proving too easy. When I was taken to see the village millet fields they were pitifully thin and barren.

'That,' the village chief's son said, pointing to the carcass of a locust on the ground, 'is what has broken our village.' The locusts had come just as the newly planted crops were sprouting and had eaten the new shoots. This circumstance, however, had not affected the villagers' spirit of generosity. When I left, the village chief's son said that he wished to give me a present of a sheep. 'I see you cannot take it on your moped,' he said, 'but you will give me your address in England and I shall send it to your family instead.'

★

The evenings and nights in the villages were often long and tedious. There was generally no illumination and, were there any, few diversions with which to entertain oneself anyway. To counter this people sometimes occupied themselves by relating stories. They gathered round a fire after eating their evening meal, made some tea perhaps, and listened attentively to each other. One night I heard many stories related by a group of functionaries with whom I had found lodgings in the village of Felou.

After finishing our evening meal of couscous we sat round a small fire and one by one the functionaries related stories about the experiences they had had in different parts of West Africa where they had gone to look for work. Most of these stories were set in the seaboard countries such as Togo, Ghana and Nigeria. These were, everybody agreed, dangerous countries, countries of corruption and bad magic. In some of these countries you could even buy parts of the human body in the market-place, so evil was their magic.

'I once went to Togo to get a job,' the teller of one story began. 'As I had no place to stay in the capital I found myself a girl and I went to live with her. After some weeks of living with the girl I was invited to come and visit her village. The thing that I could not guess, though, was that some people had paid a lot of money to the girl because they wanted to kill me for their magic.' The silence that came from the small group around the fire seemed to deepen as they listened to the man talk. 'So off I went with the girl to her village and there we had a big party and there was much drinking and dancing.

'When night came I went to sleep with the girl in the house in which she lived with her mother. Now, the girl usually slept in a small windowless room and the mother slept in a big room with a window. This night, however, the mother told her daughter that she and I should sleep in the big room with the window and she herself would sleep in the small room without one.'

'Ah, the plots of women,' interrupted one of the listeners. 'Such plotters they are.'

'For two nights we had parties and slept together in this fashion,' the man continued as he poked the fire with a stick. 'Then on the third evening the village witch-doctor called a meeting down by the river near the village and told the girl and all the villagers to come to it. At the meeting it was decided that that night was to be the one they would cut my throat; for they wanted my head for their magic, you see.

'Whilst they were having their meeting down by the river, however, I went to a small shop nearby to buy some cigarettes. It had, in fact, been my habit on previous evenings to send somebody else to buy my cigarettes but that evening there was nobody to send, of course, because they were all at the meeting down by the river.

'When I reached the shop, the old man who owned it said to me: "What things have you left at your girlfriend's house?" I replied that I had left my bags and papers there. "Listen to me well," said the old man. "I am not of this village and I will not see evil done." And then he told me what the villagers intended doing to me and said that he refused to let me return to the house even for my bags and papers, so great was my danger. I must hide in his shop, the old man said, and leave the village the next day.

'When the meeting by the river broke up the villagers returned to find that I was missing. They looked high and low for me but did not find me and so presumed that I must have gone for a walk and would return later on.' The storyteller now quickened his pace. The listeners shifted, their eyes concentrating on the fire. 'They told the girl to go to bed to wait for me. Later that night they broke the window of the room where the girl and I had slept together every night and entered to kill me; but when they found that I was still not there they cut off the girl's head instead because they had already prepared their magic and must have a head that night. The next day I ran away from the village.'

I stayed in Felou for only one night. In the morning I was given a large steaming sheep's head, inclusive of eyes, for my breakfast, of which I made the best I could for politeness' sake, then I was off towards the town of Mourdiah, a long day's ride away.

During that day I passed a number of small villages, each of which seemed as desolate and poor-looking as the burnt-out countryside through which I mostly drove. They were mere collections of mud huts huddled together like beggars. Their wells were drying, or had dried up. Their cattle had died in the droughts, and their crops had been ruined by the locusts.

And the people of those villages seemed to have more than their share of ailments. Their bodies were as ravaged as their villages. Everywhere I looked amongst the people who gathered around me when I stopped at the *bentangs* I would see bald eyes, malformed legs, mangled hands, blindness, deafness and ghastly skin diseases. They were hungry and sick but, against all odds, this did not seem to have broken their spirit.

One heard no complaints from them, only a considerable amount of laughter. It seemed as if the smallest excuse was taken to laugh. As I sat with the villagers on their *bentangs* where they sat all day long with little to do or no energy to do it, they joked and laughed. They laughed at each other's ailments, at me, at life and their fate. When one blind old man was told that I had come to take him away because he was now no use and, in retaliation, he chased his tormentors around the *bentang*, striking at them with his stick with surprising accuracy, a young boy, whose entire body was so malformed it was little more than a head propped on top of a tangle of shrivelled limbs, laughed until the tears ran down his face.

In the last of those villages I picked up a young man who wanted a lift to Mourdiah. And so with him perched on top of my rucksack on the back of my moped I drove the last stretch to that town with my front wheel barely touching the ground.

★

Mourdiah was really only a large village, not a town. A town implies streets and traffic and square stone buildings, but as Mourdiah was capital of a *cercle*, like Nioro du Sahel, it perhaps merits that title. It had the usual allocation of functionaries and administrative buildings, a post office, a chemist and a large, gravel road running beside it. But these were all separated from the main part of Mourdiah, the part that was in fact a small traditional town.

This part of Mourdiah was an old town with a reputation of being very religious. In it lived a famous marabout who ran a prestigious Koranic school and it had one of the largest mosques I have seen in a place of its size. The well-constructed earth buildings of the town huddled close around this mosque, hemmed in on all sides by dry river beds that in the wet season flooded, making the town an island.

I did not stay in the old part of Mourdiah but instead found lodgings in the rest house of a pest-control project a few kilometres away. The rest house was next to a large compound inhabited by some of the town's resident functionaries. There I was mostly separated from the life of Mourdiah and I became introspective, and in the mornings and evenings I used to sit on a verandah looking out over an empty bush writing in my diary. This is what I wrote:

The mornings in the rest house are the best times of day. In the early mornings the world is still partially the domain of nature, it still holds something of the clear depth of night: man has not fully imprinted his authority on the day; he is still busy waking himself up, dressing himself and his life in the manner he wishes to conquer it. So he is still gentle and quiet and you can go and sit and watch the day coming, and watch the animals who have been awake for a long time and are enjoying this brief spell of day which is entirely theirs: the sheep and goats, frisky and happy after their night of pegged-down inactivity; the kids and lambs jumping on walls and logs and hopping into the air like ballet dancers on their springy legs; the chickens and guinea fowl pacing about after each other and bits of food.

One morning, as I was watching, an old man from the village came to whitewash one of the newly constructed toilets. He looked happy at his work, slapping the paint on slowly, filling up the large square wall until there was only a small space left in the middle; then it was finished, the work neatly completed. When he walked past me sitting with my back to a verandah, he said to me, 'That's good, very, very good.'

Sunny evenings are like rewards for having got through sunny days. It is like the gradual lessening of pain after taking painkillers. First the shadows get long and the contrasts great. The sun is still hot and makes you sweat with much exertion, but already the sunny contrasts with the shady, colours as deep and rich as they ever will be. Then so quickly it is time to watch the sun disappear.

Of course, so often, even on clear days, the sun can disappear before it gets to the horizon, either into clouds or atmospheric mist and dust. When there are no clouds it is pure and naked, the round sun changing colour from white to yellow to red, then it is gone with a quick last wink. But the

146

best time is when there are some clouds. Then the sun may disappear before it hits the horizon but this is quite made up for by the splendour of the clouds when they catch the sun's light underneath, from where the sun has sunk beyond the horizon. There in one go you get all the colours of a sunset spread in bands along the different strata of cloud, first the dark blue of sunless clouds, maybe one or two wisps in front of them that still have some of the sun so are bright orange contrasting with the dark blue, then a strip of more ruddy orange, then deep red, then purple, and all the time it is changing and deepening and meanwhile the goats are coming slowly in from the bush, the cows as well, and men mounted high on camels. The birds in the trees are quietening down: the quiet beat of wings as they hover about their nests. The bush seems so intensely quiet: it is asleep already and its nightlife has not yet started.

Now, as you look about, you have to look twice. It is beginning to get dark, not really dark, but a little indistinct and if there are clouds everything is pastel pink in their reflected light. There are some voices far off, the cry of the muezzin or a donkey gasping for enough air to bellow, then the bellow comes and hopefully makes the donkey happy after all that gasping, but it sounds so much like a cry. Now only the last bands of cloud on the horizon have the sun and they are the deepest blood-red and anything between you and them is silhouetted, void of colour. And now it is night and out come the cats and bats and frogs.

And what of the night that falls so thick after the sun? Now it is time to find companionship, as night is not a time to be alone. Bush and nature have reverted to their own, no place left for man. He seeks his fellow humans to gather round some tea, or a fire if it is cold. When there is a good moon, of course, it is different, but still not the same as day. The cool, blue light of a moon is not a friendly light. It is stark and naked, the moon and its light. Then to bed.

There are mosquitoes in Mourdiah but I am privileged enough to have a mosquito net. It is a secure, cosy feeling to lie almost naked on my bed and hear the buzz of mosquitoes so close and yet unable to get at me in my fortress. Sometimes,

sometimes very late, long after the embers had gone, when even the trees seemed asleep, late enough for the evening to have been yesterday and the morning still tomorrow I wake, a call of nature perhaps. I crawl out of my bed, under the mosquito net, and go outside. I feel a bit of an intruder, maybe a cat thief. Here there are no crickets, no night birds. The bush around is deathly quiet. I step stealthily, trying not to wake the bush that is waiting, hovering on the eaves of the rest-house grounds, waiting for the morning.

There was no one staying at the rest house because this was a quiet time of year. The harvests were in and the locusts had done their damage. There was no locust-chasing to do although soon the hunt would be on for their breeding grounds. The only person at the rest house, besides myself, was the office clerk. He never left the rest house and did not mix with the functionaries who lodged nearby. He said he did not like to socialize. He was a solitary, dry little man and he led an intensely boring life. At this time of year he had absolutely nothing to do except to get up and wait to go back to bed.

Sunday was market day in Mourdiah and on Sunday morning the office clerk came and asked me to come with him to the village. He had a commission to fulfil with a family, he said. The market was not a particularly big one, but busy enough. There was some drumming and singing outside the commandant's compound because he was leaving his post. The new one had already arrived. We walked through the village to go to the family with whom the office clerk had a commission to fulfil and when we passed the village *bentang* outside the mosque the Imam called us over. He shook my hand politely but seemed annoyed at the office clerk and they had words.

I should explain something. The village people were not happy that I was staying over in the functionaries' area. They did not much like the functionaries – at least not the older men of the village – because they were strangers and did not fit into the village hierarchy and thought themselves superior to it. The old men knew better. But they also did not like me staying with the functionaries because they had heard that I was a historian come to study their village. I was, by rights, their property. It should be by them that I was shown the village.

This is true, of course, not that I was a historian, but that I should really have been staying in the village, not up near the functionaries. But when a stranger arrives somewhere and somebody very kindly gives him a nice room to stay in he can hardly say, 'This won't do.' I had, though, been in the habit of going into the village each day and I had made a friend of a butcher, an old but wily man with whom I would go and sit whilst he worked. In this way I had got to know quite a few of the villagers.

One day it was arranged for me to meet the Imam and all the holy men of the mosque. They knew all about history, I was told. I could ask them all my questions. So I went and sat down on a mat with the Imam and all the holy men and a great crowd gathered round. The Imam was a kind, gentle-looking man and, like all the holy men, wore a long white gown and a skullcap on his head.

I had Mungo Park's book open before me on the mat on which I sat cross-legged. It looked impressive. The Imam, by way of an interpreter, said to me, 'What does this man Mungo Park say about our village?' I flicked through the book to find the passage about Mourdiah. 'He says,' I said, 'that Mourdiah is an Islamic town and there is a house where people are allowed to drink beer from maize called *neo dollo*.' I hesitated before continuing. 'He says that he found many people quite drunk there.' The information was taken in silence by the Imam and the holy men. They fiddled with their prayer beads vigorously, waiting for me to continue. 'He says that he received extremely good hospitality in Mourdiah.'

'Ah, yes,' the Imam exclaimed happily. 'This was a good Islamic town. When El Hadj Umar, the great Jihadist, came here with his holy war he did not fight our people because he found that their Islam was pure enough. Of course Mungo Park would receive good hospitality in such a town.'

When our conversation came to an end, the old Imam simply said, '*Abana*', which I knew meant 'It is finished', so I got up and left and the butcher took me to see the old town of Mourdiah a couple of miles away. But the old town was just a wide open space with some mounds of rubble in it.

When we got to the house of the family with whom the office clerk had a commission to fulfil, we went and sat with the old head of the family in the porch to his compound, a small room like a stable where the old men traditionally sit in the afternoons. We did not say very much and soon a girl who had been sent for came and sat on a small stool next to us. She was a pretty girl, strong and brimming over with rosy good health. Her skin was oiled to a satin shine and her hair tied with coloured beads. She had a confident, sweet smile that never dropped. After about half an hour of sitting in near silence with her we simply got up and left.

As we walked away from the house, I said to my friend that she was a very pretty girl and, half in jest, asked whether he was going to marry her.

'Oh, pretty is she?' he said. He really was very dry, my friend, almost as dry as a stick. But he did laugh at my suggestion that he might marry her.

'No, no,' he said, 'her father is a friend of mine in the town of Nema and asked me to come and see her, to send his regards and make sure she is healthy.'

After this we went to the village pond and stood for a long time looking at the swarming insect life in it. There were many small black beetles that sped around on the water's surface circling round and round each other. The pond was filled with lilies and purple flowers. Next to it were vegetable plots. We went to the vegetable plots and the office clerk started a long conversation with a man who was tending a small crop of tobacco. They talked about the Civil Service, discussing certain directors, some of whom were dismissed as very bad but others who were real directors, men who when they said 'No' meant 'No' and when they said 'Yes' meant 'Yes'.

I soon left these two and went to the market and sat down with the butcher with whom I had become friendly, who had a meat table there. I watched the market: the Fulani women coming in from the bush with calabashes of milk to sell, the *jubo* truck filled with the savoury *Jubo* soup cubes everyone likes to use to thicken their sauces, and the usual babble and confusion of market-goers. When the office clerk returned from the vegetable garden he came and sat with me and the butcher.

150

I knew that the butcher disliked functionaries above everyone else in Mourdiah. 'My son,' he said, 'you are welcome to come and sit with me and my English friend. Do not feel unwelcome at all.'

'My father,' the office clerk replied. 'I always feel welcome in Mourdiah. You are too thoughtful.'

'Will you take some coffee, my son?'

'Yes, my father,' the office clerk replied innocently.

'Here you are, my son,' the butcher said with a wicked gleam in his eye, and gave the office clerk the dregs of the cup of coffee he had earlier made for me.

★

When I left Mourdiah I headed west once more on the heels of Mungo Park, and in the small and dusty village of Dalibougou, Park's old village of Datiliboo, I met a young man called Doua who had a story that went like this.

Doua knew what he wanted from life. For him there was no choice. 'Africans are tired people,' he said, 'all is hopeless for them.' He had been born in Dalibougou twenty-five years ago, although he had not now lived there for ten years. When he was still very young his father had left home and gone to live in Dakar in Senegal. When he was fifteen he had followed his father to Dakar and then, a few years later, had gone by himself to the country of Sierra Leone. He had now been living in a small town in the north of Sierra Leone for six years and he had a job there as a carpenter's assistant. Doua liked Sierra Leone. 'Everything is modern there,' he said to me. 'There's a cinema and a disco-thèque in my town, and some of my friends have cars. Food is cheap and life is good. I have an American friend as well. He has given me his address in America and one day I shall go to America because that is the richest and the best country in the world. What do I need with this village? Ha,' he laughed, 'look at my hands, look at all these blisters.'

Doua had been back in Dalibougou for only two weeks but he already wanted to leave again. He had had to work in the fields which is why his hands were blistered. This was the first time he had been home for ten years. He had no money left because he had given all his savings to his mother, but he had a sheep and he was going to walk the 80 kilometres to the town of Banamba where he could sell his sheep and buy a ticket to Bamako.

From there, somehow, he would make his way back to Sierra Leone and he would not return for another ten years, he said. His mother had been crying ever since he had told her he was leaving again. She had stopped eating because she could not stomach food, so great was her sadness.

'It is tradition,' Doua said, 'which is holding the Africans back. They are so traditional and this is what prevents them from developing. They cannot do anything as long as they remain slaves of their traditions. Look at how poor this village is. But they have nearly a hundred cattle. But, you know, they won't sell a single one of their cattle. They won't even eat them unless they are old or ill. The cattle are their wealth but they do nothing with it except to keep it in order to pass on to their sons. Even when the crops fail and they have almost no food, or when somebody is ill and needs medicine, they won't sell a single cow. I cannot understand it. There is nothing for me in this village. The people here are fools. Only the Westerners know the answer. Look at how rich they are and how useless we Africans with our traditions are.'

When I first met Doua in Dalibougou he was wearing a bomber jacket and a baseball cap and he talked to me about such things as the price of cigarettes and beer. Then he tried pretending that he hated his village by saying all these things to me. But actually he was terribly confused because he loved his village and could not stand to see his mother crying so and not eating. He was happy I had turned up because he could say all these things to me about his village.

He had said them to himself over and over again, to try and convince himself that he was making the right decision: there were no two ways about it, he was going to leave the village again and he was determined to believe all he said; and airing it to me made it somehow more concrete; it made his decision irreversible. Because, before I arrived, he was worried. He could feel himself being drawn back into the village life. His hands were blistered and he had become a part of the family again.

'I must leave very soon,' he said, 'or I know that I shall be trapped and will never leave again.' Already a girl had been chosen for him to marry. He could see the gateway to the outside world closing fast. He had to move quickly. He had to be rash and cruel if necessary and my appearance spurred him on. I stayed three days in Dalibougou and Doua decided to leave the same morning as myself.

From Dalibougou to Segou on the Niger was a long fast ride. It was as if the great water was calling me, as if I was draining into it as do the big rains when they come. As was always the case in the villages, the acquaintances I had made in Dalibougou pushed my moped a little way out of their village to see me on my way and show me the right track – all, of course, except Doua, who since four in the morning had been trudging his way southwards with his sheep and the burden of his fate.

The track I was shown died out surprisingly quickly in an old field of millet. Luckily there was a small Moorish encampment beside the field and so I obtained more directions from a man I found there. Whilst I then went off in the direction I was shown and circled round and round in the bush looking for any signs of a track, that man slowly put on his turban and his sandals and, by the time I had returned to him to ask for more directions, he had his stick in his hand and was ready to guide me. He led me to a track which I followed all the way to the village of Fanibougou.

The moment I arrived in Fanibougou I was led a little way out of the village again by a man pointing excitedly towards a large tree. Under the tree was parked a Land-rover. 'There. Over there,' said the man, 'is a person of your tribe.' And sure enough, arriving at the Land-rover, I discovered a tired-looking and unshaven European. He, it turned out, was a Dutch geologist and he was delighted to see me.

'I'm busy, very busy,' he said, when I introduced myself, 'but just a moment and we can have a good chat.' And he immediately launched into a history of the inefficiency of the organization for which he worked. He flung open the back of his Land-rover and showed me how badly organized the stowing of all the equipment had been; how so much was broken and how he had changed all that. 'It's small things like this,' he explained, 'that mean the difference between success and failure.' And then once he had got all this off his mind, for it had obviously been there for a long time and at last he had found someone to say it to, we sat down and he explained to me what he and his team were doing.

They were trying to locate good spots for the digging of wells. With the use of a network of electrical wires they sent bows of electric current into the earth and, by plotting the readings they got on a graph, determined in which spots water was most likely to be found. 'Some villages are lucky,' the Dutchman said, 'like Fanibougou here which already has three wells and more are to be dug. But others, like one I was in earlier today, are not so lucky and no matter how many wells are sunk, no water is found.'

I passed a couple of hours with the Dutchman watching him and his team work under the surveillance of a group of bemused villagers. I wanted to reach the village of Sonango that day but, having left Fanibougou and the Dutchman, later in the afternoon I began having problems with my moped. I stopped in an area of fields and, seeing that petrol was leaking from my engine at a fast rate, looked in the petrol tank to discover that it was nearly empty. There was a young Fulani herder nearby and he came over and we both looked at my engine wondering what to do. I then did all the things I knew to do to engines, which were not very many, but they had no effect on the leak. I started to take things to pieces but then, when I got lost in the intricacies of the engine, I back-tracked and stood there for a while longer looking at the engine whilst the herder went off to locate his sheep which had wandered. The sun was licking the horizon by now and soon another herder appeared, this time a lively older man who proceeded to rattle away to me in Fulani, a language of which I did not understand a word. Now and again he would stop and laugh and then I would smile because it was a beautiful evening and this man was very friendly.

Sonango was only 11 kilometres away so I decided to race there before my petrol ran out. I left the herder with his cows and drove at a great speed because whenever I slowed down the engine flooded and stalled. In and out of the bends I raced, over rubble, into potholes; branches of trees lashed me and then I hit some deep sand and fell off. But soon I was on again driving like a maniac until, dusty and sodden with sweat, I reached Sonango.

When I stopped outside the village I looked around me for the first time that evening and saw that there was a shock of the utmost beauty unfolding in the sky to the west. The intensity of it was such that it was like one of those skies designed in science fiction films on alien planets. It was as if a great hand had stirred the clouds. They were swirled around like whey, the most brilliant, fluorescent and moving purple and red, and the village of Sonango washed over, as it were, with blood, stood small and simple and strange beneath such a brilliant sunset.

In Sonango I was sat on a mat in the village chief's compound and a bag of sugar was brought, and put down beside me. 'This is a present from the village chief,' a skinny young man who was the French-speaking element of the village said, pointing to an old man sitting nearby on a prayer mat. Then the skinny young man and the people of the compound began looking concerned. At length a discussion was held, at the conclusion of which the skinny young man came over and tentatively said: 'What is your preference for food tonight?' On reporting back that I would eat whatever the family of the compound did there was an almost tangible sense of relief.

Once a year in this village, all the village men get together and come to the village chief's house to give him their blessing and thank him for being the village chief. It so happened that this took place the evening I was there. There was no great rigmarole. The men simply came and sat down in a circle and were fed couscous and meat by the village chief's wife. When they had finished they broke their circle and converged on the village chief who was sitting by himself across the compound. One man said, 'You are our father, our light and our inspiration. It is you who leads us through this life. You stand tall in the divine light of Allah. We thank you in his name.' And the others replied, 'Nba, you are our father, our light and inspiration. May God's blessing be on you.' Again the first man spoke some words and again the thick mumbled response of all the men's voices came back. In a few minutes it was all over; the men departed and the village chief was left alone where he sat, no doubt glowing with a feeling of benevolence, and thankful to the God to whom he prayed who had created the beauty of the earth.

I had been informed that evening by the village chief's son that there was somebody in the village who knew all about the reparation of mopeds. The following morning, it turned out, that somebody was none other than the village chief's son himself. And although my bike appeared to have now somehow cured itself and worked perfectly well, I could do nothing to stop the village chief's son indulging in his desire to help.

'There is probably some sand in the carburettor,' he said. 'Don't worry. It can be easily fixed.' And so the village chief's son, with the aid of many small boys, proceeded to dismantle parts of the engine until soon, there being little else to undo, a halt was called and everything was put back together again. Now, however, it was discovered that the bike, which an hour before had been quite healthy, did not work at all. This was a source of great amusement to the village chief's son and his team of small helpers and when I looked not so amused they thought this even funnier. In the end, by chance, I saw a cable that had not been re-fitted and, on replacing it, my bike once again tickered into life.

From Sonango to Segou the flavour of the land changed considerably. Here I was away from the influence of the desert and the desert people. From here on this was the land of the Bambarrans. These people were less reserved than their more formal Sahelian neighbours. There was more of the south with its lax-limbed humidity and its colour and chaotic gaiety to these people. Their villages were farmyards surrounded by fields of brown earth. Here was muddy peasantry as opposed to the more spartan life-styles of the pastoralists.

In one village a jolly family sat me down with a bunch of bananas and continued their chores, shouting to me now and again such things as, 'Hey, my friend, why don't you settle here and marry my sister?' Or, 'Tell me how rich you are, my friend, and I'll tell you how happy you are.' One young man was splitting fresh calabashes with single strokes of a machete and standing them out in the sun to dry. A woman was bathing her baby in a bucket of water, holding it by one arm and dipping it in and out like a fish, and then whirling it around in circles to dry. The village of Oualokaro which I passed late in the day was in fact two villages, one Fulani, a collection of perfect, thatched, round mud huts clustered round a minaret, the other the oblong buildings of the Bambarrans with shiny tin roofs.

As the day went by a feverish desire to see the Niger grew in me, to see a large expanse of water; to smell the humidity of it. The closer I grew to it the more people I met and the better the tracks became. In the village of Kala where I have left Mungo Park eating his fish and listening to the singing of his hosts, I passed some time trying to find out if there was anybody who knew of this story; but there was none. And then from here all tracks led to the same place, to the ferry point from where people took the boat to Segou on the far side of the river. And then, between the bushes, I saw the glistening waters of the Niger and they grew and grew, for here the river was very wide because a dam further upstream had swelled it to the size of the Thames at its mouth. Far across on the other side, low and concealed in trees, was Segou, the only distinguishable feature from here being a tall water tower. But once I had boarded a long, thin dugout boat, and my moped had been placed beside me, and we had begun to pole across this, the shallow side of the river, the town began to take shape. Even from here I could hear the humming of Mali's second largest town, and smoke and pollution hung heavy above it. I felt like a country boy coming to the big city for the first time. I was excited and could not keep my eyes from looking that way, eager for all the sights and sophistication. Soon the ferryman had to put his pole aside and paddle as the river deepened. The colours of Segou became warehouses, piers and old colonial buildings. Here was the old seat of kings, Mungo Park's primary objective, the bastion of the Bambarrans, and one of the greatest markets to be found so far from the sea, so long hidden from the eyes of any European, secreted in the heart of West Africa on the banks of the Bambarrans' 'Joliba' river.

VI

Segou

WHEN IN JULY 1796 Mungo Park first peered across the Niger river to the town of Segou, he was greatly impressed by the place, estimating it to contain 30,000 inhabitants. 'The view of this extensive city,' he wrote, 'the numerous canoes upon the river, the crowded population, and the cultivated state of the surrounding countryside, formed altogether a prospect of civilization and magnificence, which I little expected to find in the bosom of Africa.' Now Segou has grown into a city of 65,000 inhabitants, proud of its Islamic past, a great seething market town, and one that grew before my eyes as I was paddled across the Niger river.

I had visited Segou when I had been in Mali five years before. Now as I drew closer to it I began to recognize it: the cement pier with its attached, sunken barge; the township of the Bozo fishermen squatting tight and low at the top of the beach to the left of the pier, all the long, wooden boats of the Bozos pulled up along the beach to a place where it became a point; then, stretching to the right of the pier, also to a place where it became a point, the river wall on top of which was a long, dusty road dappled in shade from the large trees planted down its length that partially obscured the river-front face of old colonial buildings and the indefinite, huddled residential quarters; and straight ahead, behind the pier, a condensation of city and movement and heat.

Here was Segou, a core of colonial elegance threaded with busy, commercial life surrounded by quarters of village calm and shanties of street-side poverty, the whole place covered with a fine red dust stirred up by thronging bush taxis and an army of mopeds exactly like mine; at dusk, it rose above the town to sandwich a layer of blue cooking-fire smoke.

That time five years earlier I had been amazed by the sheer dilapidation of Segou, by the scent of creeping mould and musky

161

age mixed with the sharp, damp smell of rot. This time, though, I had no sense of that sort of thing. Now, as Mungo Park had also been, after my time in the spartan bush, I was amazed at the magnificence of the place, at the sheer profusion of sights. It was like an orgy for the eyes. Everywhere I looked there was activity: people washing themselves in the brown riverside waters of the Niger; lines of boys tugging at fishing lines at the end of the pier; brick-makers laying out their patterns of bricks to dry on the beach; clusters of merchants haggling in tiny shops bulging with boxes and sacks of goods; weavers sitting behind looms in make-shift shacks, lengths of cotton stretched out 30 yards in front of them, tossing shuttles from hand to hand; heads spinning through crowds propelled by unseen mopeds – all the coming and going of beggar boys, matronly ladies with baskets swaying on their heads, and soiled working men. I was thrilled to be in a city once again and set off to locate a hotel where I could get a good meal and a soft bed.

Sadly I did not find a good hotel that night, but ended up in a very bad one and an expensive one at that. It was the sort of hotel where you are obliged to pay for an air conditioner even though you do not want one and it does not work anyway, the sort that has a long, stone bar propped up by a line of depressed-looking waiters, and an empty dance floor bathed in garish lights and surrounded by dark alcoves from which come the whistles of the hotel's resident ladies.

I sat at the bar with the depressed waiters sipping luxuriously cool beers and pretending that I was enjoying myself. On the tape recorder a famous *griot* was singing a story about the long line of Bambarran kings who had ruled Segou before it was conquered by El Hadj Umar and became a part of his new Islamic state. He sang deep and powerfully to the accompaniment of a *kora*, or African harp. As he sang the waiters listened attentively to his words. 'Ah, Damonsong, son of Monsong,' one of them said wistfully, 'he ruled for twenty-five years.' And this seemed temporarily to lift him from his lethargy. Had he, I wondered to myself, come from the villages? Was he one of the lucky ones who had fulfilled his ambition to escape? Was this, for him, a dream gained, or a dream shattered?

My previous time in Segou I had stayed with a young student

I had met on my first day. Now, on my first morning back, I went in search of this old friend of mine. He had lodged with a family who lived on a long, dusty road which ran parallel to the Niger, one block away from it. It was a straight road, shaded down its entire length by the tall plane trees the French had planted throughout the older part of town. Down each side of it ran the uninterrupted façades of squat buildings, the red earth from which they were built worn smooth with age and rain, with small wooden-shuttered windows carved out here and there, and doorways leading to cramped family compounds. The families spilled out of their homes on to the street and dotted the thin, broken strip of tarmac that ran down the centre of it as randomly as fallen leaves.

Hardly anything had changed: each part of the street had its own flavour and life, and the part which I had known was just as I remembered it. In the small grass hut beside a tree the cloth-pressers were, as always, at work. Sitting either side of a wooden block, the two men hammered lengths of cloth with round, wooden mallets, pounding in gum arabic to starch and stiffen them up. Click, click ... click, click, the sound of their work came as precise as a metronome, exactly four hits per second, pacing the day from dawn to dusk. With his fresh straw brooms lined up against a wall for sale, the broom-maker sat beside them on his brick as though he had never moved. From the dark, sooty interior of a workshop, a smith sat filing a knife. An old tailor, the only man in the street to remember me, worked outside his doorway, bent over his sewing machine, bits and scraps of material lying at his feet. The coffee-table man was still there with his babbling kettle and trestle table.

Through the half-open doors of a garage I could see the con-vertible Peugeot that had once belonged to the President of the country but was now owned by a lean old merchant who had made his money in fish. In the tiny shops down the sides of the street there were, as always, small boys thrusting their hands clutching notes over the tall, wooden counters to buy soap for their mothers, or cigarettes and sugar for their elder brothers. And there, opposite the house of the family my friend had lodged with, were the two ancient trucks belonging to the old father of that family. Even five years ago they had looked totally wrecked, one of them sitting on blocks instead of wheels, with refuse and dogs collecting beneath them. But, in fact, five years ago at least, the old father of the family had used one of these trucks for threshing millet in the harvest season. Somehow he would get it started and drive it out to the countryside where he would be employed running it back and forth over the millet heads, in this way separating them from the seed.

This was a good street and I had fond memories of it. You could sit beside it and never get bored. In the mornings and evenings the Muslims would pass on their way to the mosque further up, walking silently and serenely as though they were drifting on an unseen current. From the same direction, but from much further up, almost on the outskirts of town, military men would come from the military garrison, striding in brisk and confident groups. And then, in the evenings, all the young men, freshly washed and clothed in their smart modern dress, would promenade as idly and slowly as the long evening permitted, chatting and joking with the groups of girls standing outside their doorways.

The family with whom my friend, the student, had lodged was large and seemed to consist mostly of women. There was the old father, even five years ago so old he rarely left his room, and a couple of young boys, but the rest were women and girls. Whether they were all part of the family, however, I never knew because the mother of the family, a strong, tough matriarch of a woman who could be as sharp as she could be sweet, ran a cloth-dyeing business and all the women and girls who were employed at this lived in the compound. In the compound there were a few huge black pots and it was in these that the material was boiled with indigo dye. All day long the women stirred the pots with large wooden paddles, or wrung the material into tight knots, or pounded it, or hung it up to dry. Rivulets of deep blue water ran between the stone flags of the compound to converge on a hole in a wall through which they trickled into the street. The compound was a busy, industrious place, the women workers stern and sweaty about their tasks, and so not a place in which to idle and get in the way.

When I entered the compound that first morning in search of my old friend, I was greeted warmly by the mother. 'It is you,' she cried almost with incredulity. 'You have returned. Ah, this makes me very happy. You have come for your friend? Alas, he is not here. For two years now he has been in Bamako where he is continuing his studies.' She took my hand and pumped it vigorously. 'There is now another young man in his room who is also a student,' she said, 'just like your old friend.'

The family had a number of rooms that they rented out to young men, as indeed they had done when I was last here. Those young men, as was so often the case with the young men throughout urban Mali, did nothing with their lives. Having finished their education and having found no employment, they passed their time sitting in the street outside the house brewing tea and chatting to their friends. They were bored and despondent but were so resigned to their fate that they remained friendly and cheerful. They made just enough money through petty street business to buy their tea and cigarettes and the batteries for their tape recorders that never ceased to be played. The mother of the family treated them kindly but sternly and if they lay about in bed in the mornings she would barge into their rooms, pull off their bedclothes and shout, 'Come, up you get you lazy beasts! It's not a man's business to lie about in bed all morning.' In fact, if I remained in bed too long, she used to come and turf me out as well.

The young man who now occupied my old friend's room was a quiet, serious person, much taken with his religion. The mother of the family said, 'Your friend may be in Bamako but you will sleep in his old room. Ahmed,' she called to the young man. 'You have a guest.' He did not seem to object, even though I got his bed and he was removed to a mat on the floor, but then he had no choice: the mother's will was not to be questioned. Sleeping in this room, passing much of my time with the young men and their socializing in the street outside the house, I passed ten very relaxing days in Segou.

★

I paid a visit to the bank one day in Segou in order to change some traveller's cheques. The banks in Mali were not remarkable for their efficiency. Sometimes they were so completely clogged

165

with hysterical customers all fighting for access to the tiny, port-
hole windows, you simply turned your back and left. At others
they were entirely empty and peaceful. The one I went to in
Segou was like this. It consisted of one very large and spacious
room cut in half by a long wooden counter with an enclosed
cash kiosk at one end of it. There were two women behind the
counter, sitting beside two small filing cabinets, the open drawers of which revealed tightly packed filing cards: rolls of paper
spilled from their tops, down their sides. At the back of the room,
sitting at a desk in a glass office, was a small, bearded man who
I presumed was the manager.

One of the women behind the counter, the one dressed in the
most beautiful green and yellow fluted dress, greeted me with a
charming smile. She took my traveller's cheques, studied them,
and then handed them to the other woman, telling me, pleasantly, to wait a moment. The room was filled with an air of great
peacefulness. I was the only customer there. The only other
member of staff, besides the two women and the manager in the
glass office, was a man methodically stamping pieces of paper in
a corner. Thump, thump, the sound of his work came across the
room as if from a great distance. From an open door near to him
came the echoes of a conversation from another part of the
building: indistinct, short bursts of babbling speech. Everything
in the bank was very mechanical: old-fashioned typewriters and
other heavy, metallic pieces of machinery – there was nothing
digital or computerized here that hummed and burred. The man
stamping the pieces of paper moved over to one of the typewriters and proceeded to type, the slow uneven clanking rhythm
only adding to the sense of peace.

The woman who had my traveller's cheques finished filling in
a piece of paper she was working on. She studied my cheques
some more. The man at the typewriter stopped his typing and
came over to study them as well. I saw the manager in his glass
office get up from his chair, open his door, and he too came over
to study my cheques. He was a neat little man with a well-cropped
goatee beard and a blue suit buttoned up to the collar.

There was a problem with my cheques. Perhaps I could go to
one of the other banks in town? I had already been to them and
they had sent me here, I explained. There was more studying of

my cheques. Did I have the receipts for buying them? No, I did not. Could I sign the cheques so that my signature could be compared to the one in my passport? Only if they would change them for me. The two men wandered off, seemingly having lost interest, the manager back to his glass office where he sat down at his desk again, and the other man back to his typing. A small, cheerful Moor had come in and had begun laughing and joking with the woman with the charming smile; she threw a quick one at me, as if to give me confidence.

The second woman, a lady of a tougher, plainer style, remarked on something she had seen outside the window of the bank: a large lady throwing sand to the wind. She laughed loudly. Sign the cheques, she said. I signed. She set to work on filling out more forms. There were four of them, each one with four copies. Sixteen pieces of paper. It took a long time.

Meanwhile two other men had entered and, having approached the counter, stood beside me, clutching cheques in their hands. The great peacefulness descended again. I saw the manager scratch his beard. The woman with the charming smile was now idly leafing through her filing cards. A car honked outside. One of the two men standing next to me was trying to get the attention of the man on the typewriter who eventually came over and took the cheque from his hand, looked at it and handed it back. The man was dismissed. His cheque could not be cashed here. The second man managed to give his cheque to the woman working on my forms. He stood meekly before her as she studied it; then it was sent off to the manager via the man working on the typewriter. Muffled voices came from behind the glass windows of the office: a negative nodding of the head; the cheque was handed back to the customer. He did not look disappointed. He never looked as though he expected it to be cashed. He left.

My paperwork was finished. I signed all copies and they were all sent to the manager with my passport and cheques. They sat on his desk for a long time before he picked them up. I watched him studying them. Soon I started to feel sleepy. A couple of other men came in and formed a line by the cashier's kiosk, which was empty. The man on the typewriter ignored them and concentrated on picking his fingers. The woman with the charming smile was now chatting to another woman who had come from the door where the echoing voices had been coming from. They slapped hands together on greeting, and laughed loudly. This new woman also wore a beautiful dress, this time a long pink one. She was a vast woman but carried her weight with great regularity.

The manager finished with my cheques. The typewriter man collected them and gave them to my woman who returned my passport. She did a few more sums and signatures on the forms and gave me a numbered tag for the cashier's kiosk. I went over to it and joined the two men still waiting there. Silence descended on the bank again. Clunk, clunk went the typewriter. There was another long wait. I got fidgety and caught the eye of the woman with the charming smile who gave me another quite sweet one, effectively dissuading me from going over to her to ask what was happening.

I waited some more, then the typewriting man finished his typing and came over to the cashier's kiosk, unlocked the door and sat down. Both the men before me had large wads of money to be counted out. Then it was my turn. Each of my sixteen pieces of paper had a place to go, four of them put through the pigeon hole for me. My money was counted out. I took it, and as I walked towards the door of the bank my frustration eventually got the better of me and I contemptuously scrunched up my four pieces of paper and flung them at a waste-paper basket. Nobody noticed. And then I opened the door and stepped out into the busy and noisy street.

★

The inefficiency of the banks in Mali was the reason why a friend that I made in Segou was having such a very difficult, and for him quite desperate time. Mike was a Jamaican who, his mother being African, as a young boy had been brought up in Africa. He was a quiet, shy person and dressed in a plain, conventional manner. He was by way of being a musician and had recently passed some time in Ivory Coast looking for a band to play with. One day, when travelling in the north of that country, he had had everything he possessed stolen, from his money down to his guitar and even his wristwatch. It so happened that he was at that time in the company of a man from Segou who, for some reason that I never quite determined, took Mike all the way to Mali. Then, shortly after arriving here, Mike's friend had had to depart again and so here Mike now was, two months later, with no money whatsoever and not a word of a common language with the Malians, for he spoke neither Bambarran nor French.

The money Mike had had stolen had been in the form of traveller's cheques and, these being refundable when stolen, he had set into motion the machinery for getting new ones issued. This was something he was attempting to do through a bank in Segou, a process that, once having been set in motion, could not be halted or altered in any way. In other words, he could not now go to Bamako to get his cheques refunded where it would be much quicker. He had to wait here, and the manager of the bank with whom he was dealing was, by his own admission, being optimistic when he estimated that it would take an entire month for there to be any fruition to the process.

A month was a long time for someone who, every day, every hour, was cut off from the people around him by his lack of ability to communicate with them, a lonely time. Also, of course, Mike had no money to buy even cigarettes. It was in fact because he was so lonely that I met him. One day one of the young men who sometimes hung out at the house I was staying in took me off across town to meet a person who, he said, desperately needed to see someone who spoke English.

Mike's situation was not quite as desperate as it may seem. He was a stranger in Mali and so, as was customary amongst the Malians, he was being looked after by them as best they could. A family related to the friend of Mike's who had originally brought him to Segou were feeding him one meal a day and giving him a bed at night. They were, if only to the barest minimum, by cause of them being quite poverty-stricken themselves, supplying his bodily needs; but for his spiritual needs they could do little. And so my appearance was, to Mike, like a rope thrown to a drowning man.

'You are my saviour,' he said to me. 'I am dying here. I'm too tired to live any longer. I have no friends and even I have no cigarettes. You are my god.'

This was strong stuff, but Mike was not the sort of person who liked to be lonely and was, indeed, very nearly at the end of his tether. And so I passed much of my time in Segou in his company. I would buy sugar, tea and cigarettes and we would sit in the house he was staying in, and through me he would ask all the questions he had wanted to ask of members of the family of that house for two months but had been unable to.

Mike's gratitude to the Malians for their kind treatment of him was very strong. He could become quite tearful when talking of the family who looked after him. 'Their kindness . . . their kindness,' he said, 'is so warm. It is as if they were my own family. The Malians are such warm and generous people it makes my heart hurt.' And indeed they were kind and generous towards him. Wherever Mike went in town people would try to console him. They would lament his bad fortune, sit him in their shops and give him tea. But they could not give him conversation or lend him any money: hard cash was in such short supply in Segou that even the price of a packet of cigarettes was a serious amount.

The only person Mike knew in Segou who could speak English, besides myself, was a Ghanaian who lived in the Mission quarter. This quarter was named after the Catholic mission which was to be found in it, and was mostly inhabited by Christians, many of whom were Ghanaian. But this man, rather than relieving Mike of his distress, added to it, for he was himself in an almost permanent state of depression. Mike would go and see him now and again, sometimes in my company, but he would always come away more depressed than before.

The Ghanaian was known as 'Bon Gâteau' because he was a cake-maker and, by all accounts, made very good cakes. He lived in a large, squalid and overcrowded compound inhabited exclusively by Ghanaians. He occupied one tiny room with his wife and baby daughter, a room cluttered with sacks of flour and cooking pots; many juju artefacts such as snake skins and birds' wings hung on its walls. The other inhabitants of the compound were all women who, like Bon Gâteau, had come to Segou in search of money and by now had resorted to prostitution to make ends meet.

Bon Gâteau was an intense, changeable character and this was not helped by the fact that he drank a lot of *neo dollo*, the maize beer. 'This stuff is very strong,' he told me, 'far too strong for a white man.' When he was drinking it he would either be highly excitable and harangue Mike and me with long implausible stories, or he would be sunk in depression with his hands clasped to his head muttering, 'There's no money here, no money, no money at all.'

One morning when Mike and I went to see Bon Gâteau we found him in a great state of excitement, as was the whole compound. 'Oh, it was such a fire,' he was saying, 'such a great fire, such a bad piece of magic.' He was covered in soot and drinking his *neo dollo* at a great pace and it took a long time to determine what he was going on about.

There had, apparently, been a fire in a small shop nearby, started by the two owners of the shop who had been brewing some tea next to two drums of petrol which had caught fire and exploded. The shop had been gutted and the two men taken to hospital, badly burnt. All morning Bon Gâteau and the people of the compound had been trying to put the fire out with buckets of water and Bon Gâteau had himself been trying to save as much of the shop's merchandise as possible by dashing through the flames and dragging things out. His hair was singed but he was proud of his work. 'Two bags of rice I saved,' he said. 'And how the flames leapt about me like very little devils themselves. What a great fire that was.'

★

One of my favourite times in Segou was the night. Most of the town being without electricity, when night descended the place was sucked into the deepest of blackness that seemed all the darker for the very fact of its being a town. The sun would disappear over the Niger, there would be a brief twilight, then, like the chop of an axe, darkness would fall and there would, seemingly, be only yourself and your immediate surroundings left. The rest of the town simply disappeared, as does the world only a few feet from the glow of a camp fire. But Segou then became a labyrinth of sounds and atmospheres. Its hidden, seething life, secreted in the darkness at points along a street, or gathered in rooms and courtyards, was quite tangible with its

171

low hum and stir of drowsy activity. The whole town quite throbbed with cosy, companionable atmospheres changing from street to street or corner to corner. Of course there was some light, especially in areas of greater commerce or affluence, and as darkness became complete oil lamps would appear one by one, dotted down the streets as randomly as fireflies, only dimly flickering with the tiniest haloes of light, or perhaps illuminating the outline of a window, or creating the ghostly shapes of shadows on the back walls of compounds seen through open doorways.

You might be walking down a street of such pitch darkness your eyes seemed to be all on their own, then, in the distance, you would hear the sounds of music and, heading for it, come across an oil lamp on a corner with the shapes of backs bowed over a brewing pot of tea, with a tape recorder of flashing red lights playing beside them. Sometimes you might look up and see the stars and then everything – the entire town, humanity, reality itself – would slip away as you lost yourself in the constellations and the great darkness between them that fell to your feet.

The best night I had in Segou was New Year's Eve, which (having, as will be seen, returned to Segou after an excursion to the north) I passed in the company of Mike. We divided our time between a bar, the owner of which claimed to be a Rastafarian and wanted Mike to join his reggae band, and a nightclub which was named after the old Bambarran king, Damonsong. There were many nightclubs in Segou. They were generally open-air places with tables and chairs spread spaciously around raised dance floors. There were dark alcoves and long, stone bars. Men would set themselves up at a table, sometimes ordering all their beers in one go to be lined up before them like a challenge, and there they would sit the night through, laughing and joking with those people who bound from table to table like balls in pinball machines, getting up to dance now and again, and generally slipping into that warm, blurred state where everybody, and especially the girls, was your best friend to whom you could say what you liked.

The bar we went to was fairly quiet that night, its only client besides Mike and myself being a small, thin man buttoned up in

172

a safari suit who was methodically making his way through a row of seven large beer bottles, taking swift glasses of pastis between them. The other people in the bar were the barman, the Rastafarian and a cheerful girl with a matter-of-fact voice. The Rastafarian was busy describing to Mike, who could not understand a word he said, the sort of music he and his band liked to play; the barman reminisced to me about a job he had once had in a big hotel in Abidjan, the capital of Ivory Coast; and the girl sat with the drinker helping herself to his beers and telling him of the dangers of mixing drinks, about which the drinker was in full agreement.

When Mike and I returned to that bar much later in the night the drinker was still there, sitting now on a stool beside the bar. There he hung like a wilted flower so completely filled with alcohol you felt that if you pricked his skin with a pin, alcohol rather than blood would come out. When he moved his arm to raise his glass to his lips he did so with irregular, jerky motions like a badly operated puppet and, looking at him, one could not help but be impressed at his perseverance, for his determination to continue drinking must have been very strong to keep him upright on his stool.

The barman did in fact treat him with respect. 'He is my very best customer,' he said, and so saying gave him a small pat on the back, but this unfortunately set the man swaying like a pendulum to such a degree that Mike had to put out a hand to steady him. The man's arm then gradually extended to clasp his glass which he raised to his lips and, with a sip, he regained his wilted composure and turned his head to survey us as though from a very great distance.

In the nightclub, Damonsong, Mike and I joined a table of people that consisted of one large and merry lady dressed as though for a ball, a tall, thin bar-girl in a short skirt and a man with a charming, toothy smile wearing a smart suit who told us that he worked for the navigation office, a government department which controlled all commercial activity on the Niger. This man, it appeared from the many stories he told me, felt a great affection for the Niger and fully understood its problems.

'Man has corrupted it,' he said, referring to the dam that had been built across it further downstream. 'It is fat and unhealthy and its fish are few now because man is too hasty. He must always try to change things and make them do his will like a man thrashing his donkey to death.'

'What use is a dead donkey?' he asked, and continued with one of his many proverbs: 'Patience is the golden route.'

'You know,' he continued, 'there are many mermaids in the Niger, but they also, like the fish, are now rare to find. In the month of Ramadan it is customary for small boys to leave dishes of couscous beside the river for the mermaids. This is one of our customs.'

Mike and I stayed late at the nightclub, taking it in turns to dance with the large lady. She was a good dancer who, one could see, loved to dance like she loved to live. She moved her weight in time to the music, naturally and harmoniously, all the while a smile of pure pleasure across her face. Then we were off across the dark town to the bar, idling our way there in order to soak up the many atmospheres we passed on the way, and to watch for a while a group of girls dancing and clapping to tomtom drums around a blazing fire. The girls stood in a large circle round the fire and each one in turn dashed into the light in the middle of the circle and there attempted to dance herself into complete harmony with the drums, letting the rhythms enter her body, to shake it and convulse it until sweat ran from her brow and she could take no more so stepped aside for the next girl.

And then, in the early hours of the morning, when dawn was creeping like a mist over the town, I left Mike at the home of his family and said goodbye, for the next day I was to leave Segou for good. Before I left him he said, 'Take this. It is the only thing of worth the robbers missed that I have to give to you.' And he offered me the gold chain he wore round his neck. 'Please take it. Take it without regret.' I managed to convince him, however, that if his money did not come through he might need it to sell, and this he only very grudgingly accepted. Mali was having its effect on Mike.

★

Tuesday was market day in Segou. And on that Tuesday, market day broke, as did most days in Segou, bright and fresh. The dust and haze of the previous day had settled and the sun, just appearing at the horizon, did not yet combine heat with its light. By now the boat and bush taxi passengers, sardined voyagers from every part of the countryside, were already unloading their goods. A small fleet of donkeys and carts with their accompanying drivers clasping donkey-bashing sticks in their hands were waiting nearby for their use. Snakes of sturdy men ferried sacks of rice or corn from the river-boats to the shore, the heavy weight of the sacks carried across their necks and backs bowing them almost to the ground. Everywhere people were setting up their stalls, and all the time more people were arriving from the countryside, some on foot or by horse, some by bicycle and cart.

On the Niger, a flotilla of small pirogues was transporting passengers from the far shore to be disgorged on the beaches: wave after wave of humanity struggling up the sands like an invasion. These small pirogues lay so low in the water that, from a distance, it appeared their passengers were afloat all on their own. On every part of the Niger I could see thin, colourful rows of people scattered as haphazardly as sticks on a flood.

The market of Segou was not, as it seemed once it was in full swing, totally disorganized. It may have been, in some ways, like an explosion with a centre of great density and intensity and shock waves of decreasing activity, but every part of it had a different function, all the parts joined to each other to give the impression of chaos.

In the most commercial street of town, where all the big-time merchant shops were to be found, were the stalls of goods that had been imported from outside Mali. One part of the street was for all the things that came from China such as scents, padlocks, mosquito coils, pens and packets of tea. In another part of it were all the goods such as nails, hammers, door hinges and bundles of steel wire that might be found in a hardware shop. And in another place were electronic goods such as radios, watches and tape recorders with their accompanying batteries and cassettes. There was the smiths' part of the market where roughly made aluminium pots, ladles, shovels and picks were to be found. Near to this was an area of all that was tin: plates, basins, mugs and tiny teapots – the huge piles of them were overwhelming with their bright, gaudy colours. It seemed that the merchants who sold these items were not satisfied to lay out only the quantities they thought they might sell, but must display their entire stocks as if by their sheer weight of number customers would be seduced into buying more of them.

The area for livestock in the market was on the perimeter. Here sad, bedraggled clusters of sheep stood about amongst groups of more lively-looking goats, seemingly unaware of their pending fate. There was the odd horse with serious-faced men gathered round it discussing its merits and some camels brought in from the bush by tough-looking Moors who stood patiently beside them, seemingly as aloof and detached as their camels from the market mayhem taking place around them.

In other areas of the market were such things as hay or chopped firewood or wickerwork baskets. There were piles of the tall bamboos used for poling pirogues, or rubber well buckets, or shiny metal buckets stacked up like castles about their owners. There were tobacco sellers, their black tobacco still in the leaf or compressed into bales; straw mats with designs woven in; huge, tumbling piles of grass scrubbing sponges; bundles of the sinuous sticks used for cleaning teeth; old and empty bottles for whatever use you liked; and tall, bendy towers of golden calabashes cut in half for use as bowls.

Another part of the market was devoted to clothes and cotton material. Young men had stalls of synthetic trousers and shirts with fake designer labels from France, women had piles of dirty, Oxfam cast-offs, and wealthy merchants had bolts and bolts of the tie-dyed and waxed materials which came from such diverse places as Sweden, Scotland, Taiwan and Nigeria and which, with all their bright colours and designs, made up the fancy style of Malian fashion.

In most of the markets of Mali one can find a great profusion of food. In fact, visiting these markets, one has the impression that this is a country well-endowed with food, not one where many people are for much of the time underfed. But this is because much of Mali still runs on the market system of exchange and barter and so it is in the market-place that the fruits of hard labour are all brought together.

Food means life, and the more food the better the life, and so the sheer explosion of quantities of naked food to be found in

176

the Segou market is a thrilling sight, even if, in reality, it does not mean that everybody is going to eat well that night. The atmosphere in the market, in the presence of all this food, is almost intoxicated, heady. It feels like a festival and on this day at least most people will in fact eat well, spending their carefully saved money and indulging themselves on all the delicious dainties that have been prepared by the townsfolk.

It is in the central market-place of Segou that the core of the Tuesday market is to be found. Here there are two large buildings housing the meat sellers. This is not a place for those with delicate sensibilities. At first it is the damp, slightly putrid smell that you notice; then the hysterical drone of thousands of bluebottle flies; then the aspect of a cavernous space darkened with dried blood; and finally the sight of a row of gory sheeps' heads staring blankly at you sends you scuttling quickly out.

I often wondered what became of all the good cuts of meat for here everything seems to be either offal or extremities. There are hooves and tails, ears, eyeballs and testicles; hearts and livers, intestines, and steaming piles of much that is unidentifiable. Cheerful, sweating men stand next to the displays of all this meat which either hangs from hooks or sits on large wooden chopping boards. Blood is on them and their cleavers, it trickles off the wooden boards and runs down little gutters in the middle of the floor.

Outside the meat market, sitting in many rows, tightly squeezed together, are the charm and medicine vendors: men who looked sharp and quick-witted. Organized on pieces of plastic before them are their wares: small, leather amulets containing verses of the Koran which most Malians wear from birth for protection against certain evils; gum arabic to be taken for a bad stomach; mango tree bark to be boiled for an anaesthetic for toothache; incenses to be inhaled for influenza; and many other powders and oils, roots and leaves to be consumed for other ailments. There are birds' wings, dried monkeys' hands, or even heads, snake skins, ostrich feathers, chicken claws, lizard tongues, milky bottled potions and all the other oddities that minister to the spiritual as well as the physical.

These men know their craft and know, more importantly, how to convince people that they know their craft. They also sell such things as beads, hair pins and plastic jewellery, and have many of the small cowrie shells that used to be the currency before the coming of Europeans. Near to the rows of these men are other tightly packed rows of women selling spices for cooking and many kinds of colourful and pungent powders.

And then there are the couscous sellers, the bean and rice, millet and corn, salt and cassava sellers, with large pyramids of their wares sitting before them. Vegetables are generally sold in small amounts. Each woman has six or seven carefully counted out piles of okra, tomatoes, carrots or onions. There are lettuces and yams, sweet potatoes and pumpkins, cucumbers and cabbage, all the fruits of the women's labours in the small vegetable plots they harvest in the river-beds beside their villages. Fruit comes in vast mounds. Mounds of oranges, lemons, guavas and blackened bananas, and other mounds, towering above the rest, of green and fleshy watermelons.

The huge, sprawling mass of women and their foods spills out from the central market-place to flatten eventually on the river's edge. Here are piles of black, dried fish, sometimes broken into flakes and compressed into balls. Onions get the same treatment, chillies form bright red domes, and round, yellow balls of peanut paste can be seen everywhere. Peanuts are perhaps the single item in the most profusion. They form a major part of the Malians' diet, either eaten roasted or put into a sauce. Women sit in front of such huge piles of them that you despair of their ever selling them.

And so, like a ball picking up momentum down a hill, business begins to flow. It becomes furious in its intensity. There is such commotion and noise, such a dense array of activity and colour, that you seek out a tea shack in which to sit stationary for a while. Now you can watch the other market, not the one stationary like yourself, but the one carried on people's heads and in their arms. These are the people with only quantities of merchandise that are portable: men with cloth and clothes draped from their arms and on their heads; people hawking bottles of colourful pills that can, they claim, perform the most remarkable feats; a boy with a torch; another with a pair of socks, perhaps acting as a satellite for his elder, clothes-stall-owning brother. You can watch the groups of blind men singing for alms; or the Koranic beggar boys doing the same; or a woman scaling and frying fish; or the bewildered-looking men freshly in from the bush with small bags, radios and wood axes clasped in their hands. Or you can watch the odd Tuareg, one of those 'blue men' from the Sahara whose skins become stained from the indigo dye of their turbans, a people who, since the dying of their land through droughts, are now often resigned to wandering in the lands of their old Bantu enemies, trying to sell their beautifully worked leather goods, such as boxes, and sheaths for long, lethal knives.

The market of Segou is an occasion of gaiety and celebration. It is a celebration of food successfully harvested and brought to market. But it is also a day of great importance, a serious day. All these peasants in from the countryside, and those townsfolk who also work the market, must make some money to buy the things they need to see them through the next week or month or even year. When they leave the embers of the market at the embers of the day, you hope they have enjoyed their market, and made profit from it enough to sustain them through the hardship that is every day but market day.

★

Mungo Park never entered the town of Segou, not on this trip, nor on his second trip when he returned to the Niger. Monsong, the king, it was rumoured, had received unfavourable accounts about him from traders and Moors who resided in Segou. They feared the motives for Park's journey, thinking, not unreasonably, that he was a spy sent by Europe. They foresaw, perhaps, that Europe had imperialistic designs on West Africa and would break their monopoly on trade. It is also possible, as I heard in Segou when I enquired of a holy man why Park had not been admitted to Segou, that Monsong, knowing that Park had been in the company of Daisy Koulibali, king of Kaarta, at the commencement of the Bambarra/Kaarta war, thought that Park was a devil sent by Daisy to kill him.

It is more probable, however, as Mungo Park himself points out, that Monsong feared that he would not be able to protect Park from the powerful and fanatical Moors of his court. Monsong certainly seems to have felt some benevolence towards Park, for, although demanding that Park depart forthwith from the vicinity of Segou, he gave him a present of five thousand cowries with which to purchase provisions in the course of his continued journey. Park estimates that one hundred of these little shells could purchase provisions for himself and his horse for a day, and so five thousand of them was a generous present indeed, especially considering that Park, having been robbed of all his possessions, was unable to give any present to Monsong.

Mungo Park's choice was now either to give up his journey and return to the Gambia or to follow the course of the Niger northwards and perhaps discover its termination point. Travelling northwards he knew would be taking him back into lands under the influence of the Moors, but Park was not a man to give up easily and so it was to the north that he travelled from Segou.

At first, being led by a guide provided by Monsong, Park travelled through a countryside which, he says, being highly cultivated, bore a great resemblance to the centre of England. He passed many small fishing villages, and then, arriving at the large town of Sasanding, his fears of being back in lands under the influence of Moors were confirmed. The town was much resorted to by Moors who brought salt, beads and coral there to be exchanged for gold dust and cotton cloth, and those Moors insisted that Park must repeat the Muslim prayers and make his devotions in a mosque. Being a good Christian, however, Park was reluctant to do this, but fortunately the chief of the town insisted that he could not see the 'king's stranger' ill-treated whilst he was under his protection. And so instead Park was made to sit on a high seat by the door to the mosque until sunset so that everybody could see him, for the people of the town had assembled in large, ungovernable numbers.

From Sasanding Park passed more villages and some larger towns, and, having on the way had a close encounter with a lion past which he rode within only a few feet, and having seen a 'camelopard', a giraffe, he arrived at Modiboo, 'a delightful village on the banks of the Niger'. Here he was much bitten by mosquitoes and became very feverish, not that he connected the two incidents closely, as the contraction of malaria from the bite of a mosquito was a discovery still a long way off. Being hurried out of Modiboo by the village chief he found himself in a bad state, barely able to walk, but not as bad as his horse which, worn out by its journey all the way from the Gambia, soon fell to the ground and could not be moved. As Park surveyed the 'associate of his adventures' lying panting on the ground, he could not, he says, suppress the sad apprehension that he should himself in a short time lie down and perish of fatigue and hunger. But on he went, leaving his horse behind, to arrive at the village of Kea, where the village chief told him that he paid very little attention to fine speeches, and would not allow Park to remain in his village. Just then, however, a fishing canoe belonging to the town of Silla appeared on the Niger and the man in it consented to take Park to a village further up the river called Morzan.

And so, having arrived at Morzan, and crossed the river to enter the town of Silla, Park came at last to the conclusion of this, his first journey into West Africa. It was here that he decided not to continue any further but to return westwards to the Gambia. Park was virtually penniless, having used up most of his cowries. He was sick and exhausted, hungry and half-naked. To continue his journey further northwards into the lands of the Moors would almost certainly, he says, mean that he would sacrifice his life for nothing and so the discoveries he had made would perish with him.

So now, no doubt with thoughts of how he might be received when he returned to Britain, Park had the prospect not only of a journey by foot of many hundreds of miles through unknown lands, but also of travelling during the rainy season which was already upon him, a season in which all travel was near to impossible and when fevers and disease were at their most potent. It is here in Silla, however, that I shall let Park remain for a while. Silla, or so I thought, had vanished from the maps many years ago.

VII
Downstream, Upstream

THE TAXI PARK in Segou was a hive of activity. It was here that the countryside spilled into the town. Bush taxis with towering loads of country produce on their roofs, which sometimes included small flocks of sheep, and with names like 'Bon Dieu' or 'Bon Chance' painted on their sides, were forever arriving and departing. One of them was called 'Super Jimmi', and it was with this ancient vehicle that I left Segou. I was headed downstream to the small riverside town of Kemacina and my moped was to remain behind, in the expectation that I would return to collect it later.

Although we left Segou early in the morning, we did not arrive in Kemacina, 150 kilometres away, until late at night. The reason for this was not solely the result of our slow speed over rough tracks consisting of one huge dry puddle after another, but because frequent and lengthy delays are endemic to bush taxi transport. Bush taxis are themselves the very epitome of unreliability. Toyota or Peugeot pick-up trucks, they become transformed over the years to conglomerations of all that has been cannibalized from other vehicles and invented by imaginative smiths, strapped, hammered and battered together to create veritable beasts of naked, shuddering steel in which passengers are housed in cages in the backs.

The owners of these vehicles can rarely afford to repair the engines properly or to purchase new tyres, so breakdowns and punctures occur with great regularity. But in fact it is not the breakdowns and punctures that are the main cause of delay: most Malians are enthusiastic amateur mechanics. Nor is it the police road blocks or the halts at prayer times either. The main causes of delay are the frequent halts that take place for reasons that are not easy to determine. Not a village can be passed, hardly even a pedestrian beside the road, without the bush taxi drawing to a halt, the driver entering into protracted conversations with

185

the villagers or the pedestrians, and any number of the passengers disappearing for lengths of time. These delays remain unexplained and mysterious but one can only presume that they stem from the desperate necessity the bush taxi owners are under to negotiate any possibility of business in the course of each journey if they wish that journey to turn a profit.

After we had crossed the Niger over the dam some 40 kilometres downstream from Segou, the countryside we drove through was open and well-cultivated. The land all round us had been cleared for the planting of crops, only the largest trees left standing. There were many of these tall, handsome trees with every few miles a small, brown village huddled beside one of them. These were the villages Mungo Park had passed on his way to Silla and indeed some of them still bore similar names such as Sibila, Park's Sibili, and Niaro, his Nyara. Kemacina itself, where I was headed for, was probably Park's village of Kea.

After darkness had fallen we came to large areas of rice cultivation. The land here was latticed with the small canals that irrigated the rice, and the air was humid and filled with insects that spiralled towards our headlights. Kemacina, when we arrived there, was just darkness broken now and again by the glow of oil lamps. One of the bush taxi passengers led me through the darkness to a rest house where I was given a small, bare room to sleep the night. I had to wait until next morning to see what sort of town I was in.

★

Kemacina bore no resemblance to Mungo Park's village of Kea. The French had come here, set up an administrative centre, and built a town. And like most of the French-inspired towns of Mali, Kemacina was constructed on a rigid grid system. What would normally have been a haphazard and chaotic collection of family homesteads was chiselled into one square block after another with a matrix of avenues dividing them up: the French had regimented the spontaneity of the African mode of living.

The avenues that ran between the blocks were wide and of uneven, bare earth. Down each side were deep storm drains and also rows of the tall plane trees the French had planted throughout the town. These trees having by now attained their full stature, the residents of Kemacina greatly benefited from them for it was possible to walk from one side of the town to the other virtually never having to enter direct sunlight. The town sat in their shade as though it had been built in a grand and majestic forest, peaceful and quiet with the Niger running beside it. There were few cars, the town's many avenues being left to the attentions of wandering sheep and small boys, who ran down them chasing hoops with sticks in their hands.

On my first morning in town I met a young man called Arsene sitting outside a small store house near to the Niger. The store house, it turned out, was the property of a European development project and Arsene was its guardian. He called me over to him when I was passing nearby and offered me some tea.

Arsene was tall and lanky and had an air of great ease and confidence. He seemed an unlikely person to be a watchman for he was well educated, and spoke perfect French. He was also worldly wise, though not, I discovered, because he had seen much of the world – in fact he had never left Mali – but because he had passed most of his life in Bamako and the sort of life he had passed there was of the type that makes one wise in the ways of the world. 'I was a bandit,' he told me. 'I finished my education, but then I became a bandit. I found a job in a night club, the most famous night club in Bamako. It was full of drugs and prostitutes and in time I became a big man there. After that I became a taxi driver for a while. But by then the police were after me, so I left Bamako and came here.'

'And you do not find life too dull here?' I asked him.

'Ah yes, it's a little dull,' he replied. 'But I do not mind. I am happy doing my job. I do not want to have anything to do with banditry now. It's a very bad thing. In fact, you know, if I saw someone stealing something I would chase after them myself. You see, I have changed my ways for good.'

When Arsene's father had died his mother had come to live with her brother, his uncle, in Kemacina and it was with this uncle that Arsene now lived. Arsene liked to claim that his uncle had himself been an extraordinary bandit in his capacity as the commander of one of the most ill-reputed regiments in the

Malian army. On retirement his uncle had come home to look after his old mother.

In some ways it was as if Arsene had also retired. He had a calm, resigned attitude and no longer cared anything for ambition. He was not, he told me, ashamed of his lowly job and in fact was prepared to do it for many years to come.

'I am a real Malian now. Even if you were to send me the money for an aeroplane ticket to America all I should do is to spend it. Real Malians,' he said, 'never leave their country.' And so Arsene sat outside his store house all day long, his long legs stretched out before him and his pot of tea bubbling incessantly beside him.

Arsene's best friend in town was a young policeman called Mohammed. He was his soul mate, his very partner in life. Whenever Arsene was not working he would be with Mohammed, either at Mohammed's house or at the post he controlled on the road that led out of town. There the two of them would talk and drink tea late into the night, passing the long hours of life together.

Arsene had great respect for policemen. 'They have to be strong. And they can make a lot of money from the merchants who must bribe them because so much of their merchandise is contraband. If they did not do this, on the wages they get, they would not be able to afford to have even a girlfriend, let alone a wife.

'But,' he went on, 'I should rather have been a soldier. And I would have made the nastiest of soldiers there ever was.'

Mohammed had indeed got himself well set up. He was a neat, quick-witted man and made good profit from his posting at a road block. He may not have been rich, but he had acquired all the things he desired and with these he was content. He had a new and pretty wife who had just produced a baby boy. He had a refrigerator and a television set in his small house with his wife. He had a smart radio, a brand-new motorbike, and a sophisticated sleeping bag that doubled up as a coat which he had bought from a tourist and of which he was immensely proud. And he also had a number of girlfriends, for he was a dashing and attractive figure, and, with his playfulness and underlying hardness, he had attained a position of respect.

'You will take me to Europe with you,' he said to me the first time he saw me. 'And you will also introduce me to Hélène, the pretty French woman who is Arsene's boss. I am deeply in love with her but I know she would not even consider a black man as a lover unless he was the friend of a white man.'

But I knew that the last thing Mohammed would like would be to go to Europe, for he was 'real Malian' like Arsene and so had no desire to tempt fate. As for Hélène, I am sure he would have loved that conquest.

The room that Arsene lived in at his uncle's compound was small and bare except for two beds and some calendar photographs of naked girls pinned to the earth walls. He invited me to stay with him and so for the week I passed in Kemacina I slept in the spare bed.

★

It was through Hélène that I eventually discovered the whereabouts of Mungo Park's town of Silla.

Hélène lived on her own in a large house on the outskirts of town. She was a tough, independent character and, like most expatriate field workers, was dedicated to her job and endured a hard, often frustrating, and sometimes lonely existence. When I turned up at her house she was in the process of logging on a computer all the villages that were in her jurisdiction and the work her project had done or needed to do in them. We drank pastis while she told me about her villagers and the plans to grow more vegetables in order to improve their diet.

'We give them seed,' she said, 'and we teach them new methods of cultivation, but these Bozo fishermen are a dead loss. In the middle of the year they just take off in their boats for months at a time leaving only the old and infirm people back in the villages who cannot care for the vegetables properly.'

A certain amount of indignation unavoidably slipped into her voice, as though it was a shame that the members of this small tribe of river people should go on their traditional migration rather than stay at home to look after their vegetables. She, I have no doubt, would have agreed with Doua from the village of Dalibougou that it was a determined adhesion to tradition that was prohibiting the Malians from improving their situation. 'We have the greatest difficulty in getting villagers to use new methods of growing crops,' she said. 'As soon as we leave them

189

to their own devices they return to their traditional methods. What can we do if they won't help us to help them? They must learn to accept new ways.'

Whilst I was talking to Hélène, an old man wearing a broad toothless smile and a long dirty gown entered the house. He was one of Hélène's agents who worked directly with the villagers, and had come to ask her to supper. 'But you do not have to ask me to supper *all* the time,' Hélène said when he invited her.

'But you are my boss,' the old man replied, as if this was reason enough. 'What is your command?'

'I already have food prepared for this evening.' Hélène sounded somewhat annoyed.

'It will be chicken, yes?' the old man continued, determined to have his way. 'What do you want with your chicken?'

A look of resignation came over Hélène's face. 'Chicken is very nice,' she said politely. 'But chicken *on its own*.'

The old man was upset because he wanted to produce a proper European meal. 'No chips?' he asked plaintively.

'No.'

'OK, just chicken, but garnished chicken for sure! You always like garnish.'

Hélène laughed happily. 'It is so nice to be in demand. What can you do,' she said to me, 'but accept?'

In his conversation with Hélène about some work he had been doing recently, the old man mentioned a small village about 10 kilometres down the Niger on the far bank called Salee, which I realized could well be Park's Silla, for it was in a similar position. A day later I went there with Arsene.

We travelled to Salee in a small dugout: its owner, a compact, gnarled fisherman, perched in the back paddling with a short oar. It was an old boat and sat very low in the water, and all along its bottom pieces of material had been driven into cracks in the wood to try to stem the leakage.

When we pulled out from the shore a line of children at the top of the bank started dancing up and down and shouting at us. I scowled back at them thinking that, like most of the children in the town, they were chanting their inevitable '*tubab, tubab*', a habit that was beginning to get on my nerves. But this time they were not chanting '*tubab, tubab*'. They were shouting 'hippo, hippo', because just then a large pair of nostrils and two beady eyes appeared nearby. Fortunately the hippo was more wary of us than we were of it and it quickly disappeared.

As we drifted on the current down the middle of the river with the fisherman using his oar only now and again to straighten us up, Arsene, sitting in the middle of the boat, began brewing some tea, and I, sitting in the front, watched the river and its life come gently towards me.

The Niger is renowned for its bird life. It is here that many of Europe's migratory birds come to winter. After crossing the inhospitable Sahara, the river is their first sight of water. And what a sight it must be, for at that time of year, October and November, it is swelled with rainwater and has burst its banks, flooding much of the inland delta. As these floods recede, large quantities of fish become entrapped in shallows of water and are easy prey for fishermen and many kinds of fishing birds; land that has been tilled by farmers for planting crops reveals a feast of invertebrates for other types of birds; and the countless herds of cattle, sheep and goats of the pastoralists that come to graze the lush grasses that sprout provide a wealth of parasitic insects for yet more kinds of birds. It is a time of bonanza and vast flocks of egrets, waders, wildfowl and herons descend on the delta. Ibises, pin-tails and ruffs also come to feast. Yellow wagtails, pied kingfishers, kites and warblers are there. Birds of prey such as harriers and kestrels feed on the thousands of mice turfed out of their homes by the floods. There are sand martins, Caspian terns, stilts and pelicans; hammerkops, swallows and swifts.

Sitting in front of the dugout on my way to Salee, I saw herons, sometimes as tall as small boys, posted at intervals along the water's edge like sentinels with their large, black wings spread to entice fish into their shade. Terns bombarded the water in seemingly reckless dives, their sleek bodies with wings folded back following their arrowing beaks to shatter the reflections of sky. Pied kingfishers hovered stationary in the air peering sharply down their dagger beaks for the movement of a fish. A couple of fish eagles patrolled their territories, gliding effortlessly on their huge spans of wing, passing with a rush of wind overhead. And there were all the many and busy birds that darted about the water's edge on matchstick legs picking at tiny holes in the sand with their ingeniously shaped beaks. The bird life of the river kept me enthralled for the hour it took to reach Salee, and also for the two hours it took to get back to Kemacina against the current.

It turned out that Salee was almost certainly Mungo Park's town of Silla. I did not expect to be able to find anybody to confirm this and indeed I did not: Mungo Park and his story have disappeared from much of Mali's oral histories, if in fact they ever became a part of them. But Salee had once been a large town, the only one in the vicinity of old Silla. Today it was a small village of Bozo fishermen on a hillock 3 kilometres away from the Niger. In front of the hillock was a dry water course that would in the rainy season become a part of the river and, when the Niger was endowed with more water than it is today, may have remained so all year round, which would account for the fact that Mungo Park took a boat to the very eaves of Silla.

The village was at one end of the hillock but the village chief showed me how the old town had once covered it entirely, and, indeed, the large amounts of broken pottery that were littered everywhere, and the outlines of old buildings, confirmed this. The village chief also pointed out where the old market-place had been and told me that before the town was destroyed in a war with the Fulani people at a time before he, an old man, was born, the town had boasted over one thousand horses. Most probably the people of old Silla had, after the war and as the water level of the Niger fell leaving their town high and dry, gradually migrated to the nearby village of Koungourou which was right on the river's edge and to Kemacina which, after the French arrived and rearranged the order of things, became the principal market town of the area.

It had been in Koungourou that Arsene and I had met the village chief of Salee. When we disembarked from our dugout he had been sitting on the river bank awaiting our arrival, quite unsurprised and full of smiles. 'But how did he know I was coming?' I asked Arsene as it had only been that morning that I had decided to come at all.

'Nobody told him that you were coming,' Arsene replied. 'But he knew that someone would be coming to see him today. These country people can feel these sorts of things.'

★

Christmas was only a few days off and so this was *La Semaine Locale* in Mali, the week in which *Le Concours National* took place.

Kemacina, being the capital of an administrative sector, had many country people come to compete in the competition all housed in the secondary school. Each afternoon there was a football match and athletics, and each evening there was a play performed in a newly built public hall on the outskirts of town called *Le Centre Nouveau*. One evening Arsene took me to see one of the plays.

Seemingly half of Kemacina had had the idea of seeing a play that night. All the way to *Le Centre Nouveau* there was a stream of people talking in excited voices and carrying torches and lanterns. At the door there was a scrummage, with two policemen trying to keep order. Once inside, there was another press of people all bunched up behind six rows of chairs that faced the stage. As all the chairs were taken, Arsene had a word with an usher who allowed us to stand in the aisle beside the chairs. This was a position of privilege, or so the usher made us feel by his treatment of anyone else who attempted to stand there. 'Get back, you oaf!' he would shout at anyone who approached his pitch, and, if it was someone smaller than himself, give them a thwack on the head.

In the front row of chairs sat the commandant of Kemacina with his wife and his highest-ranking officials. He was a tall man of cultivated appearance dressed in a khaki uniform, and he turned frequently to make polite remarks to the people in the second row, who, by the look of their starched and expensive robes, were the town dignitaries. The third row of chairs was occupied by more uniformed officials with their wives and friends, and in the last three rows sat others who at least thought themselves important enough to merit a chair. There was much shuffling and changing of places in these three rows until all pretenders had been weeded out. Then everyone settled down in a cosy aura of self-importance, only to be disturbed once more when, quite late in the performance, a lady of great stature and exquisite dress appeared. Brushing aside the usher in the aisle where Arsene and I stood, she surveyed the seated spectators with such a haughty look that one man was intimidated into giving up his seat. He was then, to his evident shame, elbowed to the back of the crowd of common folk, where small boys and girls were making a nuisance of themselves, being too short to see what was happening on the stage.

Once a spaghetti of wires had been laid carefully on the stage to service a microphone, the hall lighting was dimmed and two strip lights were turned on. These strip lights were intended to illuminate the stage, but, being poorly placed, they left it in shade and illuminated the row of judges who sat directly in front of the stage.

The play to be performed that night, Arsene informed me, was the story of a director of a large company who was caught embezzling the equivalent of £100,000. 'This is a good story,' Arsene said. 'Watch closely. Some people here tonight will not like what they see.'

At first, single actors came on, dressed in turn as a judge, a soldier and a businessman. Each threw dramatic poses and called out such lines as 'Justice for all and all shall be judges.' The audience at the back of the hall gave them a noisy reception. The businessman was booed, the soldier – not surprisingly, in view of the presence of the commandant – was loudly cheered.

Next came a series of short, fast scenes set in the director's home and office. There were few props, and the actors delivered their lines in a flat monotone as though reading a list. 'I need money for my education,' one son said to his father, the director, a fat man dressed in a Western suit. 'I have many debts,' another told him. Another had problems with the police. A daughter claimed that she must buy expensive clothes in order to attract a rich husband. In the office, lawyers and businessmen came to demand money that the director had promised them, or owed them. In fact, everybody from brothers to petty street traders all required money for one reason or another, and the director promised them all that they would get it.

The next scene was set in a seedy bar. Two or three coarse-looking characters sat round a crate drinking with the director. 'Crime,' one of them cried, 'is the only way to wealth.'

Back in the director's home a *griot* in a purple sequined tunic struck up a song to the accompaniment of a *kora*: 'A man may be strong and powerful,' he sang. 'But when he is caught by a lion, he is as helpless as the beggar. The clever man is the one who finds a way of avoiding the lion.'

The director was now seen visiting first a marabout and then a witch-doctor. The marabout, a devout-looking man sitting on a prayer mat, meditated for a while, mumbled many prayers, and then said to the director: 'You have been accused of embezzlement. This is no small problem and so you will have to pay very dearly if you wish it to be solved.' The director gave him half a million CFA francs, promising him five million more if all worked out.

The witch-doctor was dressed in all the weird and tatty garb of his profession. He chanted spells and waved a bone above a small, black bag from which he took a chicken's claw. 'Go and bury this beneath the baobab tree by the bend in the Joliba,' he said. 'If you do this all will be resolved.' When the director gave the witch-doctor *one* million CFA for his services with the promise of *seven* more if all worked out the audience laughed and jeered loudly. 'He has more faith in the witch-doctor than the holy marabout,' one man shouted from the back.

In the office once more, the director had another two visitors who, to the director's horror, turned out to be policemen. He was handcuffed and led miserably away. The last scene of the play was set in a court room. A judge with a wig sat on a dais and all the director's relations and dependants stood to one side. First a prosecuting attorney stood up and said: 'You see how the director must surely be guilty. How else could he have afforded to support so many dependants?' And he pointed his finger at all the director's relations. Next a defending attorney gave a long and impassioned speech pleading for leniency on the grounds that the director had come under such pressure from his many dependants that they in theory were as guilty as he. 'He is as blameless as the soldier who kills under orders,' he cried out. Finally, the judge boomed: 'Three years' hard labour.'

By the end of the play the bulk of the audience were bored

and restless as the play had been conducted in French which they could not understand; the judges were tired, some of them slumbering with their heads on the stage; and over the six rows of important, seated people a steely silence had descended.

One day I went to see one of the football matches which took place each afternoon in a football ground a little out of town. I had only been watching it for a quarter of an hour, when it came to a halt. A player had committed a foul and the referee had stopped the game to show the player a red card meaning he was to be sent off. But that player, with the full support of his team, was not to be so easily removed from the pitch. He picked up the football and refused to hand it over. Everybody, all the players, the referee and the audience, were by this time shouting and screaming their thoughts on the fairness of the dismissal. Then, when the team opposing the team of the fouler tried to regain possession of the football, the football was carried off and passed between the team of the fouler, and so the game of football developed into a game of rugger.

Soon, with the help of the audience who now swarmed on to the pitch, the game of rugger developed into a huge wrestling match. It was at this stage that the referee, extricating himself from the core of the wrestling, removed the whistle that had been shrilling continuously from his mouth since the onset of the problem, and announced that the team not of the fouler were the winners of the match. That team was Kemacina. To screams of 'cheats, liars and bandits' the referee and as many of the players of the Kemacina team as could disentangle themselves from the mêlée beat a hasty retreat from the pitch with a crowd of very angry people on their tail and were only saved from a beating by a charging, helmeted and baton-wielding troop of soldiers who had just then appeared at the football ground gates. Soon the chasers were being chased and individual bystanders being hit. One bystander, a young man standing next to me, said in a calm voice: 'Such a shame, because Kemacina were bound to win anyway.'

★

About 80 kilometres downstream of Kemacina, situated on some islands near the junction of the Niger and one of its major tributaries, the Bani, is a town called Mopti. I had heard much about this town which is renowned for its beauty and which, as a result of its being surrounded by lagoons and swamps, has been dubbed by the tourist industry 'the Venice of Africa'. It is an old town and an important centre of fishing and commerce. Many tourists visit it on account of its beauty and also because of its proximity to the ancient town of Djenne and the famous 'Dogon country'. In fact, along with Timbuktu, Mopti, Djenne and 'the Dogon country' are the principal attractions for the steady flow of tourists who come to Mali. All the towns have long and interesting histories and represent, especially the large mosque in Djenne, some of the finest traditional architecture to be found in this part of West Africa. And the Dogon country is famous for the unique style in which the Dogon people have built their villages into the rocky face of their country, and for their rich heritage of art and culture, especially their masked dances.

Many boats ply the waters between Kemacina and Mopti. I found one that would take me there on a Saturday, Kemacina's market day.

River transport on most of the inland delta of the Niger is monopolized by the Bozos. There are a few state-owned barges that carry rice and grain between the larger towns, and when the Niger is in flood a couple of modern, if old, passenger boats run between Timbuktu and the rapids just north of Bamako. Other than these, river transport is the domain of Bozos.

The boats the Bozos use range from simple dugouts to large pirogues made of wood imported from Ivory Coast by traditional boat-builders on the beaches of Segou and other riverside towns. These vessels can be as much as 100 feet in length and, when heavily laden, can draw up to 7 feet of water. They have elegantly pointed prows and sterns and are endowed with bamboo awnings down their entire lengths and large diesel engines bolted to planks in their bowels. Some of them are decorated with colourful designs and pictures of birds and aeroplanes on their hulls, but mostly they are unadorned and look just like the hard-working beasts of burden they are. The one that I took passage in had a hull black with tar from end to end, its bamboo awning covered in a network of ropes and a green, tattered canvas, in need of much repair.

There were many of these large pirogues drawn up to the beach beside Kemacina the day that I took passage to Mopti, ready for market day. Market day spilled over their sides and into the waters trapped between the boats and the shore where people washed their pots and did any number of unsavoury things. It crept up the beaches, spread, and dispersed throughout the town. It was an amphibious assault of bodies, bundles, sacks and wares. And then, once the boats had been emptied, the assault reversed. Now the boats were besieged by men tipping heavy sacks over their sides, by passengers with their goods and by marketeers come to sell things to those passengers already installed on top of the sacks. In the boat I chose, those sacks, containing millet flour, came level with the gunwales, and by midday much of the space on top of them had been reserved.

'I boarded and quickly found myself a place amidships. There I waited for the departure, but the departure did not take place for a very long time. Meanwhile a lady appeared in the water beside where I sat with a huge pannier of dried fish on her head. She was an old lady and the weight of the pannier was such that it seemed it must snap her thin, bony body in two. But this old lady was a tough village type who consisted, seemingly, of nothing but muscled sinew. With practised ease she flicked her pannier over the side of the boat next to me; then she was off up the beach only to reappear ten minutes later with another huge pannier on her head. Five times she repeated this exercise, each time placing her pannier next to me. I scrunched myself up into a smaller and smaller ball, but by the last delivery I had lost all my space and so moved to another part of the boat.

The boat did not eventually depart until some time after the sun had set. By then there were so many people crammed with their luggage on top of the sacks that it would have been impossible to count them, even if it had not already been dark. The only light on board came from a single oil lamp hanging from the awning in the stern above a small, clear space where the figure of a large woman could be seen busying herself over some steaming pots in a makeshift kitchen. The jumbled forms of passengers sitting and lying prone down the length of the boat were silhouetted here and there against the light, as were all the items such as shoes and radios and small personal bags that hung from underneath the awning only inches above their heads. Mumbles and bursts of talk came from those forms, and the crew shouted to each other as they tried to dislodge the boat from the shallows of the shore where it had, because of its weight, become lodged. 'This mother of beasts! She's wedged her rear end,' the huge hulk of the captain let loose. 'Tomo,' he called to a young man standing in the prow with a long pole in his hand. 'Wake up. Bring her around so we can get some slip. Fool. Not that way.' Once we were free the diesel engine was started up and we drew away from the dim lights of Kemacina towards the middle of the Niger.

Two hours later we were still in view of the dim lights of Kemacina, stuck on a sandbank, barely a kilometre downstream. A Bozo man of huge and powerful proportions who had a large, round face of reddish complexion and two almost oriental eyes, was the first into the water. Then more men followed him over the side, and they all began to push. They pushed first from one end; then from the other, gradually shifting us across the sandbank. Now and again the engine was started but each time sand spurted out behind and the engine choked into silence. Although there was no moon that night, it was not pitch dark. The forms of the men in the water, and the stretches of quiet river around us, were illuminated with that fluorescent glow that water always seems to hold within itself whenever it is away from artificial light.

Nobody seemed particularly concerned that we were stuck on a sandbank. In fact most of the passengers on board were by now fast asleep, and the men in the water laughed in their efforts to move us. But the only European on the boat, not realizing that river taxis often have difficulties to overcome, thought that the predicament must be quite severe. I jumped over the side into the cold, waist-high waters of the Niger to see if my small weight might be of some help, only to be greeted by: 'What's this, what's this? The *tubab*'s in the water. By God, the situation must be *very* serious,' and a considerable amount of laughter. But the laughter was good-humoured and not long after this the boat was suddenly floating free and the engine could be started.

Throughout that night we got stuck on sandbanks. I would be lulled to sleep by the gentle throbbing of the engine only to be awakened by the shouts and laughter of men back in the water again. In and out of sleep I drifted, at one time waking to see men unloading sacks from one end of the boat and carrying them with much difficulty through the swirling waters of the river to the other. Now the men worked silently, exhaustion affecting even their lively spirits. It was at this stage that I realized that nothing was going to prevent us from reaching Mopti. These tough Bozos would push us all the way there if necessary.

I woke at dawn to find us pulled up beside a large village. The village, I was informed, was Diafarabe, a place I had heard much talk of. Each year a great festival was held here at the time when the Fulani pastoralists brought their vast herds of cattle to cross the river, migrating with them from lands that would soon be flooded to more elevated areas where there was fresh grazing. The sight of their tens of thousands of cattle being driven across the river here at Diafarabe was one that people could come a long way to see.

'How long will we be staying here?' I asked one of the crew.

'Oh, not long,' he answered. 'Tomorrow there is a market here, and the day after that we shall leave.'

Having decided that this was rather a long time to wait, I asked whether there might be another boat that could take me to Mopti. This brought a sober response. 'Ah, that is bad, very bad,' I heard someone say. Not understanding what was meant by this I went ashore and began hassling the captains of the many other pirogues also drawn up to the beach.

Finding that nobody spoke French, however, I was left hovering and ignored on the edge of the shore. Then at last a French speaker appeared and a captain of a boat that was leaving for Mopti that day was introduced. A ticket price was negotiated and off I went back to my original pirogue to collect my bag.

The news of the switch of allegiance was taken sullenly. As I made my way to my new boat, the captain of my old one appeared by my side with an angry face. 'What about the money?'

he shouted at me. 'The recompense for the loss of business.' But I had already given the captain's son what I thought a more than reasonable percentage of the ticket to Mopti and so walked onwards to my new berth with the captain on my heels denouncing me as 'a very bad white man'. The passengers of the new boat sat woodenly looking at me as though I was indeed a very bad person; the captain and crew of the new boat could be heard giggling in the background.

For a moment I was left feeling very conspicuous and foreign, wondering whether I had broken some unwritten code by my switch of allegiance from boat to boat. But my doubts were not to last long. About ten minutes later, three other passengers from the old boat came over to the new one, the old captain bobbing and cursing behind them, and installed themselves and their bags. Amongst these passengers was the huge Bozo man who had been sitting next to me on the old boat. Now, with the simple gesture of offering me some powder to chew which turned out to be extremely hot ginger, the Bozo man indicated that all was well and muttered 'rascal', nodding towards the old captain. The world was once again a friendly place and the sullen looks of the passengers on the new boat now seemed more like looks of surprise.

My new pirogue was equally laden with merchandise and passengers as my old one had been. By steering a clever zig-zagging course the helmsman, who sat behind a tiny steering wheel in the prow, negotiated a route up the wide, blue waters of the Niger without once getting stuck on a sandbank.

The river was at this time of the year, the dry season, low. At each bend long spits of sand stuck out almost half-way across it, the beaches were deep and the river banks high. There, outlined against the bright sky, one saw herds of goats with herd boys, or the curved horns of cattle, and in places the dry scrubby bushes that grew in this dry, scrubby land bunched right up to the banks. And every so often, maybe every 15 kilometres, a grove of trees standing low above the bank in the far distance would herald a village. Soon the thin, round shape of a minaret with a moon and crescent on top of it could be distinguished; then, as you drew near to the village, the cluster of buildings pressed right up to the bank became clearly visible.

These villages were small and poor-looking, but with their tight knots of medina surrounding their mosques they seemed substantial, well-established places: places that had histories and many stories to tell. Some of them were pressed so close to the river that the bank, as it had been worn away, had taken a part of the village with it, leaving behind a perfect cross-section. There, hanging precariously, were houses sliced in half revealing small rooms and staircases, alleyways falling into open space, and trees tangled amongst them with their webs of roots exposed.

Other than these more substantial villages there were also many small encampments of Bozo fishermen, generally on spits and banks of sand. These were families come to parts of the river where the fishing was at that time good. They would pile all their possessions, their dogs and goats, fishing nets and pots and pans into their long dugouts, with the women and children sitting beneath the grass thatch at the back, and they would pole themselves up the river to set up their camps on the sandbanks. A few chickens pecked around these encampments, a child perhaps played at the water's edge, cooking utensils lay around small grass huts, and tiny kites flew above them as markers. Other than this there was nothing, only wind, sand and sun.

At most of the larger villages we passed, we stopped to let off passengers and pick up new ones. Villagers would come down to the shore to greet us, families would come to welcome relations, and women would bring roasted meats and peanuts for us to buy. At one village a madman waded out into the water shouting, 'The trees are on fire, the wind is dead, the sky is laughing. You have come to take me away.' But this was not an aggressive or unhappy madman. He laughed as he gibbered and everyone laughed with him in a kindly way and gave him things to carry back to their homes. A group of Koranic beggar boys then appeared, singing and shaking tin cans for alms. They made the Muslims aboard our boat, who had just finished their midday devotions and who ignored them, feel awkward.

In another village we took on board a woman dressed from head to toe in black, who, I was told, was 'a very special and holy person'. She had an air of authority and wealth about her but was so large and fleshy that she had the utmost difficulty in boarding the pirogue. Attempts to lift her over the side with any decorum failed, and so a long wooden plank was stretched to the shore. The woman got down on her hands and knees and, inch by precarious inch, crawled up the plank in a fashion not dissimilar to a slug.

As the woman puffed her way up the plank, there was a sudden commotion at the top of the beach: a group of men came running from the village towards us carrying a girl in their arms. She was screaming and struggling so frantically the men had the greatest difficulty in keeping a hold of her. They rushed her, wailing, to the side of the boat, but immediately they heaved her over the side she went completely limp and I caught a glimpse of an ashen and lifeless face which spoke of total despair. By now a great crowd of villagers had gathered round the boat, pointing and laughing. 'So fierce and determined!' they shouted, 'just like she always was. Look at the way she throws off her shawl,' they said as the girl angrily threw off the piece of material some women were trying to place over her head. 'That is not good behaviour for a bride, but just wait and see how a husband will take away that pride of hers,' they laughed. The girl was being sent away to Mopti to marry and obviously had no wish to leave her home. Soon her father jumped on board and, with a few firm slaps, reduced her to more wailing. Then we pulled away from the shore and the crowd of villagers stood waving and shouting their farewells across the water, but the girl snuffled, and had eyes only for the floor.

The journey into the depths of that evening was one of the most moving I have experienced. Even now it makes my heart pound. As the wash of the boat, almost at a level with the sides, curved so perfectly that it bent but did not disturb the mirror-still colours of the evening sky, an immense sense of peace and loneliness descended on me. It was not the loneliness of the individual. But gliding down the calm river between its quiet islands with flocks of brilliant white egrets homing in the still air, it was as if our small knot of humanity, close up in our slim wooden boat, was of the utmost insignificance, as tender and vulnerable as a small, warm heartbeat. It was one of those rare moments when you feel touched by the very quick of life.

Too soon darkness came and everybody slept, the night only disturbed by the steady throb of the engine, the coughs of the sleepers, the cry of a baby, and the occasional sobs of the girl being sent away to marry. A couple of times we came upon the strings of bobbing lights that were the Bozo fishermen at work. The crew called out to them, and exchanged news until their voices drifted away. And then, shortly after midnight, I woke to see many lights strung out along the top of the river bank. A little further on, I saw the shapes of buildings outlined against the star-filled sky. We had arrived at Mopti. It slid quietly past us until, with a sudden splurge of noise and commotion, a group of people burst out of a large doorway, singing and playing drums. That doorway belonged to a church and it was Christmas Day.

Coming to the end of a lagoon where there was a large river port, we squeezed our pirogue between two of the hundreds of pirogues pulled up on the beach, and, leaving the rest of the passengers who remained sleeping on the boat, I stepped ashore and went in search of a bed for the night.

★

I wandered for a long time down dark, empty streets. I was filthy dirty, tired and lost. Mopti hummed gently around me. There was almost no light and almost no people about. The odd cur of a dog slunk beside walls or picked at piles of rotting refuse. Then at the end of a street of tall, brown buildings I saw a bright light over a doorway. Arriving at that doorway I entered what a plaque beside it told me was the 'Bar Mali'. Inside there was a dim hallway with a steel grille on one side behind which sat a woman, who asked whether I wanted a room.

'Here, come here,' I heard her call a moment later from down a corridor. This corridor led to a small, dingy bar in which the shadowy figures and sweaty faces of drinkers could be discerned through the thick cigarette smoke. The place smelled of stale beer and urine. I was taken up some stairs on which slouched the forms of three or four women, and led to a tiny room the walls of which consisted of wire mesh and which smelled of mould. 'Will this do?' the woman asked. 'No,' I replied a little too bluntly. 'Tch,' the woman said, and walked off leaving me to find my way back to the street.

'You want taxi?' a voice came from the darkness nearby. 'I'm very good taxi driver of Venice of Africa.' A small, weasel-faced man appeared and ushered me to his vehicle. In this I travelled all the way back to the river port and on to a large boat moored at the shore beside a street. 'This boat does not work any longer,' the taxi driver told me, 'but now it's a very good hotel.'

It was a large boat: three storeys of rusty white steel lined with rows of small cabin doors. From it came the sounds of music. I boarded and found a man who gave me a small cabin in which to sleep. Then I installed myself in the bar room where a number of 'don't-care' bar girls were hanging out, and one drunk young man, and, in a corner, two Dutch girls talking earnestly with a man with long dreadlocks. It was Christmas Day so I celebrated it with beer. People came and went in the bar. The two Dutch girls disappeared with their Rastafarian look-alike and a large Lebanese man entered with a tall, elegant girl.

'What does my princess want to drink?' the Lebanese man asked the girl.

'Just water, thank you,' she replied.

The Lebanese man ordered whisky for himself, and, seeing me, ordered one for me as well. 'They are the bosses here,' he said to nobody in particular, referring to the bar girls. They ignored him. 'How's my princess,' he continued, 'my little calculator? That's just what one needs in life. A little calculator to return to in the evening.' The girl laughed and so did the bar girls. 'Put on a video,' the Lebanese man ordered the bar girls, and they complied. Nobody watched it, though. They were all too absorbed in their talk and drink. Occasionally it would be rewound to the beginning again. The room was hot and fumy. At around three o'clock the bar was closed but still customers, including myself, sat drinking. A feeling of great benevolence seeped over me. Later I went to bed.

The old part of Mopti stood tall and majestic on an island, the tiers of brown, crumbling buildings hemmed in by fields of lush reeds and water lilies that in the evening became filled with egrets. This part of it scented of age and history, its many genera-tions of buildings stacked up round a large, earthen mosque shaped and smooth-surfaced like a child's sand castle. Lagoons and stretches of open river surrounded it, and boats as elegant as gondolas were pulled up everywhere.

The more modern part of the town lay across a short causeway across which each evening a swarm of people made their way home with bicycles and donkeys and small hand-carts. Here were administrative buildings, a bank to which I went, and a hotel where a number of tourists were lodged. These tourists had come to see Mopti, like I had, and they could be seen during the daytime walking round it, capturing it in their cameras, peering about: the hunted couples with street-boy would-be guides on their tails; the surreptitious snappings of fishermen.

One morning there was great excitement amongst the groups of street-boy, would-be guides. 'The tourist truck is coming,' they shouted. 'The tourist truck is coming. Any time now it will be here.' And sure enough, soon a long bus turned up and seemingly half the town converged on it. But this was no ordinary bus. It had been converted into the ultimate-capacity overland travelling vehicle. All along it were rows and rows of drawers, rather like those in a morgue, in which passengers could be placed to sleep. Upstairs were chairs and tables, and a large trailer contained luggage, supplies and tents.

Having arrived, the passengers began to set up their tents and soon a small encampment had been erected. All their colourful and ingenious shapes stood about in the hotel grounds with wires and metal poles and utensils and tools and collapsible chairs and tables and steel boxes and any number of strange and shiny objects placed with such precision amongst them that the whole set-up looked like some highly complex scientific field camp. Here was a team come to dissect and analyse a subject. To the crowds of almost stupefied onlookers it must have seemed as though aliens had landed.

I met a man in Mopti with whom I went one night to a disco. He was a slim, cultivated Fulani man called Mohammed who lived in America. Having met so many young men who desired nothing more than to go to America, it was interesting to meet one who had. He had got a scholarship to study food sciences at a university there. This was paid for by an American development programme and it involved learning about the tinning of foodstuffs. The idea was that the programme would educate such people as Mohammed so that they could return to their country to help it develop. But Mohammed had no intention of coming back to Mali to live. He loved life in America and had found himself an American wife, which would ease the problems of obtaining a work permit.

'If I was to return to Mali,' he said to me, 'the government would just find a quiet and dusty shelf to put me on. They do not want people with new and modern plans to come and upset the way things are now. The men in power do very well out of the present situation. They do not want a change. They will get it soon enough, though, even if it has to be forced upon them by their own people. But that will be a bloody undertaking and I do not want to be a part of it.'

Mohammed was gentle and charming and had in fact only come back to Mali to sort out his family affairs after the death of his father. He was the oldest of the twelve children and had not been back for nearly ten years. His family were wealthy and owned 1,500 head of cattle. He and his next eldest brother had decided to sell all these cattle and to invest the money in business instead. This, for a Fulani family, for whom cattle are of immense importance and represent their heritage passed down from generations ago, was a drastic step. But after many weeks of persuasion their mother had agreed to the sale. Now Mohammed was waiting for the sale to take place before he could return to America.

Mohammed came with me to the river port when I departed from Mopti on a pirogue back to Kemacina. I parted from him and Mopti, and from Arsene whom I saw again in Kemacina. I travelled back to Segou in another bush taxi and arrived there in time for New Year's Eve and my evening with Mike, the Jamaican. And the next day, the first of 1990, I parted from him as well and, once again mounted on my moped, commenced my journey upstream towards the city of Bamako.

★

The rains had begun to fall in fat, warm drops, swelling the Niger and flooding the countryside through which Mungo Park had had to travel when he began his long and lonely journey home

from Silla. He was not to know that nine years later a very different Mungo Park would be back here at the town of Silla, sailing
past it in a boat on the Niger, a Mungo Park so distorted with
fever and frustration that he was soon to cause the deaths not
only of himself and his few remaining European companions,
but also of many of the Africans, those people for whom, on his
first journey, he had shown such respect. Perhaps it was now, on
his journey home, that there began the attrition of that respect.

By now the rumours that Park was a spy had spread far and
wide and the inhabitants of the countryside through which Park
had to travel feared to offer him their hospitality. Dressed in only
the tatters of what remained of his European dress, Park made
his way, a shunned and hungry man, back down the north bank
of the Niger towards Segou. 'Go along,' he was told in one town
when, fearing having to pass the night in the woods at the mercy
of the bad weather and the 'wild beasts', he requested permission
to enter it. In another place a village chief threatened to strike
him with a stick if he presumed to take another step into his
village. And he was only permitted to enter other villages with
the greatest of reluctance, and then often to be given poor and
damp lodgings in return for some of the few cowrie shells that
remained of his wealth.

Wading through swamps and swimming over swollen streams
and creeks with his precious notes tucked into the crown of his
hat to keep them dry, Park bypassed Segou and carried on down
the north bank of the Niger towards the riverside town of
Bamako. Food became so difficult to obtain that at one time he
had to survive for three days on raw corn alone. In a village to
which he was driven by his hunger to beg a little food by way
of charity, the village chief simply told him he 'had none to
spare'. Whilst Park was in this village he saw a slave, under the
direction of the 'sullen' old village chief, digging a deep pit.
'Good for nothing, a real plague,' the village chief was muttering
to himself whilst the pit was being dug. On realizing that the pit
very much resembled a grave and that he himself might be the
intended occupant of that grave, Park was about to depart from
the village when the slave, who had before gone off, returned
carrying the naked body of a boy by an arm and a leg. 'Money
lost, money lost,' the village chief muttered to himself whilst the

slave, with what Park describes as 'a savage indifference', threw the boy into the pit. Concluding that the unfortunate boy must have been one of the village chief's other slaves, Park hurried away.

Not all was hopeless and depressing on that journey to Bamako, though. There were people, perhaps at risk to themselves, who allowed Park into their villages, fed him well and gave him their help. In one village his horse, which he had left for dead on his way to Silla, was returned to him much recovered by a friendly village chief. Twice, as so often, it was the sympathies of women that helped him out, and in Bamako even some Moors were civil to him and sent him some rice and milk.

Bamako in those days was a small but affluent town. The Moors, on their way south from the Sahara, habitually passed a number of nights there and the town's merchants bought salt from them and sold it for a good profit. Today, Bamako, being capital of Mali, is a vast city.

★

The countryside on the north bank of the Niger between Segou and Bamako is still populous and well-cultivated. Sooboo, Sai, Yamina, Kanika, Tafara, Koolikorro, Kayoo and Marraboo were some of the places Mungo Park passed in this country. Today signposts erected outside these same places announced Souba, Sai, Niamina, Kanika, Tafala, Koulikoro, Kayou and Manabougou. The main road between Segou and Bamako, a fast, tarmacked one, lies to the south of the Niger. The route along the north bank, a distance of some 200 kilometres, is serviced by a gravel road that after the town of Niamina, roughly a third of the way, diffuses into a myriad of bush tracks that then unite again at the town of Koulikoro, another third of the way, where there is a tarmacked road that runs straight to the heart of Bamako.

The first part of the route passes through a succession of large Bambarran villages. These are substantial, partially modernized places with well-constructed school buildings, many tin-roofed shops, crops of water-pump-irrigated rice, and even tiny cinemas to which comes a travelling projectionist with a selection of karate films. Essentially, though, the villages are very traditional.

Their houses are of mud bricks, houses which each rainy season partially wash back into the large pits beside them from which the mud has been taken to make the bricks. Their inhabitants adhere so strongly to their animist beliefs that the mosques here are little visited. And their dependence upon their traditional methods of cultivation and industry is complete. They are old villages: places to which the kings of Segou have come to prepare for war, and renowned for their witch-doctors who have for centuries been a potent force in the politics of Segou. Each of them has much to connect it with the past.

I visited these villages during a period in which the inhabitants were busy about two industries Mungo Park also remarked on in this same area. One of these is the construction of the large clay water jars that can be found in any house in Mali. This is the work of the women and in many parts of the villages these women, their legs grey with clay to the knees and their arms grey to the elbows, can be found vigorously pounding the clay and stamping with their feet. Once it is pliable enough they construct the pots using the 'snake' method: curling snakes of clay round and round to form the shape. The pots, once perfected, are then fired in a large stack covered with millet husks which burn for fifteen or so minutes like an inferno and are then left to smoulder overnight. The next day the pots are sent by pirogue on the Niger to the market of Segou.

The other industry the people were busy about was the production of *shea toulou. Shea toulou* is what Mungo Park describes as a butter that is better in both keeping qualities and flavour than that made from cows' milk. It comes from the nut of the shea tree, a tree found throughout this part of West Africa. The nut is picked during the rainy season and then stored in round pits like shallow wells. In the dry season the nut is either boiled to extract the oil or baked in special ovens and pounded to a paste. The 'butter' is used either for cooking or as a body oil. Park estimated that in his day it was one of the biggest commodities of commerce. Certainly today it can be found in great abundance in the markets.

Making use of the natural vegetation that grows in the country-side is part of the villagers' heritage. There is barely a tree or bush from which they cannot derive some use. From a type of wild acacia tree comes gum arabic. The seeds of the baobab tree that Mungo Park calls *nitta* but today are called *sita* are good to eat. A type of sauce that is eaten with the stiff millet porridge, *to*, is made from the leaf of the baobab. The sap of another large tree called *Jankunani*, mixed with the leaf of wild garlic, is good for fever. *Nyuna*, a large and bitter fruit from another tree, is fermented in large wooden drums to be drunk as an alcohol at baptisms. And *tomongs*, Park's *tomberongs*, a small and sweet yellow berry, can be sucked like a sweet or baked into cakes. For most illnesses there is a remedy to be found in the bush, and the villagers' diet is supplemented by the fruits and nuts and berries to be found there. In times of famine the villagers can survive by sustaining themselves on the produce of the bush alone.

The first of the Bambarran villages I visited when I left Segou was called Farako. I was invited to it by a man I met in the pirogue I took across the Niger from Segou. It was unusual for people to travel to Bamako on the north bank of the Niger. In fact few vehicles used this route at all. So when the man sitting next to me and my moped in the pirogue asked where I was headed, and I replied, 'To Bamako', he showed signs of concern and enquired where I intended passing that night. I said I did not know, whereupon he invited me to come and stay with him in Farako.

My host was called Ibrahima and he was a teacher. He was a quietly spoken and neatly dressed man from Segou and had been posted to the village of Farako for five years. His wife and children did not live with him in Farako because the room he occupied there was too small. They remained in Segou and although the village was only 20 kilometres away from Segou, Ibrahima only went to see them once a month.

'My job in Farako does not allow me the time to go and see them more than that,' he sighed. 'That is the life of the teacher. Ours is a hard profession. We must sacrifice a lot. But this I am prepared to do for my country.'

And indeed Ibrahima was very patriotic. The earthen walls of his small room in Farako were covered with slogans and pictures of the President of Mali. One of the slogans, written beneath a picture of peasants tilling their fields, was, 'Contributing one's quota before resigning to fate'. Another one was a quotation from the President of Chad. 'Sahelians,' it went, 'I know we are a courageous people. I know we are submerged in trail. And since the track we have to follow must be beaten out of sweat and self-denial, we shall sweat it out and lead lives of renunciation.' One of the slogans was of Ibrahima's own creation: 'If everyone knew what everyone said about everyone, nobody would speak to anybody.'

Although Ibrahima was very patriotic he was no fool about the realities of his country. When one evening we were having supper with a friend of his, a simple and harassed farmer with too many children to feed, one of whom, he told me, was crippled by an injection given by a bad nurse and all of whom were squeezed into one tiny hut, his friend said in the middle of a conversation, 'There is not a single rich man in Mali.'

I replied to this, half jokingly, 'Except the President, of course.'

At this a look of concern came over the man's face and he said, 'The white people wouldn't allow the president of a poor country to be rich, would they?'

In answer to this Ibrahima said that he had once heard on the radio that a survey had been done to determine the three richest men in Africa. After the presidents of Zaire and Ivory Coast, the President of Mali came third.

'They have big Swiss bank accounts, the presidents,' he said, 'and when they cannot pay the salaries of their civil servants they get the money from the West.' But despite this, Ibrahima of Farako was still a patriotic man.

★

The second of the Bambarran villages I stayed in on my way up the north bank was called Souba, Mungo Park's Sooboo. Here the villagers had a story of how a white man had once come to their village, a long time before the French came to Mali, and sat under a tree. He wrote things on pieces of paper, the villagers told me, and 'We were honoured.'

I had been given the name of an American Peace Corps worker who lived in Souba, so when I arrived there I asked where I might find him. At first this drew a blank response, then someone said, tentatively, 'Mamadou?'

'No,' I said, 'an American, Peace Corps.'

'Mamadou, Mamadou,' was repeated.

'No, no,' I replied. But now a knowing and gleeful look had come over the faces of the people to whom I was talking, as though they had some special secret to which I was not a party.

'Yes, Mamadou,' they said happily, and led me through the village to the American Peace Corps Worker.

The Peace Corps is a United States Government agency that takes ordinary young Americans, instructs them in certain skills which might be beneficial to a developing country, teaches them about the culture of that country, and then sends them there for a two- or three-year term. They are often sent to small and remote villages where they have very little contact with the outside world. Joe, the Peace Corps worker at Souba, was young, blond and, unlike many Peace Corps volunteers who are often thrown into a state of near shock by such an extended and blunt contact with so very different a culture, still filled with wonder and enthusiasm about Mali and the Malians. He was immensely popular in Souba and he had already been there for two years. He had another year to go and the villagers by now regarded him as a son. They had given him the name Mamadou in recognition of this.

Joe lived in a small, traditional house on the outskirts of the village and there he always had many guests. He lived most of his life in the village, as did the villagers, in the presence of other people. There was little privacy in village life and Joe, hard as it must have been, did not attempt to guard that degree of privacy most Westerners are bred to be accustomed to, but was hospitable to his permanent guests. Always there were young men present with their pots of tea and idle chat. And most people when passing nearby would take time to come and greet the village's most popular inhabitant. Two of his frequent guests were a pair of dumb men. One of these men was a great joker and an excellent mime artist. 'If you were to put him on the streets of New York,' Joe said to me, 'all hell would break loose.'

Being an extrovert and having no knowledge of a formal sign language with which to express himself, this man had developed a repertoire of acts, signs and noises that could quite clearly communicate whatever he desired to say. He was forever jumping about the place making a fool of himself and contorting his elastic face. When he met me he enquired whether I had come to the village in search of gold and diamonds and then told me that he was married to the fattest girl in the village who was just then pregnant with his first child. Another of Joe's frequent guests was a little old man bent nearly double by his reputed 107 years of life. 'He talks all the time,' Joe said to me, 'but nobody understands what he says. These old men are crazy,' he said, affectionately, 'they crack me up sometimes.'

One of the more useful functions Joe performed in the village, and one of the more difficult for him to deal with, was being a confidant and problem-solver. People were always coming to him for advice on their personal problems or to air their complaints about fellow villagers. Joe, being an outsider, was an ideal recipient for these things. And there were a great many problems and complaints. 'You cannot imagine the complexities of village life,' Joe said to me. 'There are so many jealousies and intrigues. The people seem to positively thrive on them.'

A man might come to him to complain that his wife, who had gone to live with her brother because he hit her one night, was spreading malicious rumours about his innocent acquaintance with his neighbour's daughter. He wanted to warn Joe not to believe anything that he might hear about him. Another man might seek advice on whether he should inform the village chief that he suspected his neighbour of purposely allowing his sheep to stray on to his millet field each day in order to get revenge for the time he spoke against his neighbour in a palaver about the time his neighbour was accused of poisoning another man's well by throwing a dead rat into it because that man had once crippled one of his donkeys with an iron bar because the donkey had accidentally wandered on to *his* millet field. 'These are the sort of petty problems,' Joe said, 'brought to me each day. It's a pain to have to deal with them, but I can't refuse because these people are my friends.'

Even the village chief would sometimes come to Joe with his problems because Joe and the village chief had an especially close relationship. Each evening Joe ate his supper with the chief and passed the rest of the evening sitting around in his compound in the bosom of his family. They treated each other like father and son and when one day the chief's daughter, who had recently been told that she was to be married to a man from a neighbouring village, ran away, it was to Joe that the chief came for help to look for her.

For two days they looked high and low in the neighbourhood but did not find her. In fact the girl had gone to Segou with a boyfriend and when she was found there some weeks later she was brought back to the village. Now she was waiting patiently in her father's compound for the day of her marriage. When one night Joe and I were having supper with the chief, Joe asked the girl if she was looking forward to her marriage. 'No,' she said, 'no, I am not,' but the smile that came to her lips implied that she no longer cared too much.

From Souba I continued on down the gravel road that linked all the Bambarran villages on the north bank of the Niger. The countryside through which this road passed was much cleared of its vegetation for the planting of crops. Only close to the Niger where sandbanks and bogs made cultivation difficult were the trees and bushes allowed to grow thick. Here brightly coloured parrots swooped from tree to bush and bush to tree, squawking loudly as I sped by, as though they were telling me off. Once past the old riverside town of Niamina where I was given rice and coffee by a friendly albino in a crumbling medina which sat upon the mounds of the crumbled medinas of a more ancient and altogether more splendid town, the countryside became wilder. Here were the creeks and streams Mungo Park had swum across with the bridle of his horse clamped in his teeth.

The villages here were small and poor and their cultivation was not extensive enough to make much impression on the tangled forests and bushes. This area was away from the urban influences of Segou and Bamako. It was deeply rural land set between the spheres of those two towns. Here I stayed in one of Mungo Park's villages, Tafala, where I was given a live chicken as a present by the chief of the village and installed in a hut filled with the sweet, musky scent of *shea toulou*, for the hut was also used as a storeroom. That night was bitterly cold, the coldest I

215

had known on my journey so far, and there was much singing and dancing outside. When I enquired why, I was told simply, 'Because we are happy.'

Outside my hut a group of naked boys lit a large fire of dried grass and danced wildly round it, leaping through its flames. In another part of the village a *griot* played a battery-powered electric guitar and sang to people huddled round a fire with blankets wrapped about them to keep them warm. Next to them, small and naked boys sat shivering on their haunches: boys are left to fend for themselves at an early age and if they have no clothes and no blanket to keep them warm that is their problem. Youth deferred to age and even when the small, shivering children edged closer to the fire they were told to keep back and not hog the heat for themselves.

The following day I met the tarmacked road at the town of Koulikoro, a busy merchants' town with a large, concrete science college. Here in the Niger beside Koulikoro are the rapids that prevent river boats travelling any further upstream. A railway line connects the termination of the river boats with Bamako.

The tarmacked road runs straight as a die from Koulikoro across an open, hot countryside right to the very heart of Bamako. As you progress along it the presence of that town becomes ever more felt. First there are the telegraph wires that loop even to small roadside villages. Then come the co-operative plantations with their citrus orchards and modern tractors and silos; then the hoardings, petrol stations and rich men's countryside villas; then the factories and military camps. Along the road, trucks laden high with sacks of grain speed past peasants making their way by foot and bicycle to the city. These peasants have country produce in panniers on their heads or rolled into long mats and strapped across the backs of their bicycles. With the wind and sun battering them on the exposed road's surface, they step with determination towards the biggest market in Mali.

Also trudging the same way are the young men who hope to find their future in the big city. They carry small bags in their hands, their shoes slung over their shoulders to keep them neat and clean for their arrival. There are also, perhaps, a few skinny families from villages that have died in the droughts, making their way on donkey carts towards their last hope.

The road does not change right to the heart of Bamako. But the countryside beside it becomes suburban. These suburbs then become centres of commerce. Markets spill on to the road. Bush taxis and buses jam it. Street after street of red earth and rubble run away from its neat grey surface at right-angles, penetrating and dividing like a plumb-line the massed and grimy quarters of crumbling homes and green, open sewers. You think you have arrived and still the road runs on without a twist or a turn, to lose itself in the pungent and clammy maul that is the city of Bamako. With the chicken I had been given by the village chief of Tafala clucking unhappily on the back of my moped, where it was strapped to the top of my bag, I went in search of somewhere to stay.

★

The first time I had come to Bamako, five years ago, I had loved the place. Here, for me, was one of Africa's most African cities. This was not a capital like Dakar or Abidjan attempting to mimic the style of Western cities. Nor was it a capital like Lusaka or Nairobi, built from scratch by colonialists, with a hollow and soulless feel. It was essentially a huge market town, as African as any of the markets of Mali. It was a centre, an intensity of everything Malian.

Here in Bamako could be found everything I had seen in the course of my journey. Here was the market of Segou, only vastly larger and continuous. Here were the dilapidated quarters and backstreet bars of Kayes. Here could be found the penniless, resident functionaries of Koniakary and Nioro du Sahel. Here were the Moorish merchants of Tourougoumbe, the marabouts and mosques of Mourdiah, and the colonial, tree-shaded avenues of Kemacina. Here was the beauty of Mopti with its river boats and swathes of lily reeds beside the shore. And here were its districts of banks and administrative buildings. Here were the peasants of the villages with their hunger and poverty, their Koranic schools, their *bentangs*, industries and animist beliefs. Here were the mangled cripples of the villages in vast and ghastly numbers. And here also were grand and majestic colonial buildings, pockets of Western middle class peeped through double-

217

glazed patio doorways, nightclubs of gaudy prostitutes, and a single twenty- or thirty-storey hotel rising like hope from the sprawl of depressed dwellings that make up most of the town.

Here indeed was everything, crammed together, intensified and adapted for life in a city. It was a confusing jungle of burgeoning commerce, heat and dirt, oppressive streets, honking traffic and sprawling humanity. Every street, seemingly every inch of the town, was covered with people. Wherever your eye fell, there would be a person. They draped the streets, bulging out of vehicles, on roofs and doorsteps, in windows and gutters. Everywhere there were forms prone and idle that at any moment you expected to explode with the frenetic and desperate atmosphere that pervades the capital.

And this is why I now liked Bamako less. For now I saw it as a desperate and hard place. One word screamed above everything else: money. For here the desperate lack of cash and the difficulty of obtaining it that was to be found in the countryside was at its most dire, because cities scream at people to make money, then suck it out of them like blood. They suck it and if they do not have their fill they spit you out into the gutter, and the gutter here in Bamako is where people just disappear. No, this time Bamako did not appeal to me. I was in no mood to close my eyes and enjoy it. And there is no place to hide in Bamako for the travelling stranger, no corners of peace and gentility. It took me and squeezed me like a vice. It squeezed out my compassion, cruelly used it, and flung it back in my face. I did what I had to do: go to the bank and post office, sell my moped, buy maps and other supplies, mend my shoes and clothes, and check in with the immigration and police.

These few things took over a week, for nothing happens easily in Bamako. The post office had lost half my mail. The banks were reluctant to hand over the money I had been wired. The cobbler ruined rather than mended my shoes and charged me too much. The immigration and police made every conceivable difficulty in extending my visa. And the negotiations over the selling of my moped were complex and crooked and I only just avoided being palmed off with invalid bank notes. But these are all the ways of a city, ways I was familiar with. And they did not bother me unduly. What bothered me was the despair and poverty I saw in so many faces. The poverty and despair to be found in the countryside was, here in the city, a different thing. Here there was no sympathy, no glimmer of hope. Here people had lost their belief in humanity and looked out only for themselves. Cities can shine on you, and then you see only the good. And they can glower at you and then you see only the bad. It depends on your mood. This time Bamako, although still truly African, was Africa slipping down the path of self-destruction. Perhaps I was just tired.

There was one pleasure in Bamaka though. And that was the friend I had stayed with in Segou on my first visit there five years before, and who had come to Bamako to study medicine. His name was Sekouba, and he was twenty-eight years old. He had the build of an athlete and wrote ponderous poetry, some of which he used to send to me. I found him at the National Medicine School in a large building on one of the hills that overlooked the city. There was no university in Mali and so, instead of having to study for three or five years to get a degree, Sekouba had to study for nine. He was bright and studious and was now living up at the National Medicine School on the hill above Bamako, waiting for the last three years of his course to expire.

When I had known him five years ago, Sekouba had been carefree and enjoyed his studies. Now, seeing him again, the frustration and boredom at having to slow his intelligence down to the leaden pace of his course had etched lines into his forehead and given his eyes a hollow look. 'I live up here, looking down on Bamako, and I never leave this hill,' he said. And indeed other than a once-yearly visit to Segou, and occasional nightly sojourns into Bamako to see his girlfriend, he never did leave his hill. There he lived in a dormitory with his fellow students, waiting for three years to pass.

Bamako is situated where a vast, low-lying plain meets a range of hills called the Mandingo mountains. The Niger, having only recently arrived from Guinea to the south, sweeps close to these hills, hemming Bamako in close to them. From 'Point G', the hill where Sekouba's Medicine School was, one can have a perfect view of Bamako laid out directly below, as neatly as a model. Sekouba and I went and sat on the edge of the hill and watched

219

the town for many hours. It was peaceful up there, only a few madmen wandering aimlessly about the rubble-strewn hillside, and a few crows sailing in the empty spaces above the patterns of the town. The madmen were from the village which adjoins the hospital to which the Medicine School was affiliated. Some people called this place 'the village of the fools' because it was just a ragbag of the people with mental disorders who had been treated at the hospital and who had then settled on the hill next to it. Its inhabitants called it 'the village of the cured'.

Sekouba and I sat thinking about the myriad and seething life of the city below us, all those hundreds of thousands of hopes and ambitions and despairs secreted in the brown, uniform face of the town. It was like a single living entity, gently pulsing and humming, lying flat and torpid upon the earth. As evening set in, the blanket of smog and cooking-fire smoke that lay over the town cleared clean away from the older and more affluent parts of it where there were many tall, well-canopied trees. The trees breathed it away. The warrens of poorer, shanty-like quarters were naked of trees and could not breathe freshly in the evening. As dusk set in, the flashes of oxyacetylene torches rose and fell like the glow of fireflies from odd parts of the city. The smiths were hard at work.

When it grew dark I left Sekouba and the madmen on the hill looking down, god-like, on a city they had no desire to enter. I took a bush taxi from the 'village of the cured' and once again became part of a single entity. On the way back to the Catholic Mission where I had rented a room we passed a tramp writhing in the gutter, spewing froth and guttural screams as though he was having a fit. The young ticket-boy hanging on to the back of the taxi looked at him and made a thin sucking noise through his teeth that in Mali indicates something that is bad. He then turned his head and got on with his job of collecting tickets. Two days later I left Bamako.

VIII

Homeward Bound

THE HIGHLANDS OF Guinea rise to well over 1,000 metres above sea level. It is here that the Gambia, Senegal and Niger rivers all have their source. The Gambia tributaries slip away to the west and the Atlantic, those of the Niger quickly unite and head off in a north-easterly direction towards the Sahara, and the Bafing, Bakoye and Faleme rivers, which are the principal tributaries of the Senegal, flow northwards into the south-western corner of Mali. It is in this hilly and wooded corner of Mali, hemmed in by the railway line from Kayes to Bamako on its northern edges and by the Guinean border on the south, that both Mungo Park and I travelled when we departed from Bamako: we were homeward bound and this meant travelling west from Bamako, back towards the Gambia. Although this area does not perhaps deserve the same shade of green as Sierra Leone, Liberia and Guinea, which some map-makers optimistically endow it with, it would not be right to give it the same orange-yellow colour as the rest of Mali either. For it is somewhere between the two, a meeting of savannah and forest, and even if the rainfall is not profuse here, one can smell humidity on the air, and the woods, if containing few large trees, at least grow thick and in many places dominate the landscape.

The people who inhabit this corner of Mali are the Malinke. They are descendants of the old Mali Empire which was centred upon this area, a people who now, as in times past, enrich themselves by digging for the same gold that once built the Mali Empire. Their land consists of tracts of tangled, thorny wilderness, plateaux of rolling woodland, and the jungly valleys and ravines that have been shaped by the rivers and streams that culminate in the Senegal river.

There is only one road in this area, only one principal means of direct communication with Bamako and so the rest of the country. It traverses the area in a west/east direction, defying the lie of the land along which all other paths and tracks follow the valleys to the north, to the Senegal river and the railway line. But even this road is virtually impassable. Only the sturdiest of trucks and Land-rovers can negotiate it, and they have to build much of it as they go. In practice this is essentially the land of the bicycle and foot. Even horses and donkeys cannot function here on account of the presence of the tsetse fly. And so, having first travelled by train and motorbike to a village called Bafing Makana on the Bafing river, it was by bicycle and on foot that I passed through this area, my moped by now being the property of a dealer in Bamako.

Mungo Park calls Bafing Makana, Manna. This was the first of the many towns and villages Park visited after Bamako that I had been able to identify on my map. It took me two days to reach it, whereas it took Mungo Park seven months. The reason why it took Park so long was that it quickly became apparent to him that he would not be able to travel back to the Gambia in this wide and broken countryside until the rains had stopped, and so he holed up in a village called Kamalia. This, anyway, was not the sort of countryside in which it was advisable to make long journeys in anything but large groups. There was much banditry and thieving, as Mungo Park discovered shortly after departing from Bamako.

Travelling a steep and rocky path in the hills to the west of that town, Park was set upon by a group of men armed with bows and arrows who, finding that he had little of value left to steal, stripped him of most of his clothes and made off with his horse, at the last moment, fortunately for Park's sake, tossing back his hat in the crown of which were his notes. Park, after this, 'naked and alone' and 'in the midst of a vast wilderness in the depth of the rainy season', began to despair. Not for the first time did he conclude that he had no alternative but to 'lie down and perish'.

'At this moment,' however, Park writes, 'painful as my reflections were, the extraordinary beauty of a small moss, in fructification, irresistibly caught my eye. I mention this,' he continues, 'to show from what trifling circumstances the mind will sometimes derive consolation; for though the whole plant was not larger than the top of one of my fingers, I could not contemplate the delicate conformation of its roots, leaves, and capsula, without admiration. Can that Being (thought I) who planted, watered, and brought to perfection, in this obscure part of the world, a thing which appears of so small importance, look with unconcern upon the situation and sufferings of creatures formed after His own image? – Surely not.' So with his spirits somewhat revived by this comforting thought, Park picked himself up and walked onwards to the town of Sibidooloo where he was hospitably received by the chief, who told him that he would arrange for Park to have everything that he had had stolen returned to him. And a few days later, when Park was resting in the nearby town of Wonda, his horse was indeed restored to him.

Then as now, the rainy season was the 'hungry season' which comes before the crops are ready to be harvested, and so there was a great scarcity of food in the countryside. Mungo Park's appearance in towns and villages, therefore, was not always welcome. The people had barely enough food to feed themselves, let alone a stranger. In Wonda, so bad was the shortage of food, Park saw women forced to sell their sons to the chief in order to obtain some. In another place the villagers were making do on the stewed blossoms of the maize plant. So it was fortunate that in Kamalia Park met up with the man called Karfa Toure who was to take a slave caravan to the Gambia at the end of the rainy season, with which Park could travel. Park had no way of supporting himself until that time, but it was arranged that Karfa Toure would provide him with food and a hut in which to sleep until such time as the caravan departed, and Park would repay him with the value of one prime slave on arrival at the Gambia.

Karfa Toure was a man of some wealth and influence and looked after Park well. He sent him two meals a day and when Park was struck down with fever for many months he came to see him each day in his hut to console him with the hopes of a speedy recovery. He did not wane in his kindness though malicious rumours were being spread about Park by traders who resided in Kamalia and were jealous of the hospitality Karfa Toure was giving him, hospitality they, having spent all their money, were also dependent upon.

And so the better part of the next seven months was spent by Park waiting for the day of the caravan's departure. He was in a state of high anxiety, for he realized that his very life depended upon a man whose opinion of him was daily being poisoned. The rainy season began to draw to an end. The fast of Ramadan came and went, but still the caravan was not ready for departure. There were always delays and in fact Park began to fear that the next rainy season might soon begin. But on 19 April, the long-wished day eventually arrived and the caravan, consisting of thirty-five slaves for sale on the coast, fourteen freemen with wives and domestic slaves, six singing men, or 'Jilli Keas', whose talents were required to divert fatigue and obtain a welcome from strangers, and a group of scholars who were travelling in the same direction, set out on the long and hazardous road to the Gambia, having first said prayers and spoken many charms for their safety.

The first part of their journey took them across the Jallonka wilderness where for five days and 100 miles no place of habitation was to be seen, a journey in which all members of the caravan, slaves and freemen alike, suffered greatly from fatigue and hunger. On 28 April, having a short time before left that poor slave girl, Nealee, who could not keep up with the caravan, beside the road to be most probably 'devoured by wild beasts', they arrived on the banks of the Bafing river at Park's town of Manna, today the village of Bafing Makana. It is here in this village that I, having travelled from Bamako by train and motorbike, once again joined up with Mungo Park.

★

There is a stream near the town of Kita, I was told, over which a man cannot jump but must always fall in and drown. Near to the stream, I was also told, at the foot of some hills, is a place where objects can hang in the air of their own accord. 'The spirits of those hills,' the man said, 'are the spirits of this town. And this town,' he added, 'is a very magical one.'

Kita is 180 kilometres west of Bamako on the Bamako/Kayes railway line and it was to there that I took the train. I was not sure how I was going to travel on to Bafing Makana, because I knew that I would be lucky to find any bush taxis or trucks going that way. The village was 120 kilometres distant across sandy and difficult countryside, and there was little reason for anyone to go there for it was only a small village. But I had hardly arrived in Kita when a large and bearded man called Zomu offered, for a fee, to take me on his motorbike.

'This is the only way you will get there,' Zomu informed me, announcing, on introducing himself, that he was a personal friend of the town's resident judge. 'And my motorbike is a very large one.'

And so it was, on what turned out to be a very small motorbike, that I travelled to Bafing Makana. The journey consisted of five hours of extreme discomfort due to the size of Zomu and the fact that I had my overweight rucksack strapped to my back where I perched at the very rear of the machine. We passed many small hamlets and crossed many small streams. We got stuck in sand and inevitably had a puncture and a breakdown. But Zomu did indeed seem to be a man of some importance and the people of the hamlets went out of their way to give us drinks and resolve our problems. Bafing Makana, when we arrived, was a small, poor village tucked in amongst the thick, tangled vegetation that grew in the vicinity of the Bafing river.

Our reception in Bafing Makana was joyful because, it turned out, Zomu's mother lived there. Many people, all of them looking as tatty and bedraggled as their huts, gathered round us.

'See that man there,' Zomu said, indicating a man dressed in rags. 'He spent fifteen years in Ivory Coast. You should have seen him then. A real man dressed in a suit, he was.'

This man turned out to be the village chief. He was now very old and he told me he had forty children, although most likely many of them were the offspring of brothers who had either died or gone away, for in such cases one takes responsibility for one's brother's children and treats them as one's own.

Bafing Makana had been a town in Mungo Park's day, but most of the inhabitants, I was informed by the village chief, had long ago settled in satellite hamlets, creating villages out of them and reducing Bafing Makana to a mere village itself. Bafing Makana did still have one important function, though, and that was to monitor the rise and fall of the nearby Bafing river which varied according to the opening and closing of the sluices of the dam that had been built down-river near to the town of Bafoulabe.

This town, whose name means 'the meeting of two rivers', stands where the Bafing, or 'Black', river, and the Bakoye, or 'White', river unite and become the Senegal river.

The dam was part of a vast new project intended to produce a reservoir in which fish could be stocked and from which water could be pumped for drinking and irrigating crops. Bafing Makana had been provided with a radio set, and one of its young men was paid a small salary to call up Bamako every two weeks to inform the water authorities what level the Bafing river was at. The people at Bafing Makana, and especially the young radio operator, were very proud of the part they played in the mysterious doings of the outside world.

The Bafing, or 'Black', river was well named, for its waters, shaded on either side by the overhanging forests, did indeed look black. It was, in the dry season at least, a quiet, sullen river echoing to the cries of the birds in the forests, the odd splash of a fish sending ripples across its dark, still surface. In Mungo Park's day there had been a bridge across it which, each rainy season when the river swelled, was washed away and then rebuilt by the people of Bafing Makana. Although I was assured by the chief that this practice still took place today, I saw no signs of a new bridge being built even though it was well into the dry season by now.

They were cheerful and merry, the inhabitants of Bafing Makana. They had a few fields of millet not far from their village. They caught fish in the Bafing river and set traps for the many guinea fowl to be found in the forests. They had a huge and ancient baobab tree in the midst of the village, the sita seeds of which they ate, a tree quite old enough to have been witness to Mungo Park's passing. And occasionally they shot one of the hippos that came up the river and dried its meat. They took no pains to improve or clean up the structure and sanitation of their small, scrappy huts because all their efforts went into producing their meagre diet.

I passed only one night in Bafing Makana and the next morning was provided with a guide to walk with me to the village of Kouroukoto, 20 kilometres to the west. We were paddled across the Bafing river by a small boy in a rotting dugout and set off at a fast pace into a thin, patchy forest with many areas that had at some time been cleared for the planting of crops. We passed through a couple of hamlets consisting of only three or four round mud huts beside fields of millet, but then came to a larger one where we rested for a couple of hours. Here we met up with the Imam of Kouroukoto, a surprising figure for an Imam, for he wore a pair of mirror-strip sunglasses and carried a tape-recorder out of which blasted the swinging rhythms of modern Zairoise music. Once we had fed on some *to* with a delicious mushroom sauce, we continued on our way in the company of the Imam and his music. Following us at a little distance was a young boy with the Imam's suitcase on his head, a suitcase of such weight and size that the boy was soon lost far behind and we never saw him again.

Sometimes brushing through thick bamboo groves, some-times weaving through tall yellow grass, occasionally crossing muddy streams in little humid ravines clogged with jungly growth, but mostly travelling through low scrubby forests in a hilly landscape where tsetse flies chased us and sat on our backs, we made our way to Kouroukoto, where we arrived in the early afternoon.

★

Kouroukoto was not an old village and although Mungo Park passed this way in the company of the slave caravan he could not have visited it, for it did not exist in his day. This was one of the hamlets to which the people of Bafing Makana had moved, and Kouroukoto was now a village of considerable size. It was in the southern section of the vast *forêt classée*, or national park, that had recently been created in conjunction with the dam on the Bafing river. There are many of these *forêts classées* in Mali, established in an attempt to create a barrier of undamaged veg-etation to hinder the southward creep of the Sahel and Sahara.

Kouroukoto stood in a large clearing in the lee of a rocky escarpment. It was a neat place, consisting of perhaps a hundred identical round, thatched huts. Many of these huts were closed up and empty because sometimes as many as eight hundred of the village's thousand inhabitants would be absent, living tem-porarily in eighteen satellite hamlets where they tended the more distant millet fields. Around the village were dozens of tall baobab trees in which clambered troops of large, brown baboons come down from the escarpment to feast on the tasty sita seeds, baboons of such fierceness that even the village's packs of snarling dogs dared not approach them too closely.

The nearest school to Kouroukoto was 80 kilometres away, so few of its inhabitants had a modern education. They were almost exclusively animist, which probably accounted for the very un-fundamental aspect of the village Imam. In the village was one huge mango tree and at a little distance from it a pond of water beside which the villagers grew many kinds of food such as bananas, yams, peppers, cassava, rice, beans and vegetables. They had goats and sheep and some men possessed ancient, single-barrelled shotguns with which they hunted for sand partridge and small deer.

On arrival I was introduced to the village chief who gave me a chicken and with whom my guide, by way of custom, exchanged the small snuff pots most older men possess, each of them taking pinches of the coarse, ground tobacco they contain. Perhaps inevitably Kouroukoto housed a functionary, and once the news of my arrival had spread he came to greet me and to invite me to stay with him. He was virtually the only person in the village who spoke French, so it seemed the logical thing to do.

My new host was called Cesaire and he lived with his round, pretty wife and young daughter in a small and spartan cement house a little set apart from the rest of the village. He was a relaxed and well-educated man and was posted to Kouroukoto in the capacity of an agricultural agent for three years. His job consisted of helping the villagers to improve their methods of cultivation, but in practice it in fact consisted of doing virtually nothing other than waiting for the three years of his posting to expire.

Cesaire had a good, if somewhat detached, relationship with the villagers in whose affairs he had quickly learned not to meddle. This included not attempting to become too involved in the cultivation of their crops, which accounted for the fact that he had very little to do. He helped them obtain seeds for their vegetables and it was he who had encouraged them to grow some rice. But the government department that had sent him here did not have the resources or the back-up to enable employees in distant villages to offer much practical help. It could not, as with all other functionaries, even pay their wages at that time. But Cesaire was a patient man and sat out his posting in the company of his sweet, hard-working wife and his much-loved daughter with good humour. Even if he did not join in the life of the villagers, he was very friendly with them.

Cesaire was a polite man and whenever groups of people came to see him from the village, even if they were young boys, he would make sure they all had a chair to sit on. And although, posted to such wild parts and having virtually no money, Cesaire had to live in a somewhat rudimentary fashion, he always attempted to maintain the standards that he, as an educated, city man, was accustomed to.

'We functionaries,' he told me, fearing that I did not understand, 'are not like the villagers. We are accustomed to civilization and live like modern people. Even, you know,' he said, 'we can make our own choice of wife, not like the villagers who have arranged marriages.'

And so when the villagers came to see Cesaire, no matter how rough or unaccustomed to modern etiquette they were, they would be made to sit on chairs and indulge in polite conversation, sipping tea from small glasses.

One of Cesaire's more frequent guests was an extraordinarily ugly man called Soli whose nose had been eaten away by a disease and whose mouth was badly twisted, perhaps by the same disease. He was large, silent with a sweet smile and a rough look, dressed as he always was in the dirty rags of clothes, his hands and feet misshapen through a life of hard manual labour. One day, in a simple, forthright manner, Soli demanded that I give him one of the cassettes of Malian music I carried around in my rucksack. Many people had asked for my cassettes and I had given a lot of them away, but this one I had determined to keep – until I found myself handing it over, whereupon Soli formed his misshapen lips into a smile. At this Cesaire burst out laughing.

'But why are you laughing?' I asked him.

'They have used their magic on you,' he said to me. 'Soli,' he continued, 'came and told me this morning that you would give him a present today. He had arranged it, he said.'

There was an air of earthiness and spiritual healthiness about this ugly, roughened man who knew nothing of my world that made me believe what Cesaire said. In the echoing forests and rocky outcrops, and in the earth-rooted lives of the villages of this small corner of the world, one could sense the strains of something magical, something tangible but unseeable in the air. Those unrealized forces that course through the bones of the earth, pulsing into its trees and grasses and plants, and into those people with their feet planted firmly enough upon the earth, are strong in such places as Africa. This roughened man of the forests was susceptible to much that the rest of us cannot receive. I realized there and then that I was like a blind man, stumbling around in a great darkness. There was much here I could not fathom. I was like a wireless set tuned to the wrong wavelength.

'Beware,' Cesaire said. 'These people can make you do much at their will. But don't be scared,' he laughed. 'This is not magic. They are just clever men and understand many things.'

From Kouroukoto I travelled 50 kilometres, still following Mungo Park and his slave caravan, to the village of Tambafinia. This was a journey done by foot and on the backs of a succession of bicycles, using a succession of guides. The first guide was the son of the chief of Kouroukoto, a lethargic lad who did not like to walk too fast. The second, Fanga, who only had one eye, I picked up at the village of Oulala. He had a bicycle and pedalled me and my rucksack, perched on the rack at the back, over a succession of large, wooded ridges from the tops of which we had a clear view to the misty lip of this forested land over the brown, undulating heads of the trees. There were no villages or hamlets here, only a few heavy vultures which loped off at our approach. One time we saw the tiny, silver arrow shape of an aeroplane high in the blue sky. Fanga knew it well. It was the Gambia/Sierra Leone shuttle service, the only flight to pass over these parts. 'When I was a boy,' Fanga said, 'I ran away and hid myself when I saw that in the sky.'

At the village of Kouroubodala I again exchanged guides, this time for a small man with no shoes. Either being pedalled on his bicycle or walking, as I mostly did as he was too small to carry both myself and my bag on his bicycle, we crossed the Dassabola river and passed through an area in which there was much cultivation and many hamlets.

In Tambafinia, when we arrived there in the early evening, I was met by a huge, fat character who, he told me, was a business-man in Mopti and had just come home to his village for a couple of weeks to see his parents. He made me some Lipton's tea, because he said he knew how much the English liked their tea, and set me up in a hut with a neatly constructed bamboo bed. That night I sat with the village chief with whom I could not communicate and about thirty other men, with whom I also could not communicate. At one time the chief's son appeared, returned from some place away from the village, in a furious temper. He threw his bike to the ground, shouted at his wife, gave a hearty kick to a passing sheep, and then picked the unfor-tunate animal up, swung it around and threw it across the com-pound to land with such a thud I thought it must be killed. But it got up and trotted off, bleating terribly.

The following day two young men, each with a bicycle, led me into a more open and romantic landscape with a range of small mountains in the distance. They left me to the care of the village chief of Konborea who installed me in his hut in the company of a thin, sallow-faced man with extremely red eyes. Inside the hut was a large, four-poster bamboo bed, a great many juju artefacts such as dried monkey heads and ostrich feathers, a picture of the President of the Gambia on one of the walls and, leaning in a corner, a five-foot-long flintlock musket. Soon two men appeared carrying two large plastic bidons containing, I was informed by sallow-face, palm wine. Palm wine is a most gener-ous offering. It is simply the sap of a certain kind of palm tree, collected by means of a small incision in the bud at the top of the tree and the fixing of a container below the incision into which the sap can drip. It is a refreshing drink and tastes not unlike lemonade. It is naturally effervescent; when fresh, strong in alcohol, and when left to sit overnight, even stronger.

The palm wine the men had brought into the chief's hut was

233

of a good quality and now we all – the village chief, the two men, sallow-face and myself – began to drink it. There was only one cup, but this did not matter for there is a strict method of drinking palm wine that must be adhered to and only requires one cup. The cup is filled to its very brim and passed to the first man who must down it in one go. Then it is filled up and passed to the next man who must do the same. In this fashion the cup is passed in strict rotation around all present until there is no palm wine left, which generally does not take very long. Each man must always down it in one go and nobody is allowed to have anything but a full cup. If someone has had enough he just passes the full cup on to the next man. In this way each person, if he wants it, gets his fair share and receives the maximum effect from that share. And that effect is generally felt immediately after the first cup; by the third a warm, dreamy state has descended upon one.

It took about ten minutes for the two bidons to be finished by all present in the hut. Then sallow-face, his eyes more red than ever, informed me that he would now bicycle me to the nearby village of Guengore which was my destination for the day. And so once again I found myself perched on the rack at the back of a bicycle and was pedalled in a somewhat erratic fashion across a wide, sandy plain in which were hundreds of small excavations, for it is here that the gold-digging country begins. We headed north towards the range of low mountains I had seen earlier in the day, in the lee of which lay Guengore.

By the time I arrived at Guengore I was thoroughly sore, having been virtually spitted by the bicycle rack. The cumulative effects of this, the palm wine, exhaustion and, now, fever, went straight to my head and I became quite irrational. No sooner had I clambered from the bicycle than I arranged for a rather startled inhabitant of Guengore to immediately drive me on his motorbike to the town of Keniaba, 45 kilometres to the west. Fortunately, however, the motorbike broke down even before it had left the confines of the village, meaning that I ended up passing a week in one of the most delightful places I had ever visited.

★

It was a time of celebration, a time to be happy in Guengore. The work in the fields was finished and the harvest was in. And this year, as last year, the rains had been good, so the harvest was excellent. The millet was safely stored in the many small earth granaries that could be found throughout the village. The rice was sacked up. The cassava was looking good. The gardens beside the stream which came down from the hills and curved round the village were giving generous quantities of vegetables. The maize was drying well. And the groves of huge, lush mango trees which grew beside the village were heavy with ripening fruit.

Indeed it was a time to be happy. Everybody – and a great many people had come down from the hamlets in the hills to join in the celebrations – was in a good mood, greeting each other exuberantly on their way to and from huts, gardens and wells: 'Koulaballi!' 'Ha, Diabele'; 'Bandia,' 'Ahe! Dembele'. This was the time of year for everybody, their work at last completed, to come together. It was the time for families to unite. The time for baptisms, circumcisions and many other joyful rites. The time for courting, for marriage arrangements, and for the marriages themselves to take place. It was now that there was time to cultivate human relationships, rather than cultivate crops. And the celebrating of this fruitful and generous time of year, when the climate was in a gentle mood, was here in Guengore not going to be any half-hearted affair. There was much strain and stress that had to be worked out of the system, and much of it that had to be rejuvenated. Already the air was thick with expectation and the drums had begun to roll.

There was a nice blend in Guengore of Catholicism and animism: people wore crosses round their necks and juju pouches tied close to their skin on their hips. A Catholic mission had been built next to the village in 1949. It was a complex of long, stone buildings with deep verandahs and rusty tin roofs in a grove of trees: there was a school building, a church and a residence for the six missionaries who lived here. Next to it, on the edge of the grove of trees, began the village.

Guengore was a large village, a network of huts and houses of all different shapes and sizes huddled close together as if for companionship. Round rondavels of reddish earth, with conical hats of thatch, rubbed sides with oblong buildings coloured grey from the anthill earth from which their bricks were made. Always new buildings were being built, somehow squeezed in like pieces in a jigsaw puzzle. Small boys ferried pats of soft earth on pieces of broken calabash on their heads to men who packed it tight and smoothed it over the lattice of wooden struts from which the rondavel sides were made. And groups of men stood about the foundations of a new house directing each other in the exact positioning of the large, grey anthill bricks. (These long houses could cost up to a thousand pounds to build and took three or four weeks to complete.) You weaved your way through the tiny passageways, bending under a thatch, minding the chickens and children at your feet and the small boys dashing round the corners of a hut, to pop out into the large public space in the middle of which was a huge and shady tree.

On one side of the village were the broken walls of an old fort. This is where, in the days of the petty village wars, the inhabitants had concealed themselves at times of attack. They rushed inside, closed the doors, and the women hung lethal charms over the walls. Once the invaders had plundered the village and taken captive any people found without the fort, the villagers could come out again and begin to rebuild their lives. Also on the outskirts of the village were more spacious compounds for those who could afford them. One of them was a man called Alphonse, and it was with him that I stayed during my week in Guengore.

Alphonse was an educated man. He had been to the Catholic mission school and to college in Bamako, and he spoke good French and even a little English. After spending a few years attempting and failing to get employment in the field of administration, which subject he had qualified in at college, he had done something quite unusual, and that was to return to his village and try to make a life out of traditional farming. Alphonse had built his compound, a large and spacious one with three or four simple but neat and sturdy huts, he had set up a small supply shop and cultivated some fields of millet, and now he was in the process of creating an extensive vegetable garden down by the stream endowed with two deep wells which he had dug himself. He had made a go of it and was still doing so when I showed up. He had enthusiasm and energy and was, if only just, making ends meet.

Alphonse lived with his wife and four young children and his sister and her two children. They were a sweet and friendly family and when Alphonse, having met me the day I arrived in Guengore and invited me to come and stay with him, led me into his compound, they told me how happy they were to have me as a guest and set me up in one of the huts with a mat, a mattress, a sheet and a pillow with a clean pillowcase. And they, as did many other people in the village, continually gave me presents of food.

There was a lot of food in the village at that time. It was a large and essential part of this period of celebration, and the women everywhere were busy preparing many and interesting dishes of different kinds of food. People were not now going to sit around eating the same plain *to* they had been eating all year. They were going to indulge themselves in the beauty of variety and quantity. There was couscous with thick sauces of chopped cabbage or onion stalks. There were sweet puddings of rice, thin and salty bean stews, roasted goats and honeycombs. In the compound next to Alphonse's a woman had even produced a dish from a squirrel one of her sons had stoned out of the mission trees.

The village was positively bulging with food and at any hour of day or night small boys would appear at the door of my hut with presents of roasted peanuts, or small cooked potatoes, or milk, or carrots and lettuce, or even at one time with three oranges from the Gambia to which the people of Guengore would sometimes make a fifteen-day round bicycle trip for the purpose of buying such things as fruit and batteries which were cheaper there. I would be told that these gifts of food came from perhaps the village chief, who was on his deathbed and could not come to see me himself, or the sweet old couple I had met that morning who owned one of the tiny cows that were bred in this area, or from the French padre at the mission with whom I had taken some tea, but more often than not they were from members of Alphonse's family. The gifts of food piled up around my bed.

Every morning Alphonse would take me off around Guengore and its nearby brother village, Dialokoto, to meet people. 'You must meet all the villagers,' he said. 'Every one of them wants to give you their greetings. It is not often we have strangers in our village.' And sure enough, by the end of a week, I must have met the larger part of them. They would all shake my hand and say, 'How is the health of your mother and father? How are your brothers and sisters? And how are all your children?' When I informed them that I had no children they would laugh heartily and give me kola nuts as presents. 'Here, take these and chew them like the old men do. Maybe they'll put fire into your loins.' One man even gave me a huge wild boar's tusk. And then there were the old men who sat all day long beneath the tree in the village clearing, its public space. These were tall, handsome men with proud eyes and single gold ear-rings that gave them a some-what rakish look.

One of them was Alphonse's uncle, a man who, Alphonse informed me, had fought for the French army in both Vietnam and Algeria, and who had been posted to Nioro du Sahel for nine years. 'A bad town,' he said, peering at me through his sunglasses. 'No women and too far north.'

And there were the three hunters we met on the path between Guengore and Dialokoto, three small, light-footed figures dressed in leather jerkins, with sacking caps on their heads, knives and pouches of gunpowder and ball at their hilts, and long muskets carried over their shoulders like infantrymen. They were standing beside a tiny grass hut on the path's edge in which they had just placed pieces of food as an offering to the spirits of their hunter ancestors. Two months ago, Alphonse told me, a pack of hyenas had taken some of the villagers' sheep and these three men had hunted them and driven them off, killing two.

It seemed that wherever Alphonse and I went, the village sing-ing man, one of Mungo Park's Jilli Keas, would appear with his son. He was a small, bright-eyed old man with a look of great mischievousness in his foxy face. He wore a velvet embroidered tunic and gold hung from both his ears. His son was a thin young man with looks as mischievous as his father's. Whenever the Jilli Kea saw me his eyes twinkled and he pulled his white goatee beard as if in thought, then asked me to give him some money. 'But you have not sung,' I would say, at which he would laugh and wheeze as though there was something very funny about me until his face streamed with tears.

Everyone at this time of year was employed in some industrious way, the women preparing their many kinds of food, the men building and repairing houses. When one day we went to see the chief of Dialokoto, we came across a group of women making soap from peanut oil. The chief lived in a room above a large kitchen house. He was a leper and had no hands and few toes. Next to where he sat was a large rock of iron ore. Once a year, Alphonse told me, the village smiths went and found a big piece of this mineral and gave it to the chief. Later in the year they smelted it and made some special knives from the metal they obtained.

In the chief of Dialokoto's room we found two men discussing a marriage proposal. 'This man has been commissioned by someone to ask that man if he will allow his daughter to marry his son,' Alphonse said to me, indicating each man in turn. 'He has been provided with thirty kola nuts to give to the father of the girl by way of a gesture of goodwill. If the marriage is agreed on, the boy will have to pay the equivalent of ten cows, one of them specially earmarked for the mother of the girl in recognition of the pain she endured when giving birth to her. The rest of the cows, you must understand,' he said, 'are not so much in payment for the girl as though she were a piece of merchandise, but recompense to her family for the loss of her labour.' When Alphonse and I left the kitchen house, leaving the man deep in talk, we met a woman at the door muttering to herself and waving her arms about quite frantically. 'She,' Alphonse said, 'is a mad woman, but is only mad on Mondays and Thursdays.'

One day Alphonse and I found all the menfolk of Dialokoto performing a ceremony in the village clearing. They were choosing a name for a certain work group of young men, all of whom had been circumcised in the same year. The young men, who numbered 180, sat cross-legged on the ground whilst all the other menfolk stood in a great circle.

'They are good workers!' one of the village elders called out.

'Umm,' the village smith, standing in the middle of the clearing, answered him.

'The name must be of a good worker.'

'Umm,' came the consent from the smith.

'They are strong and brave and honest,' said the village elder again. 'The name must be of strength, bravery and honesty.'

'Umm,' said the smith.

'They were circumcised in the year of drought, the year our stream was as dry as the bones of the dead, our fields as infertile as the barren woman.'

'Umm,' said the smith again.

'Let the name of the group signify one who has durability, one who sneers at hardship.'

'Umm,' came the reply. And so it went on for a long time, the village elder describing the name that should be chosen for the young men's work group, the village smith always replying 'Umm'. In the end the young men's group was given the name Chaka, the name of a village chief who had died a few years before – a man, the village elder said, who stood for all the things he had described. Once the name was chosen a blessing was given by the village elder and all the men answered together, the strong, deep tone of their voices rumbling like thunder round the clearing.

To my surprise, once this was done, the smith pointed to me and said, 'See the stranger amongst us, the white man who came to visit our village. May he and his family live long and healthy lives! May he be welcome in our village! We give him our greetings!' Then a huge pannier containing, I was told, five thousand kola nuts was produced and each man given a handful.

Every night there was drumming in both Guengore and Dialokoto: people were getting themselves warmed up for the harvest festival which was to last for three days, the first of which was for the women and girls and the second a masked dance for everybody that continued on into the third. There is something about African drumming, especially by night, that irresistibly plucks at one like the chords of a double bass. It quickens the heartbeat and focuses the mind on things distant and cerebral: passion is subdued to make way for the passion of music that can hold you as firmly as a drug-induced trance. And the drumming of these three days of the harvest festival was intended to produce a high state of trance.

In Guengore the drummers consisted of five men with congas

– tall, wooden drums – and tomtoms, smaller wooden drums with, here, tin rattles tied to their sides. They drummed almost ceaselessly for two nights and three days. And this was no mere tapping of the drums. The five virile and half-naked young men poured themselves into their drums. They thickened the air, the village and the entire night with their rhythms. Their rhythms wove and rose and waned. They coiled about each other, then took sojourns of their own. The young men went far beyond exhaustion. So soon their eyes became fixed, so soon their concentration was lost to the muses that dictated their melodies. All was in their hands, blurring on the tight, dirtied drum skins. Their bodies knew nothing of sloth and laxity, every bone, sinew and muscle was alive with strain and tension. Sweat shone on their skins. Their feet and heads moved spasmodically as though not of their will. For two nights and three days the sound of their drums held anything as mundane as tiredness and wear at bay. They were the heartbeat of the celebration and could not be stopped.

On the night of the masked dance the drumming took on a more frantic tempo. And so, inexorably, everybody was drawn to the village clearing. That night was as dark as only African nights can be. The village houses through which you weaved your way to the clearing were quiet and empty, only the odd cry of a baby or the mumble and murmur of the very old and sick, who did not wish to attend the dance, coming from them. But ahead, even from within the dark network of the village houses, a great, dancing orange light could be seen illuminating the top of the large central tree. Then, coming round the last hut, you saw the thronging backs of the villagers silhouetted against the orange glow of a great fire. The air was thick with the frenetically spiced excitement that comes with the gathering of humanity on dark nights: so much is hidden by the darkness, so much can be revealed.

A huge circle had been formed round the clearing. The oldest and most respected people had chairs to sit on. At their feet huddled girls and boys and small children. And behind them stood the rest of the villagers, some on carts, some on boxes on the carts, some on benches, some on the ground. Everyone was tightly bunched, pressed close together, and everyone's face was orange in the flickering glow. The fire was beside the tree at one side of the circle. It was a fire of hay and two men had the job of keeping it continually supplied, and so continually flaming, from a large pile of hay nearby. Each time they threw on a new load, with a crack and whip the flames leapt up to scorch the lower branches of the tree and draw the circle of people back from the darkness into which they had begun to slip.

I went to the dance in the company of Alphonse who made sure I was provided with one of the privileged chairs in the circle. No sooner had I settled myself in, though, than he took me away again to a nearby hut in which a group of men were preparing to drink some palm wine. He had to knock on the door and announce his name before we were allowed in. Then the door was locked behind us. 'The village elders must disapprove of the drinking of alcohol,' I thought to myself, only to be corrected a moment later by Alphonse.

'We must not let anybody else know we have some palm wine,' he said, 'or else the whole village will be in here wanting some. The palm wine comes from far away and is not easy to get hold of.' The three bidons of the stuff were quickly put away in the correct fashion by the seven men present, then we all, in the highest of spirits, went back to the dance. Not much later a very sick and shaky-looking Alphonse came and told me he was retiring for the night because he was tired. He was not, he had told me earlier, accustomed to drinking alcohol.

The dances were a mixture of haphazardness and organization. There was a harmony of spontaneity. The young unmarried girls had their dances, the older women theirs, the masked and grass-skirted men and the acrobats theirs, even the drunks and madmen theirs. They took it in turns to dance, not organized turns, but as and when the night called for them to get up and dance, when their bodies could no longer resist, and those turns always came at the right moment.

The married women formed long crocodiles, holding each other's hips and shuffling round the circle swinging from side to side in a subdued but rhythmic fashion. They looked grand and beautiful in their long, patterned dresses and similarly patterned headdresses, and gradually more and more of them got up from their seats, for the women were privileged enough to have seats, and joined the crocodile until it had nearly joined head to tail.

The audience clapped and sang. They sang songs of thankfulness, thankfulness to anything and anyone who had helped their village: to a big merchant from Bamako who had done much business with the village; to the missionaries; to each other; to the clouds that produced the rain, to the earth that produced their crops. And to demonstrate this appreciation they brought food to the dance and placed it on the ground in front of the circle of people. One woman of every family which could afford it at some stage of the evening went to her home to collect food to bring back to the dance. Each time one of them appeared the crowd clapped and cheered and the woman would add the food to what was already there. Throughout the evening more and more was produced: millet of all different sizes and types, dried maize, couscous, beans and rice.

As the excitement and cheers of the crowd grew, so the women went to their homes again and again, two, three, four times even, to collect more food. There it was, lying in the light of the fire for everyone to see, an undeniable fact. It was a gift, a sign of generosity in response to the generosity of the earth. It would be stored and handed out to poor families in times of hardship. How wonderful it was, how good it made everyone feel to see all this surplus food, all this generosity. The crowd swayed with exhilaration.

Then the masked dancers came. They dashed into the middle of the circle, their heads entirely hidden, at the back by long sisal hair, at the front by masks of wild and fanatical looks with widespread eyes, bared teeth, and predatory eagle noses. They stepped forwards, planting their feet with aggressive thuds to the ground. They swung round, shook a leg, then burst into a run at the crowds. Children wailed and scattered in fear, women screamed and laughed nervously at their screams. Dark and ominous, unpredictable, untrustworthy, the men leapt about the circle like demons, shaking and uttering guttural cries. Something chilling came into the night. Here were fears and spirits in the throes of a drum-beat trance. Here they could be seen at last, and faced. Here they became real. Behind those masks were not men in disguise, but what cannot be reasoned with: a mask hides, like night, so that much can be revealed.

Whilst bearing the masks those men became their parts: powerful, untouchable, even cruel fears. The drummers throbbed, the crowds gazed, transfixed, the masked men became only those hideous masks which wove and thrust and spun in a whirl about the village clearing. Then they were gone, whooping and yelling into the night from whence they had sprung. Later, on many occasions, they reappeared to keep the crowds in fear of their fears.

Young unmarried girls then leapt up and, as if caught by a sudden wind, their bodies were taken by the drumming. It ran through their legs and arms, winding them up. They loosened themselves to the drumming, let it use them and take on a form of its own. Yes, they let themselves forget and blanked their minds, all the better for the music to take a hold. For fleeting seconds, if they concentrated enough, they were taken away to a different place, all about them forgotten, the drumming and their bodies numbed into one. Then with a jolt they were back, back to return to their places to let another girl take the limelight. Some of them were eager to dance and some were shy and had to be persuaded. These were the ones who danced the best.

The middle-aged women did not dance like this. They had their crocodile dance, for it would not be seemly to let their bodies become so abandoned. The most abandoned dancing was that done by old women, women past the days of caring. One of these women let the drumming take her to its limit. She did not hold back an iota of herself and soon her thin, awkward old body became stiffened and tremorous with her trance. Her eyes glazed like those of the dead. Spittle and froth flew from her mouth and she fell to the ground and writhed. She was beyond recall. Men held her down, poured water on her face, then carried her away to let time soothe her fit.

And on the dancing and drumming went. Acrobats came and jumped over each other. A man played with fire. Children formed little circles and danced. A madman entertained the crowds with a wild and gibbering dance. A call was made for the white man to dance, and so I too entertained the crowd for a short while. On and on the drummers worked, into the dawn, into the morning, and throughout the rest of that day, until a whole year's worth of temperance and toil had been exorcized from the village.

The following day I left Guengore, up into the hills at dawn. 'Don't suffer from nostalgia,' were Alphonse's parting words.

★

I climbed into the range of hills in the lee of which Guengore sat, and Mungo Park skirted them to the south. I parted from him for the last time, for I was headed for the town of Keniaba on the far side of the hills, the beginning of the end of my journey, whereas Mungo Park was headed for Senegal, where I did not wish to follow him. His journey, too, was near its end. Just over one month's march and some 450 kilometres would bring him back to Pisania on the banks of the Gambia river, where he had commenced his journey just over two years and six months earlier.

Those last stages of Park's journey, traversing the Bilali river, Park's Ba-lee, or 'honey' river, and the Faleme river, to arrive in what is today the country of Senegal through which the slave caravan made its slow and tortuous way, must have been hard. By then Park was reduced by illness, poverty and exhaustion to a pitiful state, so much so that the slaves of the caravan, amidst their own sufferings, sympathized with Park who, like so many of them, had difficulty in keeping up, and brought him water to drink and collected branches for his bed at night.

The British traders on the Gambia river, having heard rumours that Park had been murdered by the Moors of Ludamar, had long ago given him up for dead, so his arrival amongst them was greeted with much surprise. His appearance by then was so dramatically changed he was thought by one person to be a Moor. When he did put his appearance to rights, donning the English dress he had left in the care of his old host, Dr Laidley, and shaving off his long beard, Karfa Toure, the man who had taken Park under his wing and brought him to the Gambia, was as delighted and amazed by the look of him as he was by everything European he saw, such things as a schooner lying at anchor on the Gambia river which impressed him so much he sighed: 'Black men are nothing.' He was not so impressed by Park's loss of facial growth, however, and claimed that it had converted Park from a man into a boy. Park was, after all, still only twenty-six years old.

And so the tale of Mungo Park's and Europe's first penetration into the almost mythical lands of inner West Africa comes to an end, with Park, only a few weeks after his arrival at Pisania, sailing away from the shores of Africa on a slave ship bound for the West Indies, from where he could take passage back to England. Park had touched the very heart of West Africa with an innocence and tenderness that it would not often again experience at the hands of Europeans. And it, no doubt, had touched the heart of Mungo Park, as indeed it touches all who immerse themselves in it.

But West Africa had touched Mungo Park not so gently. In the same way that the flame of a candle will scorch the tender fingers of a young child experimenting with something that attracts it but which it does not understand, the harsh realities of West Africa seared and perhaps hardened the youthful heart of Mungo Park. The time was right, for Britain, in the guise of Mungo Park sent back a second time to explore the Niger, was in a forceful, impatient and imperialistic mood. The rivalries of the European powers, in the throes of the Napoleonic wars, were at their greatest height, and Britain's penetration into West Africa would now be no gentle and thoughtful thing. Now was not the time for patience and tact and it would be because of the lack of these things that Europe's dealings with Africa were to produce the same sort of sentiments, echoing right up to this day, that Mungo Park's friend, Karfa Toure, expressed: that in comparison to Europeans, 'black men are nothing'. And patience is something that is needed by the Europeans in Africa, as anyone who has visited there will tell you. Without it disaster is always the result.

What was it that took Mungo Park back to Africa a second time, abandoning perhaps for ever the beloved wife he had married on his return from his first trip, leaving perhaps to be orphaned the three children he had raised in the borderlands of Scotland? The account Park had written of his first trip, *Travels into the Interior of Africa*, had been well received by the British public. He was a national hero and the shining star of his old employers, the African Association. Perhaps it was his ambition, fired by this fame, that made him risk his life, an ambition that was certainly not being fulfilled by the life Park led on his return of a local surgeon in the borderlands of Scotland. Perhaps it was to put an end to the nightmares that were plaguing him, nightmares of his sufferings at the hands of the Moors of Ludamar. Perhaps for him it was merely an extension of his preferred career, a career that could quench his restlessness and provide a healthy income for his family. Or maybe it was just that Park had been 'bitten by the bug', as are most visitors to Africa, and for some reason that he could not fathom just felt the need to return.

Whichever, return Park did, and, just under eight years after the conclusion of his first trip, 4 May 1805 found him once again departing from Pisania with the quest of exploring the course of the Niger. This time, however, Park was not the solitary wanderer of his first journey. He was now at the head of an expedition sponsored by the British Government and consisting of forty-four Europeans: thirty-four soldiers, two sailors, two Scottish friends whom he had chosen to accompany him and six carpenters who were supposed to build the boat in which they could all sail down the Niger to its termination, wherever that might be.

The expedition was badly conceived and executed and was, it can be seen in retrospect, doomed to disaster from the onset. A fast and forceful thrust to the Niger was what it was supposed to be, though it soon became apparent that the soldiers were unfamiliar with and could not handle the numerous donkeys laden with vast quantities of merchandise and supplies that accompanied the expedition. The most fatal error, though, was that the expedition, thanks to many delays, was late in setting off and found itself travelling into the teeth of the approaching rainy season at the hottest time of year. If Mungo Park considered either cancelling the expedition or awaiting the end of the rainy season, he dismissed these options and instead rashly put his life and the lives of all his companions at risk by going ahead at such a time: within only a couple of days the first of the soldiers had died of an epileptic fit brought on by the heat.

How terrible that journey to the Niger must have been! Cutting across much the same country as Park had travelled on the return from his first trip, the cumbersome, drawn-out and disorderly expedition was from the very first preyed upon by bandits who haunted its steps, stealing from the enfeebled soldiers with the greatest of audacity: a trail of those soldiers were left dead and dying in its wake, struck down by fever, dysentery and heatstroke.

How could Mungo Park have thought this expedition could succeed? He knew only too well the effects the rainy season had had on even his hearty constitution. He knew only too well that this heavily armed and threatening group of strangers would not be received well by the inhabitants of the countryside. And he knew only too well that that countryside was infested with bands of robbers and that those robbers, and even ordinary villagers, would not be able to resist such easy and rich pickings as the expedition represented. But he was determined to succeed, determined, perhaps, not to be defeated in his purpose once again by Africa. He would pick up and carry his expedition to the Niger if necessary. And this is very nearly what he did. Regardless of his own fevers and dysentery, he behaved like a hero. As one by one his soldiers dropped off and died, and as one by one the donkey loads were stolen, he could be found dashing up and down the long line of his men, picking them up, carrying them, administering medicines to them, encouraging them. Day after day he loaded up the donkeys almost single-handedly, drove them forever onwards, and fought off the bandits. Day after day his will dragged his expedition towards the Niger. How sad that when it eventually arrived there three-quarters of the soldiers were dead and only one carpenter remained to build the boat.

The end of Mungo Park's story is an unhappy one. That strong, enthusiastic and conscientious young Scot who had originally come to Africa with simply 'a passionate desire to examine into the productions of a country so little known and to become experimentally acquainted with the modes of life and characters of the natives', had become a man quite demented with fever, frustration and a will to prevail over the land that so tormented him. There was nothing for it now but a mad dash down the Niger to success or death. He had done with the Africans, and intended sailing down the middle of the stream without landing.

And although he did relent a little and attempt some communication with the peoples through whose lands he passed, he and the four Europeans who were all that now remained alive of his companions were soon firing upon anyone who attempted to approach them on the river. Nobody knows how many Africans were killed in this fashion, but Park's passing down the Niger into what is today the country of Nigeria left a lasting and unpleasant impression on the peoples and kingdoms to be found on its banks.

There is some confusion about the final events of that fateful journey, but whether or not the army that positioned itself at the rapids of Bussa in today's Nigeria had been sent there because Park had omitted to give presents to the king of the country through which he was passing, as he should have done, or whether Park had in fact given some presents to a local chief to be passed on to that king, who, discovering that Park would not be returning his way, kept them for himself, or just what the intentions of that army were and who it was who opened fire first, is unclear. What is clear is that Mungo Park's end came when, realizing that he and his companions would surely all be killed in the boat should they remain in it, Park, grabbing one of his companions, jumped overboard and was never seen again. He, his ambitions and his demented heroism were drowned in the swirling waters of the river he had failed to explore. Africa had foiled Europe's attempts to know it this time. But Mungo Park was only the tip of the iceberg. So soon Europe would have its revenge. So soon it would prevail over Africa and have its way with it, if only for a brief time. The explorers, so many of whom would also lose their lives, would eventually explore its rivers and map it out. The traders would seduce and exploit it. The soldiers would conquer it. And the administrators would administer it and at least believe they had it tamed. Then it would break free and become the land through which I made a journey, a journey that was now so near to its end.

I climbed into the hills in the lee of which Guengore sat. It was the earliest hour of dawn, so early not even the womenfolk of Dialokoto had stirred from their huts. Each breath of air was like a draught of cool spring water. Each step, no matter how quiet, broke upon the still greyness of dawn like ripples on a pond.

I climbed into the hills, into a small, fertile pocket of existence risen above the brown plains of Africa. Here was agriculture in profusion, and busy hamlets, and cattle and goats, all tucked in amongst the tall, yellow grasses and gullies of rubble rock. Through the hills I marched and out and down the other side to arrive in the evening, all covered in dust and sweat, at the small, frontier-like town of Keniaba placed upon a scrub-covered plain. Here I passed the night in the company of an old sax-ophonist who had been sent to Keniaba to instruct the town's resident band. 'I was a factory worker in Dakar, but I am a *griot*,' the old saxophonist repeated with great regularity. The long life of this man could be read in the myriad of wrinkles that made up his face, wrinkles that when he played his saxophone, as that evening he did, took on a life of their own and expressed every hint and nuance of the music being played. We drank in a bar until late at night in the company of an array of shadowy and vociferous figures. We drank until the stars in the sky began to swim, drank until all the drinkers had found oblivion. 'I was a factory worker but I am a *griot*,' the old saxophonist mumbled to himself until a woman came and took him away to his bed.

From Keniaba I travelled fast and hard and within a week found myself back in the Gambia once more. The first part of this journey was along the road that went north from Keniaba to Kayes, a road that is infamous for it is down this long, broken and often impossible track that successive Western mining com-panies have lugged the sophisticated equipment with which they hoped to extract the gold that is to be found near Keniaba, the same gold that once helped build the empires of old. Hundreds upon hundreds of container trucks have made their tortuous way down this road, and millions upon millions of dollars have been wasted because those mining companies inevitably go bust, defeated by the intractability of the Africans and the reluctance of their land to give up its wealth.

The truck in which I travelled this road was driven by an energetic little man who stopped at every village to do some business, even if it was merely to transport some pumpkins two hundred yards. One time we saw a troop of baboons dis-appearing into the bush far in the distance. Even though they were so far away and were quickly lost to sight, the driver brought his truck to an immediate halt and, digging frantically around beneath his seat, brought out a small pistol of local design which he quickly loaded with a shotgun cartridge and fired off, only to have it fly from his hand and hit the roof of the cabin. But this was no attempt at a kill, as indeed there was no chance of that, just a reminder to the baboons that it was man who ruled hereabouts.

From Kayes, where I once again saw Michel and my two friends, Ousman and Amadou, it was the train back through Senegal and then a bush taxi to the border of the Gambia. 'Welcome to Gambia' a large sign at the border said, 'Guinness is good for you'.

Three days later I was in an aeroplane, rising up into the African night. There I sat in my window seat, letting myself become infused and saturated with that detached and savoury mood that night-time flights inspire. Here I was drawn away from one reality, not yet arrived in another. I let my mind wander over all I had experienced in Africa, let it pick delicately through all the sights and friendships, through all the good times and bad times, let it almost burst with alternating and inexplicable feelings of sadness and joy. I could imagine that Africa was a great and enticing darkness, a darkness of such depth it could drown a man even such as Mungo Park.

'Don't suffer from nostalgia,' had been Alphonse of Guengore's parting words. But that I could not promise.